AN ELEMENTARY

ENGLISH GRAMMAR

FOR THE USE OF SCHOOLS.

By R. G. LATHAM, M.A., M.D., &c.

LATE FELLOW OF KING'S COLLEGE, CAMBRIDGE:
LATE PROFESSOR OF ENGLISH IN UNIVERSITY COLLEGE, LONDON.

NEW EDITION,

THOROUGHLY REVISED AND GREATLY ENLARGED.

LONDON:

LONGMANS, GREEN, AND CO.

1875.

PREFACE.

BETWEEN the end of the third and the middle of the sixth
century a language different from both the original British
and the Latin of the Roman period was introduced into
England. It was the mother tongue of the present English.
We know the direction in which it spread; because in
Wales and Scotland the original Celtic still keeps its
ground. And we know that about A.D. 600 it was firmly
established in the Eastern half of South Britain as the
English. Two names of two divisions of the German family,
Angle and *Saxon*, are also known to us. But the date of
its first introduction, the rate at which it encroached upon
the earlier forms of speech, along with the exact way in
which it has extended itself, are points about which we
know very little.

This is, doubtless, a matter of regret. On the other hand,
however, if we look upon the study of the English Language purely and simply as grammarians, we can dispense
with the study of its external history; or, at least, the two
branches of investigation can be kept separate. As to the
essentially foreign and German character of the English, the
language speaks for itself. We know it familiarly as it is
spoken at the present moment. We have specimens of it
as old as the eighth century, and we have a rich intermediate literature. Moreover we have the present German,

and allied languages of Holland, of Denmark, of Norway, of Sweden, and of Iceland, with which we can compare it. Hence, even when loaded with additions from the Latin, the French, the Greek, and other languages, its genuine German character is undoubted.

I am not prepared to say that with this we may not be satisfied. In this case we may begin at once with the details of our language and its affinities to the German dialects of the Continent. The presumptions deduced from the little that we know of its external history may coincide with its known structure; or they may differ from it. They may lead us to suppose that our language should be as free from British or Latin elements as it actually is. Or they may lead us to expect more remains of the languages which it displaced than we find. But upon these questions we may abstain from speculation. In other words we may take our language with its German character as we find it, and pronounce it to be what it is, either with the presumptions in favour of its being so, or in spite of them.

Much may be said in favour of this mode of treatment. It is usual, however, to say something about its introduction; about the parts of Germany from which it came; about the import of the terms Angle and Saxon; about the relations of the dialects of Germany Proper and Scandinavia; and, above all, about the extent to which the blood and the language of the English nation coincide.

All this—as has just been stated—may be avoided by limiting our consideration to the language itself. Nevertheless, one thing is certain: viz., that if the question of its introduction is to be gone into, it must be gone into thoroughly. If we write about it at all, we must write fully.

In a work like the present this is impossible. But the present is only the forerunner to a larger one; in which the subject is treated more comprehensively. Still there are special pieces of evidence with which the reader cannot make himself familiar too soon, and on this principle the chief notices in the way of evidence are laid before him. Even when taken altogether they are neither numerous nor long. The selected texts in the present small volume may be counted on our fingers. They fall, however, into two classes—the first containing the incidental allusions of the *cotemporary* Latin and Greek writers; the second the account of the Venerable Beda in the eighth century. Each class has its merits, and each its weak points. But if we give one, we must give the other also: for it is certain that they do not coincide. Of this the reader should be aware; though it is not necessary that on the very threshold of his studies he should either fix upon the class he prefers, or trouble himself to reconcile the two. But—as said before—he should know from the very first the nature of the scanty materials he has to deal with.

The Saxons came from Southern, the Angles from Northern, Germany; the former introducing the dialect in which the chief works of the times anterior to the Norman Conquest are composed. The latter brought with them the dialects of the parts between the Humber and the Forth; and these culminated in the literary languages of Scotland under the first five Stuarts. The former is represented by the present dialects of Dorsetshire, Devonshire, and the West of England, and is called Westsaxon; the latter by the Lowland Scotch and the English between the Tweed and the Humber. This is called Northumbrian. Out of the intermediate dialects arose the present literary English. These, though all three *dialects* of the German of England, have as fair a claim to be called different *languages* as the Danish and Swedish, or the Spanish and Portuguese ; and each has its several stages.

But besides this there are stages of the English language in general ; and it is necessary to separate the two histories.

In Part II., which treats of *Orthoëpy* and *Orthography,* there is little which is not found in the earlier editions.

And the same may be said of Part V., which treats of *Prosody.*

In the Third and Fourth Parts, which give us *Etymology* and *Syntax,* the general principle which distinguishes them from one another is clear and precise. Where we have words like *father* and *fathers—write* and *wrote—call* and *called*—we have, in each pair, *one* word and no more. This is Etymology. The second word is a slightly altered form of the first. Still it is a *single* word.

In combinations like—*of a father—I have written—I am calling,* and the like, we have *more words than one.* This is Syntax ; *i. e.* two, three, or (it may be more) words in combination. Sometimes one of these governs the other. Sometimes they are in concord or agreement. But, in all cases, they are two words in combination. Hence the name Syntax.

On the first view nothing is clearer, or more distinctive, than this. There are, doubtless, cases where the place of a word is equivocal ; *e. g.* in compounds. Terms like *oak-tree, Thursday,* and hundreds of others are of this class ; and it cannot be denied that they may belong to *either* Syntax or Etymology. They belong to Syntax so far as they are *two* words. But they are combined together and treated as one: and, so far, may be referred to Etymology. Still the class of compounds is not the one that need detain us longer. It raises a slight objection to the principle here laid down; but not one of much practical importance. When we say *all bláck bírds are not bláckbirds*, it is easy to see that in the first pair, we have two *separate* words; in the second, two words compounded into one.

The class which has a tendency to perplex us is represented by such combinations as *the hand of a man* when compared with *a man's hand, the skin of the lion*, &c. &c. Here the words *man's* and *lion's* are, according to every test, Genitive Cases, and, as such, single words belonging to Etymology; whereas *hat of a man* and *skin of the lion* are combinations of words, and, as such, belong to Syntax. In sense, however, they are so nearly identical that we are tempted to treat them as such. At any rate, we say that *of* is the sign of Genitive case. Yet *lion* is not a Genitive case at all. The true fact is somewhat different; and the accurate expression is—not that *lion* is a Genitive Case of which *of* is sign—but that there is a combination of a wholly different character with a meaning equivalent to a Genitive Case.

In the Verb the tendency to confusion is greater, and the influence of the Latin Grammar has much to do with it—that of the Greek a little. But the Latin is sufficient for our illustration. Where the Latin gives us *scribam = I shall write*; *scribebam = I was writing*; *scripsi = I have written*, and the like, it gives us a true Future, a true Imperfect, and a true Past Tense; and, as such, a form in Etymology. The English equivalents in sense, which are all combinations of different words, in every sense, belong to Syntax.

In the Passives we get a still more decisive influence. *Amor = I am loved, amabar = I was loved, amabor = I shall be loved*; all of which are Etymological Tenses. But

in the same table *amatus sum = I am loved*, is treated
exactly in the same way. It is called the Perfect Passive
Tense : whereas it is really a combination of the Substantive Verb with the Past Passive Participle. The difference
in the way of form and expression is clear ; but the
meaning is that of a true Tense.

It is not, then, strange that combinations so accurately
coinciding in sense as *I shall write* and *scribam* should be
placed in the same class, and treated as *Tenses*.

This, perhaps, is enough to illustrate the difference
between true Inflections like *fathers, wrote, patris, scripsi,*
and the like, and combinations like *of (a) father, have
written, shall write, was writing,* &c. There is a true Case
or Tense in one series ; a combination of different words as
its substitute in the other.

It is only necessary to add that I have carefully kept
these two classes distinct ; referring the first to Etymology,
the second to Syntax ; I have done this not merely here and
there, but generally and thoroughly ; and I believe that
no competent critic will deny the propriety of my doing so,
as a matter of pure and simple Grammar ; or that he will
condemn the distinction as wrong in itself. Some, perhaps
most, of them recognise it partially ; and, perhaps, I may
suggest that they would go further in the same direction,
if the practice to the contrary were less prevalent than it
is. Sooner or later, however, the thoroughgoing character
of the distinction must prevail, and, in my mind, the
period of transition and compromise is coming to a close.

This difference between true Inflections like the signs of
Case and Tense in words like *patris, fathers, scribam, scripsi,*
&c., as opposed to combinations like *of (a) father, will
write,* &c., concerning which thus much has already been
said, has another bearing upon our grammar. We have

seen that for the former the latter may be substituted.
But are we sure that this is an accurate way of speaking ?
It is certainly accurate when we translate from Latin into
English ; for then we render an original single word like
scripsi by the combination *have written*. But what if we
translate *I have written* into *scripsi ?* In such a case the
combination is the original form, and the Inflection the
substitute. This, however, is a point upon which we need
not dwell. What we must most especially understand is
that, so far as meaning goes, certain inflections have certain
combinations by which they may be represented, and
vice versâ.

For these two modes of representation there are two
names. Forms like *scripsi, scribam, scribebam, scripturus,*
&c., where we have but one word, are called *Synthetic.*
Their substitutes, such as *I have written* or *I wrote, I shall
write, I was writing, I am about to write,* &c. are called
Analytic. Languages in which the single word prevails are
called *Synthetic*; those in which the combination of more
words than one prevails are called *Analytic.* But this is
not all. The same language which is Synthetic in one
stage may become Analytic in another; the Latin for
instance is Synthetic, its daughter (the Italian) Analytic.
More still—the change is, as a rule, in one direction. The
Synthetic stage is always the older of the two; *i. e.* Synthetic languages become Analytic as they become modern.
The converse never takes place. In the Synthetic languages
the signs of Case, Tense, Mood, Person, Voice, and the like
are numerous, and well marked; so that if we see a word
with its signs of Case and Gender, we know that it is a
Noun, even if it stands alone. And if we see it with the
marks of Person, or Tense, we infer that it is a Verb.
When this is the case it is easy to say what it is as a Part

of Speech. But when all these outward and visible signs
are gone, we have no such criterion.

Now the English is the most Analytic Language in the
world. It has so few inflections of any kind that there are
few words in it which we can distinguish from one another
as Parts of Speech, except by observing what place they
take in the construction of a sentence ; and we can only do
this by applying the rules of Syntax. Hence, it is in the
Syntax rather than in the Etymology that the differences
between the several Parts of Speech—Noun, Pronoun,
Verb, &c.—are explained.

Nearly all this, however, is already exhibited in my
earlier Editions, and, to some extent, recognised. In other
matters the alterations are limited to particular details.

CONTENTS.

PART I.—HISTORICAL INTRODUCTION.

* See under ERRATUM, p. xx.

PART II.—ORTHOËPY AND ORTHOGRAPHY.

PART III.—ETYMOLOGY.

PART IV.—SYNTAX.

b

xviii   CONTENTS.

AN

ELEMENTARY ENGLISH GRAMMAR

FOR THE USE OF SCHOOLS.

PART I.

HISTORICAL INTRODUCTION.

CHAPTER I.

§ 1. THE English Language was originally foreign to the British Islands; and *Germany* was the country from which it was introduced.

§ 2. It spread gradually; indeed, at the present moment, there are remains of the original languages in Wales, in Scotland, in the Isle of Man, and in Ireland. There was a similar fragment in Cornwall during the last century.

The English language, then, extended itself over the British Islands more than thirteen hundred years ago, just as it extended itself over North America in the Seventeenth, and over Australia, Tasmania, New Zealand, and the Cape in the present, century.

§ 3. *The names under which it extended itself.*—The two most conspicuous names in the German invasions were those of the *Angles* and the *Saxons.* From the former we get the words *England* and *English*, from the latter the syllable *-sex* in *Essex, Middlesex, Sussex,* and *Wessex=East, Middle, South,* and *West Saxons.*

B

The notices of these two names fall into two classes. The first contains those authors that speak ·about them simply and exclusively, as applying to certain parts of Germany; and without any reference to Britain. The second contains those that connect them with the soil of Britain.

§ 4. *Early notices of the Angles.*—Of these there are two, and two only.

Tacitus.

After mentioning the Langobardi, or Lombards, Tacitus writes thus :—

Then come the Reudigni, the Aviones, the *Angli*, the Varini, the Eudoses, the Suardones, and the Niuthones, protected by either rivers or forests. There is nothing remarkable in detail, for these nations; though, in common, they worship Herth, *i.e.* Earth the Mother.

Reudigni deinde, et Aviones, et *Angli*, et Varini, et Eudoses, et Suardones, et Niuthones, fluminibus aut sylvis muniuntur; nec quid-quam notabile in singulis, nisi in commune Herthum, id est Terram Matrem colunt, &c.—*Germania*, § XL.

Ptolemy.

Of the nations of the interior, the greatest are those of the Suevi *Angli* (who be east of the Langobardi, stretching northwards to the middle course of the river Elbe), and of the Suevi Semnones, who reach from the aforesaid part of the Elbe, eastward to the river Suebus, and that of the Buguntæ in continuation as far as the Vistula.—*Lib.* II. *c.* XL.

§ 5. *Early notices of the Saxons.*—Of these there is only one, that of Ptolemy; for Tacitus says nothing whatever about them.

The Frisians occupy the sea-coast beyond the Busacteri as far as the river Ems. After these the Lesser Chauci, as far as the river Weser; then the Greater Chauci, as far as the Elbe; then in order on the Neck of the Cimbric Chersonese, the *Saxons*; then the Sabalingii, &c. ; and. after the Saxons, from the river Chalasus to the Suebus, the Pharodini. —*Lib.* II. *c.* XL.

In another part of the work there is a notice of ' *Three Islands of the Saxons,*' but without comment or explanation.

§ 6. Both Tacitus and Ptolemy wrote *after* the reduction of Britain as a Roman Province; but *before* the time when the Germans became formidable to Rome, and attracted notice as enemies on the coasts both of Gaul and Britain. The interval between the Saxons of Ptolemy and the Saxons of the next writer who will mention them is nearly two hundred years; and with the Angles it is still longer. For this reason, I pause at the two earlier notices. The division is natural; for the populations of Tacitus and Ptolemy had nothing to do with Britain; and there is a considerable interval between the two classes of authorities. For the greater part of the second and third centuries the history of both the Angles and the Saxons is a blank; and when they re-appear, they are more connected with Gaul and Britain than with Germany.

§ 7. *Languages with which the English came into contact.* The original language of *South* Britain was the *British*; now represented by the Welsh of Wales, and, in the last century, by the Cornish of Cornwall.

The original language of *North* Britain was the *Erse* or *Gaelic*; now represented by the *Erse* or *Gaelic* of the *Highlands* of Scotland, of Ireland, and of the Isle of Man.

Both belonged to the *Keltic* family.

But, besides these two, there was a third: the Latin. This was because, when the Germans invaded it, Britain was a Roman Province.

§ 8. The extent to which the Latin was a spoken vernacular language now comes under consideration; for we must know not only that the German was an intrusive language, but the languages upon which it intruded.

Upon this point Beda is our authority; for, although he did not write till near the middle of the eighth century, he gives us the philology of his own time.

The first of the following extracts makes the number of languages *Five*. The second implies that the *Latin* was the language of the Church, rather than the people at large; and, so doing, reduces the true vernaculars to *Four*.

B 2

Thus much, for the present, according to the number of the books in which the Divine Law is written, explores and confesses the one and same knowledge of supreme truth in the language of five nations: viz., the *Angles*, the *Britons*, the *Scots*, the *Picts*, and the *Latins*, which from the perusal of the Scriptures is made common to all the others.

In the next he tells us what was the import of the word *Latin* :—

He received in surrender all the nations and provinces of Britain, which are divided into the four languages—that is, of the Britons, the Picts, the Scots, and the Angles.

§ 9. *Rate and date of the introduction and diffusion of the English Language.*—The *rate* at which the English spread itself over Britain is uncertain ; indeed, it is closely connected with a question which is more uncertain still, that of the *time of its first introduction.*

§ 10. The evidence upon this point falls under seven heads.

    a. The coinage of Carausius, and the notice of Mamertinus.

    b. The first notice of the Saxons in *Gaul.*

    c. The first notice of them in, or connected with, *Britain.*

    d. The notice of Eutropius as to the *Littus Saxonicum.*

    e. The subjection of the *Britains* under the Saxons.

    f. The *Angles* of Procopius.

    g. The Mission of St. Augustin.

§ 11. *a. The Franks of Mamertinus.*—In the reign of Diocletian the coast of Gaul was entrusted to a Menapian named Carausius. The enemies who seem to have been most especially formidable were *Franks.* Carausius, however, betrayed his trust, and succeeded in making himself independent of the government in Rome. As far as the Emperors Diocletian and Maximian were concerned, he kept his position ; and medals are still extant on one side of which are stamped the joint Emperors with the inscription : '*Carausius and his brothers,*' and on the other Imperial Peace, Peace of the Empire, or Peace between the Emperors. This recognition, however, was not achieved without a contest.

To this we have an allusion in the following extract from Mamertinus in a Panegyric delivered before Maximian, the colleague of Diocletian in the Empire:—

By so thorough a consent of the immortal Gods, O unconquered Cæsar, has the extermination of all the enemies whom you attacked, and of the *Franks* more especially, been decreed, that even those of your soldiers who, having missed their way on a foggy sea, reached the town of London, destroyed promiscuously and throughout the city the whole remnant of that mercenary multitude of barbarians which, after escaping the battle, sacking the town and attempting flight, was still left—a deed whereby your provincials were not only saved, but delighted by the sight of the slaughter.

This extract gives a Frank army in the parts about London A.D. 290; and its value upon this point is unimpeachable. The evidence is that of a panegyrist, and, as such, cotemporary with the events alluded to; moreover, it is addressed to hearers who had taken part in them. Whether the victory was as glorious as the orator makes it, or whether the arch-pirate Carausius, on whose side the Franks were manifestly engaged, was much injured by it, are matters of minor importance.

But the Franks, though Germans, are neither Angles nor Saxons; neither is their history in Britain from this time at all continuous. Still they are named by Mamertinus; and, what is more to the purpose, the *Saxons* are *not* named by him; either in the extract under notice or elsewhere. Neither are they mentioned by any cotemporary of Mamertinus, or by any historian under the long reign of Diocletian's successor, Constantine the Great.

§ 12. *b. The first notice of the Saxons in Gaul.*—The first notice of the Saxons *in Gaul* is the *second* notice of them *anywhere*. The only writer who has mentioned them before is Ptolemy. They are, *then*, in *three islands*, and on the *Neck of the Cimbric Chersonese* (*Holstein*), as we have seen.

The authority now is the Emperor Julian, who not only writes from personal experience, but states that he does so :—

The Franks and *Saxons* of the nations on the Rhine and the Western Sea are the most warlike of nations .... this I know, not from hearsay alone, which is unsafe, but I have thoroughly learned it by the proof itself (αὐτῇ πείρᾳ τοῦτο ἐκμαθὼν οἶδα).—*Opp.*, *ed. Spanheim*, pp. 34, 56.

§ 13. *c. The Saxons in connection with Britain.—The Limes Saxonicus.—The Notitia Utriusque Imperii* is referred, from certain points of internal evidence, to the interval between A.D. 369 and A.D. 408. It tells us that there was a tract in Britain called *Limes Saxonicus*; that it was under the administration of a *Comes Limitis Saxonici*, and that it consisted of the sea-board from the Wash to the Southampton Water:—

Sub dispositione viri spectabilis Comitis Limitis Saxonici per Britanniam—

    Præpositus numeri Fortensium Othonæ.
    Præpositus militum Tungricanorum Dubris.
    Præpositus numeri Turnacensium Lemanis.
    Præpositus equitum Dalmatarum Branodunensis Branoduno.
    Præpositus equitum Stablesianorum Garionnensis Garionno.
    Tribunus Cohortis Primæ Vetasiorum Regulbio.
    Præpositus Legionis II. Aug. Rutupis.
    Præpositus numeri Abulcorum Anderidæ.
    Præpositus numeri Exploratorum Portu Adurni.—Cap. lxxi.

There was a similar and corresponding *Littus* in Gaul, in which we find the German word *March* (= *Limes*).

    Sub dispositione viri spectabilis Ducis Belgicæ Secundæ
    Equites Dalmatæ Marcis in Littore Saxonico.—C. xxxvii. 1.

§ 14. *d. The notice of Carausius by Eutropius, &c.*—The preceding extracts have given us *cotemporary* evidence. The present will *not* do so. There are special reasons, however, for submitting it to the reader:—

    Carausius apud Bononiam per tractum Belgicæ et Armoricæ pacandum mare accepit, quod Franci et *Saxones* infestabant.—*Eutropius*, ix. 15.

It is well known that a very important use has been made of this passage. With few, if any, exceptions, the histories of England, when they treat of the German Conquest, give very little prominence to the *Littus Saxoni-*

cum; and, when they notice it at all, they generally add that *Saxonicum* need not be supposed to mean '*inhabited by Saxons*,' but simply '*harassed, or threatened, by the Saxons*,' or '*exposed to the ravages of the Saxons*.' That this meaning is, to some degree, a forced one, few deny; but it is probably admitted, on all sides, that, from one point of view, it is not unnecessary. The authority of Beda, supported by that of the Anglo-Saxon Chronicle, makes the history of the German Conquest begin with Hengist and Horsa, Vortigern and Vortimer, and their cotemporaries; and it is clear that if this be the case, the *Littus Saxonicum* must be explained away. This, to say the least, excuses a construction which, under other circumstances, might be condemned as non-natural.

This passage of Eutropius does more. It makes it almost natural. It suggests that the *Littus Saxonicum* may date from the time of Carausius, and that it was because the Franks and Saxons had to be *kept away from it*, rather than because *they occupied it*, that it took its name. Whether this would have any definite bearing on the main question is doubtful; because we have seen that, however much, *in the first instance*, Carausius was opposed to the Franks, he afterwards took them into his service.

But it is the value of Eutropius as an authority for the word *Saxon*, rather than the application of his evidence, that is now under notice; and it is the opinion of the present writer that he took the word *Saxones* as connected with the name of Carausius, not as it was in the time of Carausius himself, but according to the meaning it bore in his own time.

§ 15. There are three periods in the early history of this perplexing word *Saxon* :—

1. That of the Saxons as occupants of the Cimbric Chersonese, in which they are simply items in the geography of Germany, and in no connection whatever with the rest of Europe. This is given in the single notice of Ptolemy.

2. That of the Saxons as formidable seamen during the
decline of the Roman Empire, especially along the coasts
of Gaul and Britain.

3. That of the Saxons in Germany subsequent to the
establishment of the Frank Kingdom.

§ 16. The second period is the one under notice; and I
submit that it had *not* begun in the time of Carausius. That
there may have been Saxons among the pirates against whom
Carausius was employed is likely.   It is also likely that
the Saxons, single-handed, may have been as formidable
as the Franks themselves.   But it is certain that, in the
Panegyric of Mamertinus, no such name as *Saxon* is to be
found.   The difference between the Saxon element in a
piratical population and the other elements had yet to be
made.   As far as our evidence goes, Julian is the first who
does this.   He is the future Emperor of the *East*; and it is
in the writers of the Eastern, rather than the Western
Empire, that it is found.   By the time of Eutropius their
ravages had become frequent and persistent, and, when he
wrote, the name of Saxon had become familiar in Constanti-
nople.   Under this influence, then, it is submitted that Eutropius wrote; identifying the Saxons of his own time with
the marauders of the time of Carausius.   This is Gibbon's
opinion, who writes that Eutropius 'used the language of
his own times.'

This is why, when every other piece of evidence in the
present work has been (upon principle) given only when
it is cotemporary with the event, this notice of Eutropius
has been recognized.   It is *not* the evidence of a cotemporary.   If it were, it would be evidence of extraordinary
value; for it would put the state of both Gaul and Britain
in the time of Carausius in a much clearer light than that
under which we find it; and, what is more, it would tell us
not only that the term *Saxon* was then in use, but what
were the relations of the men who bore it to the British
and Gallic coasts.   It is *not*, however, evidence of this
kind, but of a much inferior character.

§ 17. *c. The Subjection of the Britains under the Saxons.*
—The settlement of a German population in Britain is
one thing; the evacuation of the island by the Romans
is another. Yet they are closely connected. Germans on
the soil of Britain we have already found; but Germans
as the dominant population, Germans unchecked by either
the legions or the navy of Rome, we have yet to find.

Who the Saxons of the *Saxon Shore* actually were is
uncertain. The ordinary meaning of the term is, undoubtedly, a coast *occupied by a Saxon population*; but, in
the present case, it is (as we have seen) held to mean a
coast *threatened or harassed by the Saxons, and, as such,
defended against them.*

It is nowhere suggested that this is the natural import of
the term; it is only maintained that it is, if needed, a legitimate one. And, provided we take the accounts of Beda and
the Anglo-Saxon Chronicle as genuine history, it *is* needed.
It is needed if the accounts of the Hengists, Ellas, Cerdics,
and other Anglo-Saxon heroes are to be taken not only
as permanent settlements, but as the *first of the kind*;
and that so exclusively as to make it necessary to put upon
the words *Littus Saxonicum* a construction which would
never suggest itself spontaneously, and of which no second
instance has ever been adduced.

Whether these two statements be accurate or the contrary
is a matter upon which the reader must judge for himself.
He need only understand, as a preliminary, that it is in no
respect a point of scholarship. Whether *Coast* or *Shore* be
the better translation of the word *Littus* is a matter of
indifference. '*Saxonicum*' there is but one way of trans-
lating. Hence, in respect to the import of the four words,
there is no difference. We can do nothing with the words
Littus Saxonicum in Latin, that we cannot do with *Saxon
Shore* (or *Coast*) in English. If '*harassed*' or '*threatened*' or '*frequented* by the Saxons' be a forced inter-
pretation of '*Saxon Shore*' as an English term, it is

equally forced in the Latin *Littus Saxonicum.* Those who have noticed the way in which several influential writers usher in this secondary sense of '*Saxonicum*' will not condemn the present remark as superfluous. Either consciously or unconsciously, a great many of them suggest that in the Latin phrase there is more latitude and pliability than in the English.

§ 18. *e. The Evacuation of Britain by the Romans.*—The following extract from Prosper Tiro is one that, in the mind of the present writer, has had scant justice done to it.

The date is A.D. 441.

The Britains, up to this time torn by various massacres and events, are reduced to the dominion of the *Saxons.*

Britanniæ, usque ad hoc tempus variis cladibus eventibusque laceratæ in ditionem *Saxonum* rediguntur.

I submit that these *Saxons* of Prosper Tiro are the Saxons of the *Littus Saxonicum.*

The date is earlier than that assigned to Hengist and Horsa, but it is later than that of the withdrawal of the legions by Honorius, A.D. 409. That Honorius withdrew the exclusively military legions, or rather that they were withdrawn by Constantine and the British pretenders who fought their battles in Gaul, is likely enough. The question is whether he withdrew the dockyards, the arsenals, and those sailors who chose to remain where they were; and on this point there is not a particle of evidence. Failing this, we must look to the *Littus* of Gaul; and here it seems to have been left as it was. At any rate we hear of the Saxons of Bayeux—the *Saxones Bajocassini* of Gregory of Tours, and of others—long after the Imperial character of the Littus has disappeared, and long after the Merovingian Franks had become strong enough to keep off intruders. Still, it must be from either fresh intruders from the North, or from the remainder of the *Littus,* that the Saxons of Gaul, of the Fifth, Sixth, and Seventh centuries, are to be deduced.

The word Britannia during the Fifth century means not only Britain, but Brittany, or Armorica. Hence, it is probable that these two countries are the *Britanniæ* of the extract. Still, there is in Britain a Britannia Prima, and a Britannia Secunda; while even in Gaul there is, besides the Armorican Brittany, a notice of certain *Britanni* on the Loire. It will be seen in the sequel that there are other ambiguous words connected with this period.

The gist of these remarks is to put the evidence of Prosper Tiro, *at least*, on a level with that of Beda and the Saxon Chronicle; and if the present work were one upon the general history of England during the fourth and fifth centuries, instead of a mere introduction to the details of the structure of the language, more would be said on the subject. Objections would be anticipated, and the result of the difference between the two authorities indicated. As it is, however, the solitary date of Prosper Tiro is simply preferred to the details of Beda and the writers who follow him.

§ 19. The well-known letter to the Roman general Ætius, in his third consulship, sometimes quoted as 'The Groans of the Britons,' in most works (and in none more than my own) finds its place, A.D. 449. It is now excluded from the text, and that purposely. This is to show that the omission is not accidental. It runs thus:—

To Ætius, thrice Consul, the groans of the Britons. The barbarians drive us to the sea. The sea drives us back to the barbarians. Between these arise two sorts of deaths. We are either slaughtered or drowned.

Ætio ter consuli gemitus Britannorum. Repellunt nos barbari ad mare; repellit nos mare ad barbaros. Inter hæc oriuntur duo genera funerum. Aut jugulamur, aut mergimur.

It is doubtful whether the Britons of this epistle, instead of being Britons of Britannia, are not the Bretons of Armorica (Brittany). When Ætius was in Gaul, St. Germanus was in Britain. On his return he passed through Armorica. The Armoricans at that time had offended Ætius, and he sent his ally, the barbarous king of the Alani, to chastise them. The barbarians, then, are the Alani.

Read from this point of view, the letter has a significance which it wants if we read it as an application from Britain. The Britons are pent up between the enemy on the land on one side and the sea on the other. This might, or might not, have been the case with the Saxons. The Alans, however, *must* have pressed on the Bretons from the *land* side, and the more they pressed westwards, the more the latter retreated, the more stringent the alternative of the surrounded population would become.

§ 20. *f.* The following extract gives us a new name— that of the *Frisians.* It is a name that has long been recognized, and one that we may undoubtedly add to those of the Angles, the Saxons, and the Jutes. It is not to be found in Beda. In the following notice where it *is* found there is no such word as *Saxon.* The inference from this, that some Saxons were Frisians under another name (and *vice versâ*), suggests itself at once; and, if we knew no more about the Frisians than what we learn from our present authority, it might pass without comment. Indeed, it is probable that, to some extent, such is the case. There is much, however, connected with the Frisians which points to the Angles and the Danes rather than to the Saxons.

From Procopius.

Three nations extremely populous occupy the island of Britain. One king is at the head of each. The names for these nations are *Angli,* Phrissones, and (of the same name as the island) Britons. Such is the manifest populousness of these nations, that every year, in great numbers, they migrate from thence, and with their wives and children go over to the Franks.

Βριττίαν δὲ τὴν νῆσον ἔθνη τρία πολυανθρωπότατα ἔχουσι. Βασιλεὺς δὲ εἷς αὐτῶν ἑκάστῳ ἐφέστηκεν. Ὀνόματα δὲ κεῖται τοῖς ἔθνεσι τούτοις Ἀγγίλοι καὶ Φρισσόνες καὶ οἱ τῇ νήσῳ ὁμώνυμοι Βρίττωνες· τοσαύτη δὲ ἡ τῶνδε τῶν ἐθνῶν πολυανθρωπία φαίνεται οὖσα ὥστε ἀνὰ πᾶν ἔτος κατὰ πολλοὺς ἐνθένδε μετανιστάμενοι ξὺν γυναιξὶ καὶ παισὶν ἐς Φράγγους χωροῦσιν.

Bellum Gothicum, iv. 20.

§ 21. *g. The Mission of St. Augustin.*—This is loosely identified with the introduction of Christianity in England —in *England,* as opposed to *Britain*; for into Britain, as a Roman province, Christianity had found its way before. The time is the last three years of the seventh century, say

A.D. 600. Ethelbert is king of Kent; his queen is a Frank princess. Gregory I., then Pope, enjoins a Frank mission to promulgate the Christianity of the Franks. The Frank King sends interpreters, and St. Augustin is at the head of the mission. The evidence of this is the Papal letters. They did not reach England till later, when Nothelm brought them over. Now Nothelm was an early cotemporary of Beda's, and as such belongs to the latter half of the seventh century; and, so doing, brings us to the time of Beda himself.

Hence, A.D. 697 there is no doubt as to the fact of the mother-tongue of the present English having become thoroughly established in Britain; in the southern parts at least. It was a language, too, intelligible to the Franks; at least to the Franks of the western division of the Frank kingdom.

§ 22. If full justice is to be done both to Beda and the earlier authorities with whom he is at variance, his account may be divided into three parts.

1. *The Century in which he wrote.*—Here he writes of what was to be found in England during the time of his own life; and, doing this, writes with an authority which it would be vain to impugn.

2. *The Seventh Century.*—This gives us, within a few years, the introduction of Christianity and several of its immediate results, one of which would be the use of the Latin language as that of the Church, and (unless it existed before) the use of the alphabet. Under these conditions we get the elements of a truly historical record; and, although *we* have no remains of it, it is probable that Beda may have had the opportunity of availing himself of it. More than this, for the latter half of the century, there were the early cotemporaries of Beda, to whom he may have applied. This we know to have been the case. We know, too, that there was a fair amount of literary activity during the period. One of the Christian duties of the recent converts to Christianity in England was that of

preaching the Gospel to their near kinsmen on the Continent, who, in the parts north of the Rhine and Ems,
were still pagans. This they performed honourably. They
called the Germans of these districts *Old* Saxons; an important name, because it shows that the descent of the
English from them was recognized. It is also a convenient name, because it means the Saxons of the Continent
as opposed to the Saxons of England. These latter, even
in Beda's time, are called *Anglo*-Saxons.

Between Beda and his cotemporaries we get trustworthy evidence for at least the latter half of the seventh
century, especially as the cotemporaries whom we appeal
to are not imaginary or merely possible ones. Beda
himself tells us, not only that there were some of them to
whom he applies, but he tells us who they were and upon
what points they instructed him. Thus he mentions by
name Albinus and Nothelm for Kent; Bishop Daniel for
Sussex and the Isle of Wight; the monks of Lestingham
for Mercia and part of Essex; with Cyneberct and others
for Lincoln. For the province of Northumberland Beda was
his own authority.

For the *first* half, however, of the century the value of
Beda's statements decreases, though not to any great degree.
There is still, without doubt, some learning in the country,
and some records. Hence, when Beda writes that Eadwin,
king of Northumberland, defeats Ethelfrith, and soon after
invades the little kingdom of Elmet (in the West Riding
of Yorkshire), and that Elmet is, then, not only independent, but British, we should not only not demur to
his evidence, but adopt it as one of the best statements we
have for calculating the *rate* at which our language extended itself.

This, then, is a *third* point in the history of our language upon which Beda speaks with authority. The other
two we have are (1) the four (or five) languages of Britain,
and (2) the existence of the Jutes in Kent and the Isle of
Wight (for which see § 25).

The *fourth* point, however, is the most important of all. It is in Beda that we first meet the word *Angle* in connection with England and the English.

§ 23. *Beda's Evidence for the Sixth and Fifth Centuries.*— For what Beda tells us here, especially for the *fifth* century, we must look less to the account he delivers than to the question as to how he got his information. The middle part of the period is one of almost total darkness. The time for the influences of the early English Christianity with its concomitant civilization has not yet come; and the time for information from the Latin writers of the last days of Roman greatness has gone by. That Beda took more than ordinary pains to obtain his information from his older cotemporaries we have seen; but we know-nothing of the sources on which *they* relied. The century and a half under notice is nearly destitute, not only of historical records, but of statements capable of either contradiction or confirmation. To say that nothing whatever can be found for the period would be an overstatement.

§ 24. Farther than this in the way of cotemporary evidence we cannot go. But Beda must also be considered as a geographer; for it is manifest that, in the following extract, there are two questions involved—viz. that of the particular Germans who came over to Britain, and that of the particular districts of Germany from which they came:—

Advenerant autem de tribus Germaniæ populis fortioribus, id est de Saxonibus, Anglis, Jutis. De Jutarum origine sunt Cantuarii et Vectuarii, hoc est ea gens quæ Vectam tenet insulam, et ea quæ usque hodie, in provincia Occidentalium Saxonum, Jutarum natio nominatur, posita contra ipsam insulam Vectam. De Saxonibus, id est ea regione quæ nunc Antiquorum Saxonum cognominatur, venere Orientales Saxones, Meridiani Saxones, Occidentales Saxones. Porro de Anglis, hoc est de illa patria quæ Angulus dicitur, et ab eo tempore usque hodie manere desertas inter provincias Jutarum et Saxonum perhibetur, Orientales Angli, Mediterranei Angli, Mercii, tota Northumbrorum progenies.

The extent to which these notices by Beda were recognized, not merely as sufficient but as standard authorities,

may be seen by their reappearance, in the same form, in
Alfred and elsewhere; even out of England. Nor were
there, until the tenth and eleventh centuries, the data for
criticizing them, even in the parts which were most open
to objection; these being the parts connected with the
geography of the Angle and Jute districts.

§ 25. That there may have been *Angles* in the *Angulus*
is not unlikely. But the *Angulus* of Beda is the present
district of Anglen, a nook of land, no larger than the county
of Rutland, lying on the *eastern* side of the duchy of Sles-
wick between the Slie and Flensburg. *Some* Angles may
have come from this district, but it would be wrong to treat
it as the true Angle part of Germany, when both Tacitus and
Ptolemy, our only authorities, place it on the middle Elbe.

The Jutes of Beda, in the opinion of the present writer,
were not Jutlanders from Denmark, but *Goths* from the
opposite coast of Gaul, then a powerful *Gothic* kingdom.

The chief point, however, in the comparison of the
evidence of Beda and that of the earlier writers, is the
extent to which one *excludes* the other. If the Saxons of
the times of the Hengists and Ellas are to be not only so
many Saxons on English ground, but so exclusively the
first of their nation as to justify us in putting constrained
constructions upon cotemporary texts, the criticism is sure
to become unduly one-sided; and that this one-sided character characterizes the early history of England throughout
few deny.

§ 26. *The Danes, or Northmen, in Britain.*—The importance of the Danish influence in England may be measured
by the trouble it created in the reigns of Alfred and his
successors, and the culmination of the Danish power in
that of Canute.

Who were the Danes? What was the date of their first
settlements? In what way have they affected our language? These are the questions that are more especially
connected with them.

In respect to the first, we may say that they were the Danes of Jutland and the Danish Isles. But they were this and a great deal more. They were the Danes of Denmark proper, and they were the Norwegians of Norway as well.

The date of their first recorded inroads is to be found in the Anglo-Saxon Chronicle, A.D. 787.

How far they have affected our language is the third question, and it is full of difficulties. It would be no difficult task to make lists of one, two, three, four, five, or even more, hundreds of words which are either Norwegian or Danish. But, unless it can be shown that they are not German, such lists would be worthless; and the proof upon this point is the proverbially difficult task of proving a negative proposition.

This, however, applies to *common* names only; with *proper* names it is different. The termination *-by*, in words like Grims*by*, &c., is a *Danish* word. *Caster*, in the place of *Chester*, is a Danish form. *Skip-*, *Carl*, *Orm-*, and *Kirk*, imply Danish occupancy. Hence, where the English parts of Britain give us Charl*ton*, Dor*chester*, *Shipton*, and *Wormshead*, the Danish forms are *Carlby*, *Ancaster*, *Skipton*, *Ormshead*, and *Ormskirk*. Any ordinary map supplies the list of these. They are the most numerous in Yorkshire, especially in the East and North Ridings; but Yorkshire is an inordinately large county. For its size, Lincolnshire gives us the most. Then, at a great distance, Leicester, Nottingham, Derby, and Northampton. We lose the word *by* in the south at Rug*by*, and on the north in Durham—Ra*by*. It is to be found, in patches, in Norfolk and Suffolk. Elsewhere, on the eastern side of England, they are either undiscovered or undiscoverable. From Yorkshire, however, they follow the western feeders of the Ouse to its watershed, which they cross, and then reappear in Cumberland, Westmoreland, Lancashire, Cheshire, the Isle of Man, and North Wales; at least in such names as *Orm's* Head.

c

In Ireland, we have a new instrument of criticism. In Carling*ford*, Strang*ford*, and Wex*ford*, the final syllable has not its ordinary import. It means an arm of the sea; in short, it is the Norwegian *Fjord*. And so it is in the *Firth* of *Forth* in Scotland. In this country the distribution of the *bys* is remarkable. We have it at Duncans*by* Head in the extreme north, and we have it in Eskdale and Annandale in the south-west. Otherwise the *bys* are exceptional. As *proper* names, these give us a long list. But they are not *common* names. They are all proper names, the names of geographical localities.

It may be expected that where we find these, we shall find *common* names also. But such is not the case. If true Danish common names exist in one part of Great Britain more than another, it is in Scotland; but that is just where the local names give us the fewest signs of Danish occupancy. This anomaly, however, has been explained. Mr. Worsaae, in his ' Danes and Northmen,' has shown that it is only the Danes of Denmark proper that exhibit this inordinate partiality for villages ending in -*by*, and that in Norway they are rare. In Iceland, pre-eminently a Norwegian colony, they are not to be found. The admitted inference is that it was Norwegians who assailed and circumnavigated *Scotland*, but Danes who assailed *England*; and, from the parts about Kirk*by* Lonsdale, &c., crossed the watershed, and gave us the numerous -*bys* of Cumberland and Selkirkshire.

This, at least, is the inference from the distribution of the termination. It is far more Danish than Norwegian, as may be seen from comparing a map of Iceland and Norway with one of Jutland or Denmark.

With this division in geography between the proper Danish and the Norwegian settlements, we no longer expect that, as a matter of course, they will agree in time. Lincolnshire is preeminently Danish.

In parts of Caithness, and the Orkneys, the language was Norwegian. In Shetland a Norse dialect was spoken in the last century.

§ 27. The earliest specimens of the English language, so far as they are dated at all, belong to the first half of the eighth century. They are known as the *Fragment of Ceadmon* and the *Death-bed Verses of Beda.*

Ceadmon was born at Whitby. The long and important poem which has come down to us in his name is in the *West-Saxon* dialect; and this has engendered the notion that the original has been lost and re-cast. The following lines, however, which have been preserved by Beda, are admitted to be genuine; for of Beda Ceadmon was an early cotemporary.

Older Text.			*Later Text.*
Nu scylun hergan	.	.	Nu we sceolon herigean
Hefaen ricaes uard	.	.	Heofon-rices weard
Metudæs mæcte	.	.	Metodes mihte
End his modgithanc	.	.	And his modgethanc
Uerc uuldur fader	.	.	Werc wuldor fæder
Sue he uundra gihuaes	.	.	Sva he wuldres gehwæs
Eci drihten	.	.	Ecê drihtin
Ord stelidæ	.	.	Ord onstealde
He ærist scopa	.	.	He ærest scóp
Elda barnum	.	.	Eorðan bearnan
Heben til hrofe	.	.	Heofon tó rofe
Halig sceper	.	.	Hálig scyppend
Tha middun-geard	.	.	Da middangeard
Moncynnes uard	.	.	Moncynnes weard
Eci drihten	.	.	Ece drihten
Æfter tiade	.	.	Æfter teóde
Firum foldu	.	.	Firum foldan
Frea allmectig	.	.	Freá ælmihtig.

The Death-bed Verses of Beda.

Fore the neidfaerae	.	.	Before the necessary journey
Naenig uuirthit	.	.	No one becomes
Thoc snottura	.	.	Wiser of thought
Than him tharf sie	.	.	Than him need be
To ymbhycganne	.	.	To think about
Aer his hionongae	.	.	Before his hence-going
Huaet his gastae	.	.	What for his spirit
Godaes æththa yflaes	.	.	Of good or evil
Æfter deothdaege	.	.	After death-day
Dœmed uuieorthae	.	.	Doomed shall be.

These, however, partly from their shortness, and partly from their containing few of the inflections which give us the best characteristics of the Northern dialect, are of more importance in the history of Anglo-Saxon Literature in general than as specimens of any particular dialect: though the dialect of both Beda and Ceadmon was the *Northern* or *Northumbrian*.

§ 28. That this Northumbrian dialect was the first cultivated is probable. By the end, however, of the Ninth Century, it is, as compared with the West-Saxon, obsolete as a vehicle of literature. Nearly all that we know of it is from *Glosses*. Of these:

1. The Glosses of the *Rushworth Gospels* are referred to the end of the Ninth or the beginning of the Tenth Century.

2. The Glosses of the *Durham or Lindisfarn Gospels*.

3. The Glosses of the *Durham Ritual*.

4. Inscriptions in Runic characters near Ruthwell in Dumfriesshire, and Bewcastle in Cumberland.

5. Glosses on the *Psalms*—known as the '*Psalter*,' but not universally admitted to be *Northumbrian*.

§ 29. For nearly the whole of the eleventh, twelfth, and thirteenth centuries no specimens of any dialect north of the Humber are known: yet the Northern boundary of Northumberland is, not the Tyne, but the Forth. After, however, an interval of 300 years it will, again, appear in the County of Durham. The Northern Version of the '*Cursor Mundi*' is a valuable specimen of a literature which is common in the Old English period, viz., an adaptation of the dialect of one part of England to that of another part. We can scarcely call works of this kind translations, yet they are more than mere transcriptions. The work under notice is one of these; and that without doubt, since the author expressly tells us as much.

> In a writte this ilke I fand
> Himself it wroght, I understand,
> In suthron Englys was it drawn,

And I have turned it till urr awn
Language of the Northern lede,
That can non other Englis rede.—*Cursor Mundi.*

This, for its date and place, is easy to read: in other
words it is very modern. But it is also very Scotch. Indeed, the classical time of the true national literature of
Scotland is now about to begin. During the Thirteenth
Century, however, the Northumbrian dialect of the middle
period will still continue to be represented by compositions
from the district between the Tyne and Humber, rather
than between the Tweed and Forth. I write between the
'Tweed and Forth,' rather than between the 'Tyne and
Forth,' because, in the way of records, Northumberland, as
the *County* so called, contributes little or nothing. Yorkshire belongs to the old Northumberland; and of this
Durham is the representative County. This means, of course,
that what is here treated as Northumbrian English is, to a
great extent, Lowland Scotch. To distinguish this from the
present Gaelic of the Highlands, the Scotch themselves
called their language *English*; and that during the Fifteenth Century; when, as far as politics and nationality went,
the difference between the Scotch and the English was a
matter of life and death. At the time of the Reformation
the word *Scotch* took its present meaning—not much before.

A little later than the Cursor Mundi in its Northern
form comes Hampole's Pricke of Conscience, along with
other works by the same writer. These represent the
Northumbrian of Yorkshire, for the parts about Doncaster,
and they are quite as Modern, and English, and quite as
North British, or Scotch, as the Cursor Mundi.

§ 30. With the Fourteenth Century begins the classical
time of North British literature; English by name, Scotch
in reality. This is introduced by James I., the cotemporary
of Henry IV. in England. Dunbar, who divides with
Burns the honour of being the great poet of Scotland,
continues it; and it is further continued till the times of

the Reformation, by Gawain Douglass and Sir Thomas
Lyndesay; but it begins to be called *English*. After this it is
Scotch, more or less Anglicised. Wyntoun, Blind Harry,
and Barbour, are early cotemporaries of James the First.
No known Scotch *manuscript* is older than 1397.

The Northumbrian dialect has been considered at
length, because it has certain perplexing peculiarities of its
own. It begins early, but it breaks off early. It then
presents us with a long blank. It then comes to its climax
of cultivation in the fifteenth century; after which it
begins (in Scotland) to be Anglicised. Moreover, though
it is in politics, nationality, and geography Scotch, it is
called, and is, *English*.*

§ 31. *The West-Saxon Dialect.*—This, as the dominant
and classical language of the times before the Norman
Conquest, began with the latter half of the ninth century.
The few examples of our earliest English that go further
back have been noticed already, and they were Northumbrian rather than West-Saxon, though not in a very decided
form. Rich as the West-Saxon is in detail, the greater
part of its literature is dateless and anonymous. But two
great names represent it, those of Alfred and Ælfric.

Its ascendancy begins with the reign of Alfred. It ends
in wholly displacing the Northumbrian. It is continued with
diminished lustre till the thirteenth century, when we first
meet with undoubted *Midland*, or Mercian, compositions.
It is continued through the thirteenth and fourteenth
centuries, concurrently, however, with the Northumbrian
and Midland. It passes into the condition of a provincial
form of speech about A.D. 1550, or, to speak more generally, at the time when the two new influences of the
Printing Press and the Reformation came into action.

---

* All the complications connected with the thorough *English* character of the *Northumbrian English* of the *South of Scotland* are
admirably unravelled in Dr. Murray's *Dialect of the Southern Counties
of Scotland*, 1873.

The West-Saxon chief works of the thirteenth and the earlier part of the fourteenth centuries are :—

Layamon's Brut ; from Worcestershire, or the Worcestershire and the Gloucestershire border.

The Ancren Riwle ; from Wiltshire.

Robert of Gloucester ; from Gloucestershire.

Trevisa, a cotemporary of Chaucer's, is also West-Saxon in its original form. But when Caxton reprints his work, he has to adapt it to the current form of speech ; though not to any very great extent.

Chaucer is West-Saxon (we may now say Western) ; at least as opposed to Northumbrian.

There are other West-Saxon writers of this period of less importance. But one work is of special importance. It was written in Canterbury A.D. 1340. It shows that, though Kent is the most eastern county south of the Thames, its dialect was *Western*. The *Ayenbit of Inwit*, or *Remorse of Conscience*, is its title. It is, doubtless, to some extent, a provincial, rather than a classical, composition. The spelling, however, makes it look more provincial than it really is ; for it is that of the present provincial spelling for Devonshire : *i.e.* with *z* and *v* for *s* and *f*.

§ 32. *The Midland, or Mercian, Dialect.*—The *Ormulum* is the work of a writer named Orm ; and this points to the Danish parts of England.

Havelok the Dane does the same. Neither are either strictly West-Saxon or strictly Northumbrian. But the Mercian, or Midland, characteristics are of a negative rather than a positive character.

Robert of Bourne was a native of Lincolnshire. He is a cotemporary of Robert of Gloucester and of Hampole, so that the three together represent the three dialects, now written concurrently. They all belong to the reigns of Henry III. and Edward I., *i.e.* the beginning of the fifteenth century.

What the Midland, or Mercian, literature more espe-

cially resembles (for we have already remarked that its
characters are negative, and may now add that its geographical position is intermediate between the two extremes)
is the literary, classical, or standard English of the present
time; though as a standard literary language it does not
take its place until later.

This is only another way of saying that the present
literary English is not the lineal descendant of the classical
West-Saxon. And we may go further. We may add that it is
less like the West-Saxon than it is like the Northumbrian,
but it is not Northumbrian. It is Midland or Mercian.

§ 33. These three leading dialects have each their own
history. With the dialects of Shropshire, Cheshire, Lancashire, Westmoreland, Cumberland, and the West Riding of
Yorkshire this is not the case. None of them have ever become classical. Neither is their relation to the other three
groups manifest. Nor should we expect it to be so. It varies
with the frontier. They have been called *West Midland*.
The name, however, is merely provisional. It is only certain
that they have mixed and heterogeneous characteristics.

§ 34. It is customary to cast the English language into
chronological divisions, or, as they are called, *Stages*. At
first the process began with the broad distinction between the
times of Alfred and his immediate successors, and those of
the modern writer. This made to some extent the Anglo-
Saxon one language, and the ordinary English another.
The difference, however, was that the former was what is
called a Dead, the other a Living language. But where the
history of a language, and indeed the language itself, is continuous, the distinction between the two vanishes. No one
who bestows any thought upon the subject can imagine that
because one language is called Dead and the other Living,
or because one is called Anglo-Saxon and the other English,
they are different languages in the way that Latin differs from
the German, or the German from the French. The English
of the present time is simply the Anglo-Saxon in a later,

the Anglo-Saxon the English in an earlier form or stage. Nevertheless, the fact that the one is understood at once, while the other has to be learned, is a fact that conveys (along with a considerable amount of likeness) a difference of some kind or other. It is not, however, the difference between two parallel and distinct languages.

As languages begin to be studied in their intermediate stages, this difference ceases to be felt; and when any notable changes take place, divisions and sub-divisions suggest themselves, and *stages* of a language are the result.

When this takes place there will always be two questions. Where is the division to be made? and what is the name to be applied to it? It is too much to expect that any line of demarcation, or any series of names, can be wholly satisfactory, or wholly permanent. The characteristics by which one stage is determined may change their value; or new principles of division may be established. There is, beyond all doubt, a tendency to change either the actual divisions, or the names which indicate them (one or both) at the present time.

§ 35. The divisions and names, however, which were adopted by the scholars of the last generation should be known; and, whether they are to be upheld or rejected, the principles upon which they were given should be understood. These were—

1. The *Anglo-Saxon* stage, from the earliest known compositions, of English origin, to the Norman Conquest and a little beyond it.

2. The *Semi-Saxon.*—Middle of the 11th to the middle of the 12th century (there or thereabouts).

3. *The Old English.*—This means the English of the latter part of the reign of Henry III., and the reign of the first two Edwards (there or thereabouts).

4. *The Middle English.*—From Chaucer to the time of Henry VIII. (there or thereabouts).

5. *The New, or Recent, or Modern English.*—From Henry

VIII. (say Sir Thomas More) to the time at which the divisions were suggested.

Of these terms, *Semi-Saxon* is the newest.

§ 36. We may approve of these or we may not; but, as they are still current, we must understand them. Otherwise there will not be a work on English philology of ten years' standing that we shall be able to read with ease.

We must know, too, how certain works, especially for the three middle periods, are to be distributed.

§ 37. The first important composition which is called transitional or Semi-Saxon is *the concluding part of the Anglo-Saxon Chronicle*—especially the reign of Stephen, the last of the kings it contains. This is reasonably referred to the earlier part of the reign of his successor Henry II. But it is a difficult work to fix. In the first, it may be somewhat more Anglo-Saxon than it would be were it not the continuation of a genuine Anglo-Saxon composition. In the second, it is considered to be, to some extent, Mercian rather than pure West-Saxon.

Layamon's Brut.—*West*-Saxon (as we have seen) in dialect, *Semi*-Saxon in date.

The Ancren Riwle.—West-Saxon (as aforesaid) in dialect, *Semi*-Saxon in date.

The Ormulum.—Mercian in dialect, generally considered *Semi*-Saxon in date. It has been thought by some that its language is too modern for the antiquity assigned to it. The modern character, however, may be due less to date than to the dialect.

§ 38. *Of Old English*, as opposed to *Semi-Saxon*, the *Proclamation of Henry III. to the People of Huntingdonshire* passes for the earliest specimen. The date is 1258.

The following are the titles of the more important ones. They are selected from a Glossary* especially dedi-

---

* *A Glossarial Index to the Printed English Language of the Thirteenth Century.* Published by the Philological Society. Edited by H. Coleridge. 1859.

cated to English of the *thirteenth* century; which shows how decidedly the term *Old English* excludes the *Semi-Saxon* on one side, and English of Chaucer's time on the other.

Havelok the Dane	The Owl and Nightingale
The Early English Psalter	Robert of Gloucester, &c.

Havelok the Dane is Mercian; the Early English Psalter is Northumbrian. The rest are chiefly Western.

§ 39. This division is very artificial; and it is not likely that it will be permanent. Neither will the term *Old English* as applied to it: inasmuch as those who disapprove of the word *Anglo-Saxon* propose the word *Old English* as its substitute. However, the Proclamation to the Men of Huntingdonshire gave a convenient date; while the scantiness of our literature in the reign of Edward II. made the conclusion of the division pretty definite. This is about all that can be said in favour of it.

§ 40. *Middle English.*—This division, so far as it gives us such writers as Chaucer and Mandeville in contrast to Robert of Gloucester and Layamon, is natural; and it is probable that, as Chaucer is read by the English of the present period, the division is a convenient one. But when Chaucer dies, England, as compared with Scotland, is, at least, on the decline. The time of the three Henrys is one when the West-Saxon has ceased to represent the Anglo-Saxon period, and when the Midland has yet to become the literary English of the present time. For the time of the four Henrys (or that of the five Jameses), the best middle English is the English of Scotland. This is doubtless compatible with the use of the term; but it was not the meaning that was given to it by the scholars who originally applied it.

§ 41. It is probable that this arrangement will not satisfy many of my readers—least of all those who have gone through the preceding remarks on the Dialects of our language. Indeed, more than thirty years ago it was complained of by the earlier investigators of them; and now, when each of our three leading dialects is acknowledged to have a corresponding literary language, the impropriety of massing them together as one, and treating them as uniform in their continuity, is manifest.

§ 42. What we know of the English *in general* is that it is the mother-tongue of three well-marked forms of speech out of which three literary languages have grown. One of these is the West-Saxon, one the Scotch, and one the present literary English. There is also a fourth class of indefinite limits, but which has never culminated in a literary language; viz., that of the north-western counties of South Britain. Each of those has its peculiar and proper history, which may or may not be susceptible of divisions in the way of growth or development.* But the stages of the *three* cannot be dealt with as if they were *one*.

§ 43. Still we know something akin to the stages of our language in general. We know that there are certain epochs at which the language in mass of the whole island was, or might be, affected.

Such a one is the time from the reign of Diocletian, at the end of the third century, to the middle of the fifth, when we know that some Germans of some sort or other had set foot in our island.

Such a one is the time from the middle of the fifth century to the beginning of the seventh, when the history of our language was a blank. But we know that it was to a great extent German.

Such a one was the time from A.D. 600 to the death of Beda; for which we have a few lines in English, and these we know belong to the *northern* rather than to the *southern* form of speech.

Such a one is the time from the death of Beda to that

* For the characteristics of the Middle English Dialect, see Dr. Morris's *Specimens of Early English*, and Prefaces to his Editions in the 'Early English Text Society.'

of Alfred, where we know that the northern literature is declining. Under Alfred and his successors the classical *West-Saxon* literature was formed. But a fresh influence was introduced by the Norman Conquest.

§ 44. From the Norman Conquest to the death of Richard II. there is a period out of which many subordinate stages may be made. There are the reigns of the two Williams, Stephen, Henry II., Richard, and John, in which the West-Saxon still is the predominating dialect; but there is very little of it. Then, under Henry III., there are compositions other than West-Saxon. Those that are Northumbrian are representatives of an old, though diminished literature in a new shape after a long arrest. Hence we have the Northumbrian form of speech re-appearing, but with no continuity in its history.

There are, also, Midland dialects, which are represented in this century, but they have no anterior history.

Meanwhile the West-Saxon declines.

For this period there is no continuity for any one of the forms of speech of which the English language consists; nor can we expect one of the language in general.

§ 45. In the Fifteenth Century—under the three Henrys —the English Language is no longer represented by the West-Saxon, but by the Northumbrian of Scotland; which is itself destined to be displaced by the Mercian of the middle district of England.

Upon both of these the Invention of Printing acts as an influence of inordinate power, and brings us to something like the present English. But this is the history of a third form of speech, in the history of which the Northumbrian and West-Saxon forms of speech are left out of sight.

§ 46. '*Anglo-Saxon*' *as opposed to* '*Old English.*'— '*Anglo-Saxon*' has till within the last half century been used generally, and perhaps universally, as the name for that stage of the English Language which preceded the Norman Conquest.

It has meant the English of England in its oldest known form, and it has meant nothing more. That it has denoted a different language from the most modern form of the present language has never been imagined. But, of late, there has arisen the opinion that it has a tendency to engender the notion that the Anglo-Saxon is one language, and the English another; or, at least, that it is a term which disguises the identity and the continuity of the two. It is difficult for a mere looker-on to say how far this error ·is real, or how far imaginary; whether it is held by the many or the few; and finally whether it is held by those whose obliquity of understanding need be humoured. It is certain, however, that no small amount of attention has been paid to the question; and that the claims of the term 'Old English' have been advocated with some learning, and with much zeal.

As early as 1852 a writer in the Gentleman's Magazine (April and May) proposed the following change : that—

1. From A.D. 550 to 1150 the Language should be called *Old* English.
2.   „   1150 to 1350   „   „   *Early* English.
3.   „   1350 to 1550   „   „   *Middle* English.
4.   „   1550 to 1852   „   „   *New* English.

That the use of the term *Anglo-Saxon* in its *original* sense has any chance of being abandoned, is, in the opinion of the present writer, improbable. Its original sense was the 'Saxon of *England*' as opposed to the 'Saxon of *Germany*;' and this last is called *Old* Saxon, or the language *Antiquorum* Saxonum, by Beda himself. Paulus Diaconus uses *Anglo-Saxon* for the *Saxon of England*.

As the name of the English of Alfred and Ælfric— the classical or standard English of the times before the Norman Conquest—it can be more easily dispensed with; and so it can for the few extant remains of the *Northern* dialect. For these the terms *West-Saxon* and *Northumbrian* may be used with advantage; and Kemble, for one influen-

tial writer, has already used them.   For the *Midland*
dialects the word has never been used; inasmuch as there
are no early Midland compositions.

§ 47. But, besides this, there is the new term *Semi-
Saxon*. The class itself being divided between two different
dialects (for the Ormulum is Mercian, while the other two
are West-Saxon), is so little likely to be permanent that
the merits of the name scarcely claim investigation.

That the term *Anglo-Saxon* will always be opposed to
Old Saxon is probable; and it is also probable that, where
the more special terms West-Saxon or Northumbrian are
unsuitable, it will hold its ground as the most convenient
term in numerous general and indefinite questions. What
these are is best known to those who have to investigate
them.

When the matter is thus put in the simple form of a
question of convenience, there should not be much to say
about the comparative merits of the two terms in the
abstract. That the existing name for the language is
English is beyond doubt; but whether it is applicable to
every stage and form of the language represented by the
occupants of South Britain is a matter on which the Scotch
and Americans, not to mention the philologists, have something to say.

That the Lowland Scotch was called English in the
fifteenth century to distinguish it from the Gaelic of the
Highlands we know; but we also know that it is not
called *English* now.

Semi-Saxon is, in my mind, a useful word. It certainly
favours the notion that *Anglo*-Saxon is more of a different
language from the current English than it really is; but, on
the other hand, it indicates the connection between the two.
It also gives us the first undoubted instance of a Non-
West-Saxon composition (the Ormulum) interfering with
the predominance of the *West*-Saxon. The period itself,
too, is a convenient one. It is separated from the *concluding*

part of the Anglo-Saxon Chronicle by the whole reign of
Henry II.; and it contains, at least, three works of bulk
and importance with well-marked transitional characters.

There is another period, also, which is certainly more
natural than either the *Old* or the *Middle* English : the reign
of the three Henrys; or the interval between the brilliant
reign of Edward III. and the Invention of Printing. It
coincides with a marked decline of English, and a rapid
culmination of the Scotch. It begins with the deaths of
Chaucer and Gower; the latter of whom is the last writer
who composed a work of any magnitude in French. It
coincides with a decided preponderance of Northumbrian
and Mercian compositions over West-Saxon.

§ 48. The English as a member of a family of languages
is only one of a large group.

Of the allied forms of speech on the Continent, the *Old*
Saxon of Westphalia is the nearest. Only, however, so far
as it is known; and this is but imperfectly. The Old Saxon
should be compared with the English in its West-Saxon form.

Next to this comes the *Frisian*. This we know in three
stages—the Old, the Middle, and the New. It is only the
Old Frisian and the Old English that need be compared.
Any one who can read the English of the times before the
Norman Conquest can read the Old Frisian. It is more
like the *Northumbrian* English than the West-Saxon. Where
it differs from the West-Saxon, it, in many points, agrees
with the Norse or Scandinavian. This is what we expect
from its geographical position.

The *Norse* or *Scandinavian* includes the literary languages
of Denmark and Sweden, with their several dialects. It is
best represented in its oldest form by the Icelandic. The
Feroic of the Farö Isles belongs to this class. The affinities
between the Norse and the Frisian, and of both with the
Northumbrian of Great Britain, have introduced many complicated questions in the history of the English in general;
especially in reference to the Northern dialects.

§ 49. The Old Saxon area is bounded by the Frisian and Danish on the North and West, and by the *High German* on the South and East.

This means that the Old Saxon is *Low* German. It lies nearest to the *Dutch* of the Netherlands, and to the *Platt-Deutsch* dialects of Northern Germany.

The present literary language of Germany, or the High German, is less closely allied to the English than the *Platt-Deutsch* forms of speech.

All these forms of speech are divided into stages; and it is in their oldest stages that they are most advantageously compared with the English in *its* oldest stage—Northumbrian or *West-Saxon*, as the case may be.

§ 50. The Norse differs from the languages of Germany Proper and England by having a Passive Voice, and what is called a *Post*-positive Article. Thus:—*a. En* Sol is *a* sun. Sol-*en*—*the* sun. *Et* Bord is *a* table. Bord-*et*—*the* table.

This is not a mere *transposition* of the same Article. The *Indefinite en* is the Numeral; *et* is its Neuter form. The Definite Danish *en* is the English *he*; *et* is the English *it* (*hit*), *i.e.* the Masculine and Neuter forms of the Demonstrative Pronoun.

b. Jeg kall*e*=*I call.* Jeg kalle-*s*=*I am called* ;—as voco and voc*or* in Latin.   The final *s* is the Reflective Pronoun *sik*, abbreviated and incorporated.

§ 51. *The Mœsogothic.*—There is another branch of the German family which, notwithstanding the opinion that it is to be classed as *Low* German, I prefer to place in a class by itself. Of its importance there can be no doubt.

It is the oldest of all the German forms of speech: for it was written as early as the last quarter of the 4th century. This applies to the mere date of the earliest specimens of it.

It is equally the oldest if we look to its structure.

But it is known in one stage only. It begins with the

D

Fourth Century, and by the end of the Seventh every vestige
of it has disappeared.   There is no dialect throughout the
whole of Germany of which we can say, 'This is a modern,
or middle form of the Gothic ;' for so the language under
notice is named—Gothic or Mœsogothic.

Moreover it has never been definitely and unanimously
traced to the soil of Germany.   It is German, but in what
part of Germany it originated no one knows.   At least
there is no unanimity of opinion.

Nevertheless, it is the representative of the German
Language in its oldest form, and there is no language in
the German family which can be explained in some of its
important details in the way of Inflection without a reference to it.

Such is a sketch of its general character, and such the
reasons for giving it what at first may appear an undue
prominence.

What we know of its external history is as follows :—

At the beginning of the Third century a German population was known on the northern side of the Lower Danube,
in what was then called the Province of Dacia; now the
Danubian Principalities, or Wallachia, Moldavia, and
Bessarabia.   The Goths became formidable to the Romans.
They crossed the Danube, and invaded the north-eastern
provinces of the Empire.   They defeated the Emperor Decius
in a great battle.   They ravaged the coasts of Greece and
Asia Minor.   They continued formidable ; and the Province
of Dacia, to the North of the Danube, was surrendered by
the Emperor Aurelian to the so-called Barbarians.   Here
the Goths establish a Kingdom ; and we know, in respect to
its geography, that the valley of the river Dniester belonged
to it :—that it was probably the central part of it.   They
break up into two divisions—each with three names.   They
were called Ostrogoths or Visigoths from their geographical
positions; Amalungs or Baltungs from the name of the
royal dynasty ; and Grutungs or Thervings from the names

by which they seem to have designated themselves. However, collectively, they are called, by the Romans, Goths.

In the last quarter of the fourth century they cross the Danube; nominally by permission of the Romans, but actually as a nation of warriors going forth to conquer. By A.D. 412 they have sacked Rome under Alaric; and initiated one Kingdom in France, and another in Spain. This division is that of the *Visigoths*.

In the latter half of the century the Ostrogoths, under *Theodoric*, make themselves masters of Italy.

But, though conquerors in three countries, they lose their language in all. It is smothered (so to say) by the Latin of the three conquered countries.

They are never heard of, from first to last, in Germany.

By the end of the Fourth Century these Goths were converted to Christianity—the Christianity of the Greek Church and of the Arian heresy.

This conversion was accompanied by a translation of the Scriptures: the Alphabet being founded on the *Greek*.

Of the translation, dating from the last quarter of the Fourth Century, we have remains, viz., the greater part of the Four Gospels.

The particular division of these Goths who seem by their conversion to have been transformed from warriors into peaceful villagers, settled in a district near Philippopolis in the Roman Province of *Mœsia*. The translation of their Scriptures is attributed to their Bishop, Ulphilas.

Hence, *Mœsogothic*, or the language of their *Ulphiline Gospels*, is the ordinary name for the chief fragment (the most important, though not the only one) of the language of these great Gothic conquerors.

§ 52. Its exact place in the classification of the German forms of speech is of less importance than the structure of their language.

1. It has a sign for the Nominative case; like the Greek and Latin. The Old High German and the Ice-

landic have the same.   But it is wanting elsewhere.   However, in both the High German and the Icelandic the sign
is -r.   In Mœsogothic it is the older form -s.

2. It has a reduplicate Perfect Tense also, like the
Latin and Greek.

3. It has a Passive Voice.   So have the Scandinavian
languages.   But this (as aforesaid) is really a Middle,
which was originally a Reflective.

§ 53. The German Class, although so large and compre-
hensive, is itself but a single member of a large Class,
Group, Family, or Order: the oldest name for which was
Indo-Germanic; the next in order Indo-European; the
newest Aryan.

Of this group there are, at least, five divisions besides
the German which are referred to, as a matter of course, in
all works upon any German language; and, *vice versa*, works
upon the Slavonic, Lithuanic, Latin, Greek, or Sanskrit
refer to the German.   These members of the Indo-European Class not only mutually illustrate each other, but are
so frequently used in illustration that even in so special
a work as the present they must be noticed.   About the
exact dimensions, however, of the class nothing will be said.
There are certain points connected with it upon which
there is no absolute unanimity of opinion.   Upon the place
of the six groups under notice there is no doubt whatever.

§ 54. *The Slavonic.*—The Slavonic division is represented
by the Russian and the Polish, as the languages of which
the general reader hears most.   But the *native* language
of Bohemia, the *Czekh* (pronounced *Tshekh*), as it is called
in opposition to the Germans, is one that has, of late years,
greatly risen in both political and literary importance.   Then
comes the *Servian*, from which, notwithstanding the close
geographical contact, we must separate the *Bulgarian*, which
is a very well marked form of speech.   Like the Russian
and the Servian, it is written in an alphabet of Greek origin.
To the languages of this division belongs the *Old* Slavonic,

or the language in which the first translation of the Scriptures was made. The Servian language is one that is not so definitely divided from the Russian on one side, and the Slavonic dialects of the Austrian Empire, as the other languages of the family are from each other; and when we trace the Servian of the Eastern Church westwards, we find that the division is political rather than philological. The alphabet, however, of the Austrian Slavonic is of Roman, as opposed to Greek, origin. The Austrian provinces here under notice are Istria, Dalmatia, Carniola, and Carinthia. In the two latter the people call themselves Slovenzi (or *Slovenians*), and this word may be used for the whole group, though from its resemblance to *Slavonic* it is not a convenient one. These Slovenians to the south of the Baltic must not be confounded with the *Slovaks* and *Ruthenians* of Upper Hungary and Gallicia. The *Slovak* is a form of the Tshekh (Bohemian) of Moravia; the *Ruthenian* is Russian.

Besides these languages there are two others which, like the Cornish of Cornwall in the last century, are mere fragments of an older language; which in the ninth century was spoken over the whole of the districts to which they belong. The first is the *Sorb*, or *Sorabian*, of Lusatia and part of Brandenburg, falling into two dialects. The second is the *Kassubic*, spoken in a few villages of the eastern part of Pomerania. This is wholly separated from the great area of the rest of the family.

Lastly, there was spoken in the last century, in the parts about Kostrow, Lüchow, and Danneberg, a fragment of the old Slavonic of the Duchy of Lunenburg.

§ 55. *The Lithuanic Language.*—This class falls into divisions: (1) the Lithuanic, and (2) the Let.

(1.) In the fifteenth century the Lithuanic language extended as far westwards as the Vistula, so that *East Prussia*, at least, was Lithuanic. Of the Lithuanic of East Prussia, or the *old* Prussian, we have only a Catechism, the Lord's Prayer, and Creed, dating from the time of the

Reformation. The great centre of the Lithuanic language at present is Samogitia, or the Russian Government of Kovno. The next great Lithuanic occupancy is the north-eastern part of East.Prussia, the parts about Insterburg, Gumbinnen, and Tilsit. There are also fragments of the language in the governments of Vilna, Vitepsk, Polotsk, and Grodno.

(2.) Courland, Livonia, and parts of Estonia are the Let districts.

§ 56. *The Latin Family.*—Important as is the Latin in itself, it is still more so in its descendants; for the Latin is the mother-tongue of the following forms of speech.

The *Italian*; of which some of the dialects are *philologically* languages, e.g., the Sardinian, and more than one of the Piedmontese dialects.

Of the *Languages of the Spanish Peninsula* the chief are the Spanish and the Portuguese; but between these as *languages*, the difference is political rather than philological. Meanwhile the form of speech in Catalonia and Valencia is provincial rather than either Spanish Proper, or Castilian, or Portuguese.

The French.—Politically this includes all the so-called dialects of France; but the Provençal of the south is, philologically, a different language from the true French of the north.

The *Rumanyo.*—This is the language of the Danubian provinces (Wallachia and Moldavia), Bessarabia, and parts of Transylvania and Buckovinia, *i.e.*, the old Roman province of Dacia.

The *Romance*, Rumonsch, of the Grison districts in Switzerland.

§ 57. *The Greek.*—Upon this it is not necessary to enlarge. In its modern form it is called the *Romaic.*

§ 58. *The Sanskrit.*—This is the literary and religious language of *Brahminical* India: the literary and religious language of the *Buddhists* of Ceylon, Burma, Siam, Pegu,

Cambojia, and Tibet being the *Pali*, a closely allied form of speech. The *Zend*, or language of the Zendavesta, the great canonical book of the old Persian creed, is another member of this group. From the antiquity of its structure, and from the richness of its literature, a very high value is put upon the Sanskrit. Its form, or stage, is that of a language of great antiquity, and so is that of the Pali and Zend. Upon the extent to which this class illustrates the change from an older stage to a newer, there has of late risen a difference of opinion; and it is clear that the matter is an important one. Is the Sanskrit a language like the Latin, the Greek, or the English, which we can trace through a long series of periods and point to certain recent forms of speech as its lineal descendants, or is it a language, like the Mœsogothic, that ends in the same condition as it begins, with no lineal descendants, or no languages that stand to it in the same relation as the English to the Anglo-Saxon, or the Italian to the Latin ? Are the existing languages of Northern India derivatives of the Sanskrit, like the French from the Latin, or are they languages of a different origin into which an inordinate amount of Sanskrit elements has been introduced ? The older opinion, and the opinion at present of a decided majority, is in favour of the former of these views; that of a recent and comparatively small minority is in favour of the second. In the present work it is sufficient to speak of this very important class as constituted by the *'Sanskrit and its derived languages, whatever they may be.'*

§ 59. Something has been said about the original languages of Britain as opposed to the alien language introduced from Germany; and more would have been said if the work were a larger one. Something, too, has been said about the language of the Roman conquerors who held the island for upwards of four hundred years. With both these the Germans, or English, came in contact. What came of this contact ? What was the action and re-action between the languages thus brought side by side ? Was it

much or little? Was it attended with intermixture of blood?
If so, to what extent? It is well known that on this point
there are extreme opinions, and that some of them run far
beyond the domain of philology. Are we a mixed race? Were
we conquered wholly, or only half denationalized? Does
our language help us in the investigation? If it do, what
does it tell us? This is a question with which the present
work has, fortunately, little to do. Upon the character,
however, of the language which resulted, either through
or in spite of the contact, there is but one opinion. The
English is not an equivocal or ambiguous language; it is
not Keltic and German mixed in such proportions as to
make its character indefinite. It is, in this respect, scarcely
a mixed language at all. Nothing short of the minutest
philology can trace any Keltic element in it. It contains
much that is not German. But this is not Keltic; and
neither the other extraneous elements nor the Keltic besides
can make the speech of England other than English—and
English means German.

PART II.

ORTHOÉPY AND ORTHOGRAPHY.

§ 60. In *speaking*, we represent our ideas and thoughts by means of *words*; which words are composed of certain elementary *sounds*. In the word *go* there are two such; in the word *got*, three; and so on. As long as we limit ourselves to speaking, these elementary sounds are all that require notice. They address themselves to the *ear*.

They are capable, however, of being represented by certain signs called *letters*; by which we are enabled not only to speak, but to *write*. Letters address themselves to the *eye*. In the word *go* the letter *g* is the sign of its first, the letter *o* the sign of its second, sound.

Orthoépy signifies the right *utterance* of words. It deals with language as it is *spoken*, and determines how a word is to be *pronounced*. *Orthography* signifies the right use of *letters*. It deals with language as it is *written*, and determines how words should be *spelt*.

All languages were spoken long before they were written; and, at the present moment, there are numerous forms of speech which have never been reduced to writing at all. Hence, letters come later than the sounds they express, and orthography is subordinate to orthoépy.

But as a picture never exactly represents the object from which it is taken, so the orthography of a language never exactly represents the orthoépy; in other words, there is always some difference between language as it is spoken and language as it is written. Sometimes there are more

sounds than letters. Sometimes words change their pronunciation as they pass from one people or from one generation to another; whilst no corresponding change is made
in the manner of writing them. Sometimes fresh sounds
from other languages are introduced; and, as no fresh
letters are brought to represent them, they must be represented, as they best may, by the letters already in use.

§ 61. The elementary sounds in the English language as
at present spoken are as follows :—

Vowels.—*A.*—1. The sound of the letter *a* in *ah, father,*
&c.

2. The sound of the letter *a* in *fate, bate, ale, pale, bait,
ail, snake, snail,* &c.

3. The sound of the letter *a* in *fat, pat, bat, that, hat,
patting,* &c.

E.—4. The sound of the *e* in *bed, beck, less, net, netting,*
&c.—This is a short quick sound. It is expressed by the
letter *e.*

I.—5. The sound of the *e* in *feet, need, seed, seek, leak,
seat, beat,* &c.—This sound is often considered as allied to
the preceding one and as a long variety of it. It is, however, the long form of the vowel sound next about to be
mentioned; namely,

6. The sound of the *i* in *tin, pity, pitted, stick, kick,* &c.—
This sound is often considered as allied to the sound of *i* in
pine, shine, &c., and as a shortened variety of it. It is, however, a shortened form of the sound of *e* in *feet.*

U.—7. The sound of the *oo* in *cool,* and of the *o* in *move,
prove.*

8. The sound of the *u* in *bull, full, pull,* &c.—Although
these two last-mentioned sounds are expressed in spelling
by different letters, they are evidently allied in utterance.
They are both varieties of one and the same sound, pronounced rapidly in the one case, and slowly in the other.
The two sounds bear the same relation to each other as the
a in *fate* bears to the *a* in *fat,* and the *ee* in *feet* to the *i* in
fit.

O.—9. The sound of the *aw* in *bawl*, of the *au* in *haul*, and of the *a* in *hall*, *all*, *talk*, &c.—This sound is generally expressed by the letter *a*, either alone, as in *all* and *ball*, or combined with some other letter, as in *haul* and *bawl*. The expression, however, is faulty, and conceals the true nature of the sound. Its real relation is to the two sounds that will next be mentioned, to which it stands in the same relation that the *a* in *father* does to the *a* in *fate* and the *a* in *fat*.

10. The sound of the *o* in *note*, *boat*, *float*, *no*, *so*, &c.

11. The sound of the *o* in *not*, *knot*, *knotty*, &c.

12. The sound of the *u* in *but*, *nut*, &c.

Semi-Vowels.—13. The sound of the letter *w* in *wo*, *will*. —This sound is evidently allied to the sound of the *oo* in *cool*. Some writers consider it identical, and assert that the words *will* and *oo-il* are sounded alike. It is, however, convenient to consider the *w* in *will* as a separate independent sound.

14. The sound of the letter *y* in *ye*, *yes*, *yet*.—This sound is evidently allied to the sound of the *ee* in feet. Some writers consider it identical, and assert that the words *yet* and *ee-et* are sounded alike. It is, however, convenient to consider the *y* in *yet* as a separate independent sound. The sounds expressed by *w* and *y* are called *semi*-vowel (*i.e. half-vowel*) sounds, or *semi-vowels*.

Mutes.—*P, B, F, V.*—15. The sound of the letter *p* in *pin*, *pit*, &c.

16. The sound of the letter *b* in *bin*, *bit*, &c.

17. The sound of the letter *f* in *fin*, *fit*, &c.

18. The sound of the letter *v* in *van*, *vans*, &c.

T, D, TH, DH.—19. The sound of the letter *t* in *tin*, *tip*, *teal*, *neat*, &c.

20. The sound of the letter *d* in *din*, *dip*, *deal*, *need*, &c.

21. The sound of the letters *th* in *thin*, *thick*, *through*, *cloth*, *moth*, &c.—It is here necessary to mark the difference that exists between the speaking and the spelling. The

sound of the *th* in *thin* is a simple single elementary sound, and, as such, should be expressed by a simple single elementary letter. Instead of this, it is expressed by two letters, or by a combination; so that, although a simple sound to the ear, it has the appearance of being a compound one to the eye.

22. The sound of the letters *th* in *thine, them, than, clothe.*—Respecting this sound the reader's attention is called to two points:

1st. That like the sound last mentioned, it is a simple single elementary sound, expressed, not by a simple single elementary sign, or letter, but by two letters, or a combination.

2nd. That, although different from the sound last mentioned, it is spelt precisely in the same way.

The *th* in *thin* is allied to the sound of *t*, as in *tin*.

The *th* in *thine* is allied to the sound of *d*, as in *din*.

K, *G.*—23. The sound of the letter *k*, as in *kill, keep, oak,* &c.

24. The sound of the letter *g*, as in *go, gun, log, egg,* &c.

25. The sound of the letter *s*, as in *sin, seal, yes,* &c.

26. The sound of the letter *z*, as in *zeal, buzz, blaze,* &c.

27. The sound of the letters *sh*, as in *shy, shine, short, ash, bush,* &c.

28. The sounds of the letter *z* in *azure, z* in *glazier,* and the *s* in *pleasure* are identical.

NG.—29. The sound of the letters *ng*, as in *king, sing, ring,* &c.

H.—30. The sound of the letter *h*, as in *hot, hear, hop,* &c., consists of a simple breathing.

Liquids.—31. The sound of the letter *l* in *leg, kill,* &c.

32. The sound of the letter *m* in *mat, cram,* &c.

33. The sound of the letter *n* in *net, none,* &c.

34. The sound of the letter *r* in *row, bear,* &c.

Here ends the list of the *simple* single elementary sounds in the English language.

Compound Sounds.—Of these, there are six; four are compounded by means of a vowel, and two by means of a consonant.

The compound sounds formed by vowels fall into two divisions.

Compounds formed by means of a vowel and the semi-vowel *w.*—These are two in number:

1. The sound of the letters *ou* in *house, mouse*, &c.—The nature of this compound is disguised by the spelling. It consists of the sound of the *a* in *father*, followed by that of the *w* in *will*, rapidly pronounced.

2. The sound of the letters *ew* in *new*. The nature of this compound is disguised by the spelling. It consists of the sound of the *i* in *pit*, followed by that of the *w* in *will*, rapidly pronounced.

Compounds formed by means of a vowel and the semi-vowel *y.*—These, also, are two in number:

1. The sound of the letter *i* in *pine, fine, find, mind.*—The nature of this compound is disguised by the spelling; since it is represented by means of the single letter *i.* The real elements of the sound in question are generally considered to be the sound of the *a* in *fat*, followed by that of the *y* in *yet*, rapidly pronounced.

2. The sound of the letters *oi* in *voice, noise.*—The nature of this compound is sufficiently, although not exactly, represented by the spelling. Its real elements are the *aw* in *bawl*, and the *y* in *yet.*

The compound sounds formed by the union of a *vowel and a semi-vowel* are called diphthongs.

The compound sounds formed by the union of two *consonants* are two in number:

1. The sound of the letters *ch* in *chest.*—This is really the sound of *tsh* rapidly pronounced.

2. The sound of the letter *j* in *jest.*—This is really the sound of *dzh* rapidly pronounced. The letter *g*, as in *gibbet*, also represents this sound.

§ 62. When the passage of the air is either free, or only partially closed, the stream of air passes without interruption, and so forms the sound which we call the *vowels*. The vowels can all be pronounced with the mouth partially open and with the breath in an uninterrupted stream.

The elementary sounds called *consonants* have the following peculiarity. They are unable to form even the shortest word or syllable without the aid of a vowel. Thus, the vowels *a* or *o* are capable of being used as syllables, and so are the combinations *ba* or *lo*. But the single sounds of *b'*, or *l'*, if taken by themselves, cannot form a word, or even a syllable.

In order to understand this difference, it is necessary to take some mute consonants and to pronounce them as independently of any vowel as it is possible to do. We must try to give a sound to such single consonants as *p'*, *t'*, &c. In attempting this, we shall succeed in making an imperfect sound.

Now, if the mute consonant so taken and uttered be one of the following, *p, f, t, th* (as in *thin*), *k, s,* or *sh*, the sound will be that of a *whisper*. The sound of *p,' t'* is that of a man speaking *under* the natural pitch of his voice.

But if the mute consonant so taken and uttered be *b, v, d, th* (as in *thine*), *g, z,* or *zh*, the sound will be that of a man speaking at the *natural pitch of his voice*.

§ 63. Those that are sounded like *p'* and *f'*, &c., are called the *Surd* mutes.

Those that are sounded like *b'* and *v'*, &c., are called the *Sonant* mutes.

Surd.				Sonant.			
p . . f	k . . —			b . . v	g^2 . . —		
t . . th^1	s . . sh			d . . th^3	z . . z^4		

Rule.—When two mutes of different degrees of sonancy come together in the same syllable, they form a sound that is incapable of being pronounced.

¹ As in *thin*.   ² As in *gun*.   ³ As in *thine*.   ⁴ As in *azure*.

This rule may be verified by practising a few combinations according to the arrangement of the preceding table; wherein it may be observed that the surd mutes are arranged on the left, the sonant mutes on the right hand. Having clearly recognized the distinction between the two, let us proceed.

	Surd.				Sonant.	
p . . f	k . . —	‖	b . . v	g² . . —
t . . th¹	s . . sh	‖	d . . th³	z . . z⁴

Taking whatever letter we may from the one side of the double line, and joining it immediately, in the same syllable, with any letter whatever from the other side of the double line, we find the combination unpronounceable.

aba,	*avt,*	*abth,*	*avth,*
agt,	*agp,*	*agf,*	*ags.*
apd,	*afb,*	*apv,*	*afd.*
atb,	*akd,*	*akz,*	*akb.*
asd,	*ashd,*	*asg,*	*ashg, &c.*

Of course, combinations of this sort can be *written,* and they can be *spelt;* they cannot, however, be pronounced, each sound remaining unchanged.

In order to become *pronounced,* a change must occur; one of the sounds must change its character, and so accommodate itself to the other. This change takes place in one of two ways; either the first of the two sounds takes the degree of the second, or else the second takes the degree of the first. Thus, *abt* becomes pronounceable either by *b* becoming *p,* or by *t* passing into *d;* in other words, it changes either into *apt* or into *abd.* So on with the rest.

av	becomes either	*aft,*	or *avd.*	*apd* becomes either	*apt,*	or *abd.*
abth	„	„	*apth,* „ *abdh.*	*asd*	„	„ *ast,* „ *azd.*
agt	„	„	*akt,* „ *agd.*	*ashd*	„	„ *asht,* „ *azhd.*
ags	„	„	*aks,* „ *agz.*	*asg*	„	„ *ask,* „ *azg.*

This change is necessary and universal. It holds good not for the English alone, but for all languages. The only

¹ As in *thin.* ² As in *gun.* ³ As in *thine.* ⁴ As in *azure.*

difference is, that different languages change different letters; that is, one language accommodates the first letter to the second, and so turns *agt* into *akt;* whilst another accommodates the second letter to the first, changing *agt* into *agd.*

§ 64. There is no fact that requires to be more familiarly known than this; since there are, at least, three formations in the English language where its influence is most important. These are the Possessive forms in -*s*, the Plurals in -*s*, the Preterites in -*d* and -*t.*

The *s* in the word *stage* is surd; the *g* in the word *stags* is sonant. Notwithstanding this, the combination *ags* exists. It exists, however, in the *spelling* only. In *speaking*, the *s* is sounded as *z*, and the word *stags* is pronounced *stagz.* Again, in words like *tossed, plucked, looked,* the *e* is omitted in pronunciation. Hence the words become *tossd, pluckd, lookd,* &c. But this combination exists in the *spelling* only; since the preterites of *pluck, look, and toss,* are, in *speech,* pronounced *pluckt, lookt, tosst.*

§ 65. Next to knowing that two mutes of different degrees of sonancy cannot come together in the same syllable, it is important to know that two identical sounds cannot come together in the same syllable.

In illustration of this, we may take a word ending in *p, t,* or *s,* such as *tap, bat,* or *mis.* To add a second *p,* a second *t,* or a second *s,* is impracticable. At the first glance this statement seems untrue. Nothing, apparently, is commoner than words like *tapp, batt, miss.* However, like the combinations indicated above, these are, in reality, combinations in *spelling* only; they have no existence in pronunciation. We have only to attempt to pronounce *bat't, sap'p,* &c. to prove this.

§ 66. To express these twenty-eight sounds in writing, there are, in English, the following twenty-six letters: *a e i o u w y p b f v t d k g s z h l m n r j c q x.* It is, therefore, easy to see that there are in English more sounds to be expressed in writing than there are letters to express them by.

From these twenty-six letters, however, we must subtract the following—

1. The letter *j*, as in *jest*; since it is not one of the twenty-eight *simple* elementary sounds that this letter is the sign of. The subtraction of the letter *j* reduces the number of letters expressive of the *simple* sounds to twenty-five:

2. The letter *c*; since it expresses only what is as well expressed by either *s* or *k*. The words *city* and *can* are pronounced *sity* and *kan* respectively. The subtraction of the letter *c*. reduces the number of letters expressive of the simple sounds to twenty-four:

3, 4. The letters *q*, and *x*; since *q* is only *kw*, and *x* is only *ks*. The words *queen* and *box* are pronounced *kween*, and *boks*, respectively. The subtraction of the letters *q* and *x* reduces the number of letters to twenty-two.

We have now seen that for* twenty-eight simple elementary sounds there are only twenty-two simple elementary letters; consequently, six of the simple elementary sounds have no sign or letter corresponding to them. These are,

    1. The *u* in *but*.
    2, 3. The *th* in (*a*) *thin*; in (*b*) *thine*.
    4. The sound of the *sh* in *shine*.
    5. The sound of the *z* in *azure*.
    6. The sound of the *ng* in *king*.

§ 67. The English Alphabet is,

1. *Redundant.* It contains three superfluous letters, *viz. c*, *q*, and *x*.

2. *Deficient.* It wants signs for the six sounds mentioned in § 66.

3. *Inconsistent.* It expresses the double sound of the first letter in *jest* (*dzh*) by a single sign, and the single

---

* See § 68. Here the list gives *forty* sounds: eleven of the vowels, however, are reducible to modifications of *a, e, i, o,* and *u*; whilst the last six sounds are *Diphthongs.*

E

ɔunds of the first letters in *thin*, *thine*, and *shine*, by two
igns (*th* and *sh*).

There are other faults in the English Alphabet and the
nglish method of spelling, which it is not necessary here
ɔ enlarge upon. For many of these a sufficient, though
ot satisfactory, reason can be exhibited.

§ 68.   RECAPITULATION.

Vowels.	1.	The sound of the letter			*a*	in	*father.* ⎫
,,	2.	,,	,,	,,	*a*	,,	*fate.* ⎬
,,	3.	,,	,,	,,	*a*	,,	*fat.* ⎭
,,	4.	,,	,,	,,	*e*	,,	*bed.* ⎫
,,	5.	,,	,,	,,	*e*	,,	*glebe.* ⎬
,,	6.	,,	,,	,,	*i*	,,	*pin.* ⎭
,,	7.	,,	,,	,,	*o*	,,	*prove.* ⎫
,,	8.	,,	,,	,,	*u*	,,	*full.* ⎬
,,	9.	,,	,,	letters	*aw*	,,	*bawl.* ⎭
,,	10.	,,	,,	letter	*o*	,,	*note.* ⎫
,,	11.	,,	,,	,,	*o*	,,	*not.* ⎬
,,	12.	,,	,,	,,	*u*	,,	*but.*
Semivowels.	13.	,,	,,	,,	*w*	,,	*well.* ⎫
,,	14.	,,	,,	,,	*y*	,,	*yes.* ⎭
Mutes.	15.	,,	,,	,,	*p*	,,	*pain.*
,,	16.	,,	,,	,,	*b*	,,	*bane.*
,,	17.	,,	,,	,,	*f*	,,	*fane.*
,,	18.	,,	,,	,,	*v*	,,	*vane.*
,,	19.	,,	,,	,,	*t*	,,	*tin.* ⎫
,,	20.	,,	,,	,,	*d*	,,	*din.*
,,	21.	,,	,,	letters	*th*	,,	*thin.*
,,	22.	,,	,,	,,	*th*	,,	*thine.*
,,	23.	,,	,,	letter	*k*	,,	*kill.* ⎫
,,	24.	,,	,,	,,	*g*	,,	*guns.*
Sibilants.	25.	,,	,,	,,	*s*	,,	*seal.* ⎫
,,	26.	,,	,,	,,	*z*	,,	*zeal.* ⎬
,,	27.	,,	,,	letters	*sh*	,,	*shine.*
,,	28.	,,	,,	letter	*z*	,,	*azure.*
Nasal.	29.	,,	,,	letters	*ng*	,,	*king.*
Breathing.	30.	,,	,,	letter	*h*	,,	*hot.*
Liquids.	31.	,,	,,	,,	*l*	,,	*low.* ⎫
,,	32.	,,	,,	,,	*m*	,,	*mow.* ⎬
,,	33.	,,	,,	,,	*n*	,,	*no.*
,,	34.	,,	,,	,,	*r*	,,	*row.* ⎭

Diphthongs.	35.	The sound of the letters	*ou*	in	*house.*	
„	36.	„	„	„	*ew*	„	*new.*	
„	37.	„	„	letter	*i*	„	*pine.*	
„	38.	„	„	letters	*oi*	„	*voice.*	
Sibilants.	39.	„	„	„	*ch*	„	*chest.*	
„	40.	„	„	letter	*j*	„	*jest.*	

The last two sounds of this list are *Compound Sibilants*; inasmuch as they are made up out of those of *tsh* and *dzh* respectively. They are, in fact, *Consonantal* Diphthongs, though the term Diphthong is generally limited to *Vowel* combinations.

§ 69. *Accent.*—The following words are accented on the first syllable—*ánchor, árgue, hásten, fáther, fóxes, smíting, húsband, márket, vápour, bárefoot,* &c.

In *brigáde, preténce, harpoón, reliéve, detér, assúme, besóught, beréft, befóre, abroád, abóde, abstrúse,* &c., the accent is on the last.

I. Words where the unaccented syllables are to the accented syllables as one to one:

a. Accent on the first syllable,—*ánchor, árgue,* &c.

b. Accent on the second syllable,—*harpoón, brigáde,* &c.

II. Words where the unaccented syllables are to the accented syllables as two to one:

a. Accent on the first syllable,—*fórtify, mérrily, cheérily, pítiful, déstitute.*

b. Accent on the second syllable,—*disáble, endeávour, repúlsive, replénish.*

c. Accent on the third syllable,—*cavaliér, disembógue.*

d. Words with their accent on the *fourth syllable from the end* are rare; because, quadrisyllables have generally two accents, as *Européan;* or one on the third syllable from the end, as *inquisitive.* Still, there are a few words, like *orthodoxy,* &c., where the accentuation is *órthodoxy,* and not *órthodóxy.* *Three,* however, as a general rule, is the greatest number of syllables for which a single accent is sufficient.

§ 70. Words like *harpóon* and *cavaliér,* where the accent

is on the last syllable, are comparatively rare in English. This is because the ordinary place of the accent is on the most fundamental syllable of the word to which it belongs; secondary additions, whether affixes, like the -*ly* in *mánly*, the -*ness* in *neárness*, &c., or prefixes, like the *be-* in *bespéak*, the *with-* in *withóut*, &c., being unaccented.

As *affixes*, or additions to the end of a word, are commoner in English than *prefixes*, or additions at the beginning of one, the tendency of our grammar is to throw the accent *back*, *i.e.* towards the beginning of words of more than one syllable, rather than towards their end.

§ 71. The same was the case in Latin; where, as most words ended in an inflectional, or some similar superadded syllable, the accent was thrown back. In the Latin, however, before it became French, many of these unaccented syllables dropped off; and words like *civíl-is*, *natión-is*, and many others, became *civíle*, *natión*, and the like. The French, then, abounds in words whereof the last syllable is accented; and, hence, it will be found that most of the words like *cavaliér*, *brigáde*, and the like—words with their accent on the last syllable—are of French origin.

The derivatives of the word *týrant* well illustrate the conflict between the claims of the most fundamental part of the word to keep the accent, and the difficulty of throwing it as far back as the fourth syllable from the end : (1) *týrant*; (2) *týranny*, not *tyránny*; (3) *tyránnical*; (4) *tyránnically*. Nevertheless, we say *tyránnic*, not *týrannic*; probably on the precedent of *tyránnical*. Here we have as many as *three* manifestly superadded syllables.

§ 72. Certain words, in other respects identical, are Nouns when the accent is on the *first*, Verbs when it is on the last, syllable—*e.g.*, *an ábsent man* as opposed to *I absént myself*; *aúgment*, *augmént*; *cómpound*, *compoúnd*; *súrvey*, *survéy*; *tórment*, *tormént*; &c., &c.

PART III.

ETYMOLOGY.

§ 73. *Etymology of two kinds.*—There are two kinds of Etymology.

(1.) One treats of such connections as that between words like *pater* and *father; patres* and *fathers.* These belong to different languages, and are not derived from one another. The *-s* in both is the sign of the same case; and the radical parts of the two are the same. But their history is that of two *concurrent* forms; and the common origin must be sought in some older form of speech. This is Comparative Etymology.

(2.) The other treats of such connections as *patres* and *pater; fathers* and *father.* Here one of the two words is derived from the other, and both forms belong to the same language. This is Grammatical Etymology; with which the present treatise will have the most to do.

Etymology deals with *single* words and the various forms they may take. It is, in doing this, opposed to *Syntax,* which treats of two or more words in combination.

§ 74. But, as two words are often combined into one, we have a department of grammar intermediate to the two divisions. This is called Composition. It is sometimes difficult to say where the combination of two separate words ends, and the fusion of the two into one begins. Composition, however, is generally and properly considered to belong to Etymology.

Composition takes place when two separate words are
joined together so as to form a single word, as

day-light	dog-star	English-man
nut-brown	father-like	pea-cock.

§ 75. *Derivation* takes place when a word is either
changed by the addition of some new elementary sound, or
by the alteration of one previously existing.

hunt-*er*	drunk-*ard*	*be*-spoke
wood-*en*	. spin-*ster*	chick-*en*.

Composition implies the addition of *whole words*; Derivation, the addition of *parts of whole words*, either real or
possible.

§ 76. Certain Derivatives are called *Inflections*. These
present themselves in nouns and verbs only. They are the
forms by which we determine gender, number, case, voice,
mood, tense, and person, and will be considered in detail in
the sequel.

The Inflection of a noun is called its *Declension*. Nouns
are *declined*.

The Inflection of a verb is called its *Conjugation*. Verbs
are *conjugated*.

§ 77. *Transitional forms.*——All these divisions run into
one another; though not to an extent which should em-
barrass us if a few preliminary notices are borne in mind.

Grammatical combinations may be made in such a manner that it is difficult to determine whether two separate
words are in contact with one another, and combined by the
rules of Syntax, or in a state of Composition. Thus in *all
black birds are* not *blackbirds*, what is *blackbird?* Is it a
pair of separate words or two words combined into one?
Again in *Thursday*, is the combination one like *man's hat*
in which the -*s* is the sign of a genitive case, and the case is
one of Syntax; or is *s* a mere connected link by which the
two elements of a compound are united? It may be either.
In questions of this kind it is the *accent* helps us. In the

COMPOSITION. 55

ordinary syntactic combination each word keeps its own
accent, as *bláck bird*. In composition one gives way to
the other—*bláckbird, Thúrsday*.

Composition often simulates derivation when, after the
union of two distinctly separate words, one of them either
changes its form or becomes obsolete. Thus *manly* looks
more like a derivative than a compound. But it is only a
shortened form of *manlike*. Again, the *ric* in *bishop-ric* is
no longer current as an ordinary term in English. Yet,
when it was first attached to the word *bishop*, it was as
truly a separate word as *kingdom, domain*, or *jurisdiction*,
or any other substantive.

With instances like those just given the process of re-
ducing derivation to composition is an easy matter. All
that is required is a certain amount of knowledge of the
language in its earlier stages. This is wanted for *bishopric*.
But in the word *manly* less than this will be enough. We
have only to *consider* a little, and its connection with *manlike* strikes us at once. The words *gentlemanly* and *gentle-
manlike* are still more to the purpose. With a little knowledge, then, and a little consideration, we can do much—so
long as the word is a *dis*syllable—for we can separate its
component parts, even if we do no more. But *mono*syllables
may also be, in respect to their origin, compounds. Here
the analysis is more perplexing. Words like *not, such*, and
which are not easily picked to pieces. Yet, common words
as they are, and monosyllables as they are, they are *compounds*. *Not* is a compound of the negative element *n'*, and
whit (as in *not a whit*). It is *n' aught*, which is again
compounded of a prefix *á-*. *Which* is, in Scotch, *whilk*;
in German, *welch*; and *such* is in Scotch *swilk*, and in
German *solch*, where the *lk* (*lch*) is the word *like*. Here, we
get derivation, as opposed to composition in its most characteristic form.

In Frisian the form is simpler still; the elements *so*
and *like* being reduced to *sok*. From *thilk=the like*, found

both in Scotch and our provincial dialects, the *l* is similarly ejected, and *thec* in the local dialects of the South-western counties represents the compound.

COMPOSITION.

§ 78. Substantives preceded by Substantives.—*Day-star, land-slip, light-house, fir-tree, goose-grass, sea-man, collar-bone, earth-nut, fire-wood, moon-light.*

Substantives preceded by Adjectives.—*Blind-worm, free-man, half-penny, grey-beard, quick-silver, holy-day.*

Substantives preceded by Verbs.—*Turn-spit, dare-devil, turn-coat.*

Substantives preceded by the form in -*ing.*—*Turning-lathe, sawing-mill.*

Adjectives preceded by Substantives.—*Sin-ful, thank-ful, blood-red, eye-bright, coal-black, snow-white, nut-brown, heart-whole, ice-cold, foot-sore,* &c.

Adjectives preceded by Adjectives.—*All-mighty, two-fold, many-fold,* &c.

Adjectives preceded by Verbs.—*Stand-still, live-long.*

Verbs preceded by Verbs.—*Hear-say.* Rare.

Present Participles* preceded by Adjectives (with an adverbial power).—*All-seeing, all-ruling, soft-flowing, fast-sailing, merry-making.*

Past Participles preceded by Adjectives.—*New-born, free-spoken, fresh-made, new-made, new-laid.*

Present Participles preceded by Substantives.—*Fruit-bearing, music-making.*

Past Participles preceded by Substantives.—*Heaven-born, bed-ridden, blood-stained.*

Verbal Substantives preceded by Substantives.—*Man-eater, woman-eater, kid-napper, horn-blower.*

Verbal Adjectives preceded by Substantives.—*Mop-headed, chicken-hearted.*

* See §§ 140–144. These will explain a difficulty which is only indicated here, viz., the ambiguous import of the termination -*ing.*

Verbal Adjectives preceded by Adjectives.—*Cold-hearted, flaxen-haired, hot-headed, curly-pated.*

§ 79. Adverbs entering into composition are of two sorts:

1st. Those that can be separated from the word with which they combine, and, nevertheless, appear as independent words; as *over, under, well,* in *over-do, under-go, well-beloved,* &c.

2nd. Those that, when they are separated from the verb with which they combine, have no independent existence as separate words; *e.g.* the syllables *be-, un-, a-,* in *be-hove, be-fit; be-seem, be-lieve, be-lie, be-smatter, be-smear, be-get, be-labour, be-do, be-gin, be-gird, be-hold, be-mourn, be-reave, be-deck, be-think, be-mire, be-rhyme, un-bind, un-do, un-loose, un-lock, un-wind, a-light, a-rouse, a-rise, a-wake, a-wak-en, a-bet, a-bide.*

DERIVATION.

§ 80. Addition of a Vowel.—*Ba-by* from *babe—Dogg-ie, lass-ie, mous-ie, wif-ie.*

Addition of L.—*Gird-le—mick-le—spark-le.*

Addition of R.—(1) *Laugh-t-er, slaugh-t-er;* (2) *gand-er;* (3) *lay-er, fodd-er;* (4) *hunt-er, sinn-er.*

Verbs—*Hind-er, low-er.*

Addition of N.—Substantives.—*Maid-en, mai-n* (as in *might* and *main*). That the *-n* is no part of the original word in *mai-n,* we see from the word *may.* The idea in both *may* and *mai-n* is that of *power.*

Adjectives.—Words of this sort express the circumstance of the object to which they are applied, being *made of the material of which* the radical part of the derivative is the name: thus, *gold-en* is a derivative from *gold,* the material of which *golden guineas* are made. So, also, *oak-en, ash-en, beech-en, braz-en, flax-en, gold-en, lead-en, silk-en, wood-en, wooll-en, hemp-en, wheat-en, oat-en, wax-en.*

Addition of the sound of O, originating in *-ow* or *-ov,* and spelt in the present English *-ow.*—By comparison with *shade* and *mead*, the forms *shad-ow* and *mead-ow* are shown to be derivative.

Addition of T.—1. Substantives.—*a.* Words which in A. S. ended in -*t*, *gif-t*, *shrif-t*, *thef-t*, *wef-t* (*weave*), *rif-t*, *drif-t*, *thrif-t*, *fros-t* (*freeze*), *gris-t* (*grind*), *fligh-t*, *sigh-t*, *draugh-t* (*draw*), *weigh-t*.

b. Words which in A. S. ended in -*ta.* The compounds of the word *wright* (from the root *work*, in the old past tense *wrought*); such as *cart-wrigh-t*, *wheel-wrigh-t*, *mill-wrigh-t*, &c.

2. Adjectives.—*Tigh-t* (*tie*).

Addition of D.—Substantives.—*Bran-d* (*burn, brenn,* obsolete), *floo-d* (*flow*), *mai-d* (*may* in Lowland Scotch), *see-d* (*sow*), *bur-d-en* (*bear*).

2. Adjectives.—*Col-d* (*cool*).

Addition of TH (A. S. þ as sounded in *thin*).—Substantives.—*Dea-th, bir-th* (*bear*), *heal-th, leng-th, bread-th, heigh-t, dep-th, mir-th, tru-th, weal-th, fil-th, til-th* (*tillage,* or *tilled ground*), *ki-th* (as in the phrase *kith and kin*).

2. Adjectives.—The syllable -*cou-th* in the compound word *uncou-th.* This word originally means *unknown,* originating in the word *ken*=to *know.*

Addition of TH (A. S. ð) as sounded in *thine.* *Bur-th-en,* derived from *bear.*

Addition of the sound of the Z in *zeal* and the S in *flags* (*flagz*).—Verbs.—*Cleanse* (*clenz*), from *clean.* In A. S. *clæn-s-ian.*

Addition of the sound of K.—*Hill-ock.*

Addition of the sound of the vowel E (as in *feet*), originating in -*ig*, and spelt in the present English -*y.*—All the derivative adjectives that now end in -*y*, ended in A. S. in -*ig*; as *blood-y, craft-y, drear-y, might-y, mist-y, mood-y, merr-y, worth-y,* of which the A. S. forms were *blôd-ig, cræft-ig, dreôr-ig, might-ig, mist-ig, môd-ig, myr-ig, worth-ig.*

Addition of -*en*, or -*in.*—*Vix-en* = *female fox.*

Addition of the syllable -*ing.*—*Farth-ing* ($\frac{1}{4}$), *rid-ing**

* As the *Three Ridings of Yorkshire.*

($\frac{1}{3}$, a corruption from *thrith-ing*). Also, *cleans-ing*, *dawn-ing*, *morn-ing*. In these words the -*ing* was originally -*ung*; as *clœn-s-ung*, *dag-ung*, A. S.

Addition of the syllable *Ling*.—*Gos-Ling* (*little goose*), *duck-Ling* (*little duck*), *dar-Ling* (*little dear*), *hire-Ling*, *found-Ling*, *fond-Ling*, *nest-Ling*, &c. The words of this class are generally diminutives, or words expressive of smallness.

Addition of the syllable -*kin*.—*Lamb-kin* (*little lamb*), *man-i-kin* (*little man*). Words ending in -*kin* are chiefly diminutives.

Addition of the syllable -*rel*.—*Cock-erel* (*little cock*), *pick-erel* (*little pike*).

Addition of the syllable -*ard*.—*Drunk-ard*, *stink-ard*.

Addition of the syllable *old*.—*Thresh-old*.

Addition of the syllable -*ern*.—*East-ern*, *west-ern*, *north-ern*, *south-ern*.

Addition of the syllable -*ish*.—*Child-ish*, *Eng-lish*, *self-ish*, *whit-ish*. The original form was -*isk*; *cild-isc* (*child-ish*), *Engl-isc* (*Engl-ish*), A. S.

Addition of the syllable -*ness*.—*Good-ness*, *bad-ness*, *wicked-ness*, *bright-ness*, *dark-ness*, *weari-ness*, *dreari-ness*, &c.

Change of the sound of a *consonant*.—*Price*, *prize*; *cloth*, *clothe* (pronounced *clodhe*); *use*, *use* (pronounced *uze*); *grass*, *graze*; *grease* (pronounced *greace*), *grease* (pronounced *greaze*). In each of the pairs of words given above, the former is a substantive, and the latter a verb.

Change of the sound of a *vowel*.—*Rise*, *raise*: *lie*, *lay*: *fall*, *fell*: *sit*, *set*. The generality of these words are verbs. There are, however, a few nouns; as *top*, *tip*; *cat*, *kit*. Here the sense is generally that of a Diminutive.

§ 81. The termination -*ry* in words like *rookery*, *fishery*, &c., presents some difficulty. It is clear that the -*r* forms no part of the original word; for, though there is such a word as *fisher*, *fisherman*, there is no such word as *rooker*. Neither does *fishery* mean a collection of *fishermen*, but one of *fishes*. *Yeomanry* and *Jewry* are words of similar origin and meaning. They carry with them the idea of a collection, or assemblage. The words *Englishry*, *Danishry*, and *Welshery* are to be found in old authors. They are, however, at present obsolete. *Eyrie* is generally said to mean the nest of an eagle. It rather means a *collection of eggs*, or *eggery*; for such is the old form of the word.

What, however, is the *-r* ? In the old Dutch and other allied dialects, we find a kind of plural in *-r*. Thus *cealfru*= *calves*; *lambru*=*lambs*; *eggru*=*eggs*. Indeed, in one word it occurs in provincial and archaic English, viz. *childer*= *children*. Out of this *-r*, with the addition of the sound of *-y*, has the termination *-ry* in the words above given originated.

In other words, however, this origin is inadmissible; and the idea of collection or assemblage is either obscure or non-existent. Such are *foolery*, *prudery*, *bravery*, *slavery*, *witchery*, *stitchery* (*needlework*), &c. In all these the *-ry* has originated out of a false analogy.

§ 82. Derivation by means of the addition of the syllable *-ster*.—*Song-ster*, *pun-ster*. Originally words in *-str-* were limited to the names of females, and were opposed to the substantives in *-er*, the names of *male* agents. Thus, in A. S.,

sangere, a male singer		sangestre, a female singer.
bæcere, a male baker		bæcestre, a female baker.
fidelere, a male fiddler	were opposed to	fidelestre, a female fiddler.
webbere, a male weaver		webbestre, a female weaver.
rædere, a male reader		rædestre, a female reader.
seamere, a male seamer		seamestre, a female seamer (or *seamstress*).

The single word *spin-ster* still retains its feminine force.

INFLECTION.

§ 83. Inflection is a special part of Derivation. It consists of (1) the Declension of Nouns, and (2) the Conjugation of Verbs. We begin with Nouns.

The declension of a noun gives its signs of (1) Gender, (2) Number, (3) Case.

The words *boy* and *girl*, *father* and *mother*, *horse* and *mare* are the names of living beings of different sexes—*boy*, *father*, and *horse*, the names of males; *girl*, *mother*, and *mare* of females.

In grammar, however, instead of saying that the word *boy* is a *male* word, and the word *girl* a *female* word, we use the terms *masculine* and *feminine*; and we say that *boy* is a word of the masculine gender, and *girl* a word of the feminine gender. But besides such objects as *boys* and *girls*, which are either male or female, there are in the world a vast number of objects, such as *swords*, *bows*, *shoes*, *iron*, &c., that are neither male nor female. These objects have names, and these names are very often neither masculine nor feminine, though they are sometimes supposed to be endowed with sex, and made either males or females. Words of this sort, that are neither masculine nor feminine, are said to be of the neuter gender. We may say then that there are three genders; the masculine, the feminine, and the neuter. The masculine denotes males; the feminine, females; and the neuter *things*, or objects that are neither male nor female. We can now apply this to the words mentioned above. In the English substantives and adjectives there is no true Inflection indicative of Gender; words like *man*, *woman*, *he-goat*, *she-goat*, &c., being approximations only. In Anglo-Saxon, however, this Inflection existed, and even in the language as it is spoken at the present time, exists among the Pronouns. Thus—

The two words *him* and *her* are of the same number, in the same case, and from the same nominative. Yet they are different words, and they differ in meaning; the first being applied to *males*, the second to *females* only.

Have you seen your brother?—Yes, I have seen him.
Have you seen your sister?—Yes, I have seen her.
Now this difference of form gives a true inflection of

gender, and it is one of the peculiarities of pronouns to be
changed, not only in the way of case and number, but in the
way of gender also.

§ 84. *Number.*—In the following phrases we speak of a
single object; that is, of one object and of no more than
one; *a father, my father, this father, one father; a son, my
son, this son, one son; a horse, this horse, that horse, my horse,
one horse.* Here the words *father, son,* and *horse,* appear
in a simple form, without the addition of any letter or
syllable whatsoever. But this is not the case with words
like *these father-s, these son-s, these hors-es,* &c. Here we
speak of more objects than one; that is, of *two* (or more)
fathers, of *two* (or more) *sons,* and of *two* (or more) *horses;*
and hence the letter *s* is added to the words *father, son,*
and *horse* respectively. Now in the Latin language the
word *singularis* means *single;* so that the forms without *s,*
such as *father, son,* and *horse,* denoting respectively *one
father, one son, one horse,* and no more, are called *singular*
forms, and are said to be in the *singular* number. On
the other hand, in the Latin language the words *plus* and
pluralis mean *more* or *many;* so that the forms with *s,* like
father-s, son-s, and *hors-es,* denoting respectively *two* (or
more) *fathers, two* (or more) *sons, two* (or more) *horses,*
are called *plural* forms, or are said to be in the *plural*
number. In the English language we may therefore say
that there are two numbers, the singular and the plural.
The singular speaks of one (*a father*), and the plural speaks
of more than one (*fathers, books*).

§ 85. *Case.*—We may arrive at a knowledge of the
nature of cases by examining the structure of the following
propositions.

He is striking him;—these words form a proposition, of
which *he* is the subject, *is* the copula, and *striking him* the
predicate. Now *he* and *him,* although the same parts of
speech, of the same gender, and of the same number, appear
in different forms. In one there is the presence, in the

other the absence, of the letter *m* (*he*, *hi-m*). The reason of
this is because the two words are in different cases. The
same takes place with *they are striking them*. We cannot
say *him is striking he*, nor yet *them is striking they*. We
cannot even say, *him is striking, them are striking*. If we
examine farther, we shall find that *he* and *they* can, by themselves, form terms; since we can say not only *he is striking,*
but *this is he*, and *these are they*. On the other hand, *him*
and *them* can only form *parts* of terms : as *he is striking
them, they are striking him*. Such is the difference in
meaning between the words *he* and *him*.

When the words differ from each other in meaning in
the way that *he* and *him*, *they* and *them* differ, it is the habit,
more or less, of languages to express this difference of meaning by a difference of form. This is done with the words
just quoted ; where *he* and *they* take one form, and *him* and
them another. Differences of this sort, expressed by difference of form, are said to constitute cases. The word *he* is
in one case (the nominative), the word *him* in another (the
accusative or objective). So it is also with *they* and *them*.

A noun is said to be in the nominative case when it can
by itself constitute a term. The words *he* and *father* are
nominative cases ; since we can say, *he is speaking, father is
coming, this is he, this is father*.

They fought with a sword.—Here there is the substantive
sword accompanied by the word *with*. In many languages,
however, the word *with* would be omitted, and the word
sword change its form. The Anglo-Saxon for *they fought
with the sword*, was *feohton sweord-e*, where no such word as
with appeared in the sentence, but where the additional
syllable *-e* served instead. This constituted in Anglo-Saxon
a particular case.

This is a picture of John.—Here there is the substantive
John accompanied by the word *of*. In many languages,
however, the word *of* (or its equivalent) would be omitted,
and the word *John* would change its form. This would

constitute a fresh case.   The meaning of the sentence *this
is a picture of John* is, *this is a picture of which John is the
subject* (or *original*).

§ 86. These three inflections, viz. Gender, Number, and
Case, belong to the declension of nouns.   They are true
Inflections, which the following are *not*.

Difference of sex expressed by composition.—

Male.	Female.
he-goat	*she*-goat
cock-sparrow	*hen*-sparrow
man-servant	*maid*-servant.

Here objects of different sexes are expressed by *partially*
different words, and the result is a compound.

*Difference of sex expressed by derivation.—*The words in
the first column are the names of males, those in the second
of females.

Male.	Female.	Male.	Female.
actor	actr-*ess*	duke	duch-*ess*.
lion	lion-*ess*	peer	peer-*ess*.

Here the names of females are formed from those of
males by the addition of the syllable *ess*.   The result is an
ordinary derivative; of *French* origin.

When we come to the *conjugation* of *verbs* we shall meet
with other Inflections, viz., those of Person, Tense, and
Mood. Of these the first two are the most truly Inflectional,
in the present English.   The Infinitive Mood has lost its
original termination -*en*; and so has the Conjunctive. Of
this mood the signs for all the Persons except the Third
Singular are the same as those of the Indicative.   The
difference between *he speaks* and *if he speak* is neglected;
and, even adhered to, it gives us only a *negative* sign of
Mood, i.e., the omission of the *s* of the Indicative.

INFLECTION, ETC., OF PRONOUNS.

§ 87. *The Pronouns—why considered first.—*The pronouns
come first under notice on account of the fulness of their
declension.   They are not, however, in this respect all alike.

Words like *some, same, each,* &c., have no more signs of gender, numbers, or case than the adjective; and this means that they have none at all. *Self, one,* and *other* are declined like substantives.

But the (1) demonstrative, (2) interrogative, and (3) relative pronouns, which are all declined on the same principle, have a true distinction of gender, and, at least, three oblique cases.

The demonstrative, interrogative, and relative pronouns have all a neuter in *t*, a possessive in *s*, objectives in *m, n,* or *r*, according to the gender; *it, what, his, whose, him, whom, when, her, where. I-t, tha-t,* and *wha-t* are true neuter signs; *t* being the original sign of the neuter gender. In the present Danish, Swedish, Norwegian, and Icelandic, and in the old Norse and Mœso-Gothic, *all* neuter *adjectives* as well end in *-t.*

§ 88. Demonstratives.—The demonstrative pronouns derive their name from the Latin word *demonstro*=*I show,* or *point out.*

Of demonstrative pronouns there are three varieties, viz. :

1. True demonstratives.—*This, that, yon.*

2. Demonstratives which partake of the nature of the personal pronouns—*he, she.*

3. The definite article, *the.*

True demonstratives.—*This* applies to comparatively near; *that* to comparatively distant; *yon* to remote objects.

Yon is undeclined. *This* and *that* are declined in respect to number only.

The old and proper plural of the demonstrative and definite article þe, þio, þæt, was þá, þæ, *tha, thea* or *tho,* without any sound akin to that of the semivowel *y*, as in *they.* This was when *he* had a plural number (*hi, heora, heom*) of its own; now superseded by *they, their, them.* When this plural of *he* became obsolete, a double change affected the plural of þe: (1) the vowel *á* became -eჳ, -ei, or -ey—

þeȝȝ, *thei*; (2) þá, þo took the affix -*s*, the forms *they* and *those* being the result.

He is found in the singular number only.

	Masculine.	Feminine.	Neuter.
Nominative:	he	—	it.
Possessive :	his	her.	it-s.
Objective :	him.	her.	it.

She is now undeclined.

The nature of the demonstrative pronouns is only understood through their history. In the older stages of our language, the words *this* and *that* were fully declined and had both possessives and objectives. More than this, they had two other cases; the dative and the instrumental. To say that this inflection is wholly lost, would be inaccurate. It still exists, though in an altered form and as a different part of speech.

Certain words, which at the present time are adverbs, were originally demonstrative pronouns. Thus :

There was a dative case, of the singular number and feminine gender, meaning *in that direction ;* the word *direction* being understood.

Then was in the objective case, masculine gender, and singular number. It meant *at that time ; time* being understood.

The word *the* in such expressions as *all the more, all the better, the more the merrier,* is more remarkable still. It means *by so much ;* and was, originally, an instrumental case. The Anglo-Saxon form was þy (*thy*) ; corresponding in power to the Latin *eo* (*eo majus*). Its present identity of form with the definite article is accidental ; the origin of the two words being different.

In like manner, *here* was the dative feminine of *he ;* and meant *in this direction* or *place.*

It, in its present form, has no evident connection with *he ;* of which, however, it is the true neuter. The older form is *hit.*

Its is a strange word and a new word. The original neuter possessive was *his* for the masculine and neuter genders. From a comparison by Mr. Watts of the different versions of the Bible it appears that ' so lately as 1611— the date of the issue of the authorized version—the word did not exist, or, at all events, was not considered to belong to that elevated portion of the language regarded as suitable for the translation of the sacred writings.'

And thei shulen take the iacyntyn mantle with the which thei shulen cover the candelstik with the lanterns and *her* (*their*) toonges & snyters.—*Wicliffe.*

Thei schulen also take a meatie of iacynt, with which thei shulen hile (cover) the candelstike with these lanternes and tongis and snytels. — *Purvey.*

And they shall take a cloth of jacyncte and cover the candelstick of light and *her* lamps and *her* snoffers and fyre pans and all *hir* oyle vessels which they occupy about *it*, and shall put upon *her* and all *her* instrumentes a coueryage of taxus skin and put it upon staues.—*Tyndale*, 1530.

And they shal take a yalowe clothe and cover the candelsticke of light therwith, & *her* lamps with *her* snoffers, and outquenchers.—*Coverdale,* 1535.

And they shall take a cloth of iacincte and cover the candelstycke of lyght and *her* lampes and *her* snoffers and fyre panes and all her oyle vessels which they occupy aboute it, &c.—*Mathews,* 1537.

And they shall take a cloth of blue and cover the candlestick of the light and *his* lamps & *his* tongs, and *his* snuffdishes, and all the oil vessels thereof wherewith they minister unto it.—*Authorized Version.*

The feminine of *he* was *heó*. This has been lost. In Anglo-Saxon, however, the inflection was—

Masculine.	Feminine.	Neuter.
He	*heó*	*hit.*

Beside which there was an accusative form *hine. Him* was originally dative.

In the plural the changes have been greater still. Instead of *they, their,* and *them,* the Anglo-Saxons said *hi, hira, hem ;* all of which forms were true inflections of *he,* and all of which are now lost. To make up for them, the existing plurals have been borrowed from another quarter.

F 2

She was originally the feminine of *se*, and served as the definite article; as *se hlaford=the lord; seo hlafdige=the lady.* At the present time the masculine *se* no longer exists, whilst, in the feminine, *she* stands in the place of the Anglo-Saxon *heo.*

These changes being understood, it is easy to see how inaccurate it is to talk of *she* being the feminine, and *they* being the plural, of *he.* The different words belong to different systems, and are no more the masculines and feminines of one another, than (to use a well-known illustration) *puss* is the vocative case of *cat.*

§ 89. Of the two powers of the pronoun *who*, the *Interrogative* is the older; its use as a *Relative* being secondary.

The neuter form is *what;* the possessive, *whose;* and the objective, *whom*

The adverbs *where* and *when* were originally dative and accusative cases from *who;* in other words, the remarks that applied to *here*, *there*, and *then*, apply to *where* and *when.*

Again,—*why* was originally the instrumental form *hwi;* meaning, *for what reason;* in Latin, *quâ causâ?*

Which is no true neuter, no true inflection. It is a compound of the radical of the relative and the adjective *like.*

The Scotch form still possesses the *l;* as *whilk.* So does the German *welch-e. Such* is a similar compound from *so-like*, in Scotch *swilk*, in German *solch.*

Whose.—This is the way of writing *whoes* or *who's.* It disguises to a slight extent the nature of the word, which is, in respect to its sound, as regular a possessive case as *father's* or *man's.*

The relatives, as already stated, differ from the interrogative only in their syntax.

§ 90. *The true personal pronouns.*—*I, me,* and *we* denote the *speaker. Thou* and *ye* the person *spoken to.*

I is found in the nominative case and singular number only.

Me has no nominative case. Its possessive is *my*, its objective *me.*

Forms of the *first* personal pronoun, *singular—I—me, my.*

Forms of the *first* personal pronoun, *plural—we, ours, us.*

Forms of the *second* personal pronoun, *singular—thou, thee, thy.*

Forms of the *second* personal pronoun, *plural—ye, you, your.*

The true possessive pronouns.—This is my book; this is a book of mine. In each of these propositions we make an assertion as to the nature of a *book.* We state what the book is in regard to ownership or *possession.* We assert that it is *my book,* that it is a book belonging to *me,* that it is a book of *mine,* and not any other person's.

Between, however, the words *my, thy, our, your, her,* and *their* on one side, and *mine, thine, ours, yours, hers, theirs* on the other side, there is the following difference. *My, thy, our, your, her,* and *their* signify possession, because they are possessive *cases.* *Mine, thine, ours, yours, hers, theirs* signify possession for a different reason. They partake of the nature of adjectives, and in all the allied languages are declined as such.

In opposition to the words *my, thy, our, your, her, their,* they may be called the true possessive pronouns. Respecting the difference between these two classes of words, more may be seen in the Syntax. Those who are familiar with the classical languages may at once comprehend the distinction. *My* and *thy* are the equivalents of *mei* and *tui; mine* and *thine,* of *meus (mea, meum)* and *tuus (tua, tuum);* and, like *meus (mea, meum)* and *tuus (tua, tuum), mine* and *thine* were once declined.

In *hers, theirs, ours, yours;* or *her-s, their-s, our-s, your-s;* the analysis is *he-r-s, thei-r-s, ou-r-s, you-r-s.* Although adjectival in meaning, these *forms originated as cases;* and that since the Anglo-Saxon period. The *-s* is the *s* of the genitive case; so that, in these words, we have a case formed from a case.

§ 91. *One* and *man*.—These are what are called the indeterminate pronouns. The latter has been entirely superseded by the former. Yet they both have the meaning. The one, however, is a word of French, the other of German origin.

a. One is the French *on*, as in *on* dit = one (*i.e.* the world at large, or Man in general) says. The older form is *homme*, which is the Latin *homo*=man.

b. Before the Norman Conquest, or during the true Anglo-Saxon period, the word was *man*, just as it is at the present time in German, where *man sagt*=*dit*=*one says*= they say. It presents itself as *me;* the vowel being changed and the *n* dropped; the dropping of the *n* being conspicuous in the Frisian as a rule, and of the West-Saxon in this particular word; where it is *me.*

The *reflective* pronoun *self* is chiefly connected with syntax. In respect to their etymology, *self, other*, and *one* are declined as *substantives.*

	Singular.		
Nominative	self	other	one
Possessive	self's	other's	one's
	Plural.		
Nominative	selves	others	ones
Possessive	solves'	others'	ones'.

That some of these forms are rare is certain. Such expressions, however, as *one is unwilling to put one's friend to trouble,* or *my wife and little ones are well,* or *these are my two little ones' playthings,* are common.

§ 92. The *-s* in *this, these,* and *those.*—These three words are *compounds* of the roots *the* and *se;* both Demonstrative. In the word *those* (§ 88) the *-se* is a late addition. In *this* and *these,* however, it is found in the oldest specimens of our language.

NUMERALS.

§ 93. *Cardinal Numbers.*—It rarely happens that the whole of the Cardinal Numbers are, in any language, declined throughout. *One* is naturally singular; so that it has no need to take any particular form in order to distinguish it from a plural. In like manner the rest of the numbers are naturally plural, so that words like *five* and *six* have no need of taking any particular form to distinguish them from singulars. These facts do away with the necessity of any forms expressive of number. The expression of case and gender is not so naturally superfluous; and, hence, in many languages the earlier numerals are declined. In the present English all the cardinals are undeclined. One antiquated word, however, preserves a trace of an earlier Anglo-Saxon declension. The word *twain* was originally the Accusative masculine of *twá* (*twá-n*, A. S. *twegen*).

§ 94. As a *Number*, the word *first* is the ordinal of *one*. As *words* they have no connection. There is no such word as *on-th*; while *fir-st* is a derivative from *fore*. This difference between the Cardinals and the Ordinals of 1, *as words*, is common throughout the class to which the German class of languages belongs. German *ein*, *erste* (derived from *ere*=before); Latin *unus primus*, Greek εἷς πρῶτος.

As a *Number*, the word *second* is the ordinal of *two*. As *words* they have no connection. *Second* is the French *second*, from the Latin *secundus*; which is, itself, a form of *sequundus*, from *sequor*=I follow. In English there is no such word as *two-th*. There *is*, however, in German *zwei*, *zweite*. Hence the difference: the Cardinal and Ordinal which we have noticed as very general in the *first* numeral, is less so in the second.

In the word *third* and those that follow, no such differences will occur. The Ordinal will be formed from the Cardinal by the addition of *d* or *th*, subject to slight variations.

§ 95. *Numerals from* 13 *to* 19 *inclusive.*—Here the affix *-teen* is another form of *ten*. It denotes *Addition: i.e. thirteen*=3+10.

§ 96. *Numerals from* 20 *to* 90 *inclusive.*—Here the affix
-ty is, also, connected with the word *ten*, though not so
closely. The fuller form of *ty* is *tig-;* and the *g* in *tig* is the
κ in the Greek δεκ-*a*, and the *c* in the Latin *dec*-em.

Tig means a Collection of Ten, or a Decad, and, so doing,
denotes multiplication; *i.e. twen-*ty$= 2 \times 10$, or two tens.

Nom. Fjórir tigir manna$=$4 decads of men.
Acc. Fjóra tiga manna $=$4 „ „
Dat. Fjorum tigum manna$=$to „ „
Gen. Fjögurra tiga manna$=$of „ „

§ 97. *Possessive and Objective as names of English cases.*—
Possessive is the English name for the *Genitive* case in Latin,
Greek, and other languages; and, in English, the two terms
are sometimes used indiscriminately. But the alteration is
an improvement. In the vast majority of cases the English
form in *-s* denotes Possession; thus the *man's hat* means
the hat of which the man is in *Possession.* The case is
sometimes, perhaps often, used in other senses; but to this
of Possession it is *mainly* restricted. It ends in *-s, i.e.*
takes '*s* as its sign; and, if this were all, there would be
nothing more to say about it. But this is not the case.
Practically the *man's hat* means the *hat of the man,* and
vice versâ. Confusion comes out of this. The word *of* passes
for the *sign* of the Possessive Case; and there are few who
have not considered it as such. But the true sign of the
Possessive Case is '*s*; and, in the combination *hat of the
man,* the word *man,* whatever else it may be, is *not* a Possessive Case.

The fact is that in *the hat of the man* we have no case
at all, but a combination of words instead of one—which is
a very different thing. This, alone, is an instance of confusion. But it may be said that *of* governs a Possessive
Case, and that, for this reason, the Combination is as truly
Possessive as the Inflection. It may or not be this. If it
were, however, we should expect, instead of the form *man,*
the Possessive form *man's*—which we do not find.

This will be further considered in the sequel. At present it is enough to say that *of* is not the sign of a Possessive or Genitive Case, in the way that *'s* is.

§ 98. *The Objective Case.*—Objective, like *Possessive*, is a new name. The innovators, however, who introduced it showed good judgment. They preferred it to the old word Accusative. This was because, though the Objective Case *in the main* coincided with the Accusative, it was, to a considerable degree, made-up out of other Cases as well. The Objective, then, is an Accusative and something more.

§ 99. *Virtual Inflections.*—There was, then, a time when the single case which is now called *Objective* consisted of two, three, or perhaps more cases, each with a name of its own. One of these was, certainly, an Accusative; and another Dative. Indeed, at the present moment, a third case still survives, though only found in Pronouns—*he, his, him.* This last word is called an Accusative. In Anglo-Saxon, however, it was no Accusative, but a Dative; and of the Dative rather than the Accusative *m* was the sign. The sign of the Accusative was *n.* Hence, the form that corresponded with the Latin *eum* was *hene*, whereas *him* =*ei.* Again, in a few old words a genuine Instrumental Case is to be found. All these are now massed together under the general name Objective. Still, there are times when it is necessary to ask to what particular division of the Objective such or such a word should be referred. Few would deny that in such phrases as *give it him, it is like him*, the original Dative character of the form still maintains itself. Such cases may be called Virtual.

SUBSTANTIVES.

§ 100. A Substantive is an *invariable* name, capable of forming, by itself, either the subject or the predicate of a proposition. The Pronoun, as we have seen, can do the same; but the Pronoun differs from the Substantive in being a variable name. See §§ 192–200.

The Declensions of the Substantive are those of (1) Number, and (2) Case.

The Numbers are two—the Singular and the Plural.

The only *Case*, with a distinct sign, is the Possessive; and even this does not distinguish it from the Plural Number—not, at least, in the language as it is *spoken*. This is because both the Nominative Plural and the Possessive singular end in *-s*; so that, when a word like *fathers* or the like stands alone, we have no means of knowing of what the sound *s* is a sign. When it stands in a sentence, and in the relation with other words, its import is more easily seen —for the context helps us. Still there is always the possibility of ambiguity of some kind. In *writing* we remedy this by the insertion of the so-called Apostrophe, *i.e.* an inverted comma. Hence, whilst the *fathers of the families* gives us a Plural Number, the *father's children* means the *children of one father*, and is a Possessive Case. This, however, is not so much a process of Language as an artificial contrivance in the way of a substitute. In unwritten languages it can have no existence.

But the ambiguity in the spoken language did not always exist. The Anglo-Saxon sign of the Possessive was -es, *e.g. cyning=king—cyning-es, king's;* while that of the Plural was -as, *e.g. cyning-as, kings.*

§ 101. *The Possessive Plural.*—This, like the Apostrophe in the Possessive Singular, is, to a great extent, artificial. In the Anglo-Saxon there was, certainly, a sign of the Possessive Plural; but it was -a—not -s, as *cyninga=kings'= of kings=reg-um.* Here the present English again addresses itself to the eye, and by altering the place of the Apostrophe we get such forms as the *fathers' children=the children of different fathers.* But between this Plural *s'* and the Singular *'s* there is this notable difference. The Singular *s* is a real one. The *s'* of the Plural has no existence at all; for the *s* in words like *fathers'* is simply the *'s* in the *s* of the Nominative. If there were a true sign of a

Possessive Case, the full forms would be the *father-s-es children*; the *master-s-es men*, &c. It is probable that if such combinations existed, we should soon drop them, on account of the accumulation of *esses*. But it is also probable that they never existed. In the few words where the Plural does *not* end in the sound of *s*, we have a true Possessive sign—*e.g.* *men's*, *children's*, *oxen-s*; and, so far, they are real, rather than artificial.

§ 102. The result of these uses of *s* is that, with few exceptions, it stands for two cases and two numbers. Indeed, as a sign of Inflection, it is the only one which the Declension of the Substantive supplies. Even here, it speaks more to the eye than the ear. We spell it as if it were *s*; but, in the great majority of cases, we sound it as *z*.

In some cases we are obliged to do so—

1. Thus: *slabs, slaves, lads, blades, dogs*, &c., are words which we can spell, but which we cannot pronounce. We pronounce them *slabz, slävz, ladz, blädz, dogz*, &c.

2. Words like *hills, drums, hens, bars, days, fleas, bows*, &c. we *can* pronounce as they are spelt; but we do not. The *s*, in all these words, and in all words like them (*i.e.* all words ending a liquid or a vowel), is sounded as a *z*.

3. If the last sound of the singular be that of *s*, *z*, the *sh* in *shine*, or the *z* in *azure*, the addition is that of the sound of the syllable -*ez* (spelt -*es*); as *loss-ez, kiss-ez, blaz-ez, haz-ez, blush-ez, lash-ez*, spelt *loss-es, kiss-es, blaz-es, haz-es, blush-es, lash-es*.

The true rule, then, for the Inflections of the Substantive is that it consists of the addition of the *sound of s modified according to the termination of the root*.

§ 103. *Plural of certain words in f.*—The following words end in the sharp mute *f*—*loaf, half, wife, life, calf, leaf*. Now, according to § 102, their plurals should be formed by the addition of the sound of *s* in *seal*, and so be *loafs, halfs, wifes, lifes, calfs, leafs* (pronounced *loafce, halfce, wifce, lifce, calfce, leafce*). This, however, is not the case. Their plurals are formed by the addition of the sound of *z* in *zeal*, and are *leaves, halves, wives, lives, calves, leaves* (pronounced *loavz, halvz, wivz, livz, calvz, leavz*) ; the sound of the *f* being changed into that of *v*. Respecting these words we must observe :

1. That the vowel before *f* is *long*. Words like *muff*, where the vowel is short, form their plurals by means of the sounds of the *s* in *seal;* as *muff, muff-s* (pronounced *muffce*).

2. That they are all of Anglo-Saxon origin. In the words *mischief, chief, handkerchief, grief, relief*, the plural is formed as in *muff*; that is, by the addition of the sound of *s*; *mischiefs, chiefs,* &c.

Putting these two facts together, we can use more general language, and say that

When a word ends in the sound of *f*, preceded by a long vowel, and is of Anglo-Saxon origin, the plural is formed by the addition of the sound of the *z* in *zeal*.

To this rule there are two exceptions.

1. *Dwarf;* a word of Anglo-Saxon origin, but which forms its plural by means of the sound of *s—dwarfs* (pronounced *dwarfce*).

2. *Beef*; a word *not* of Anglo-Saxon origin, but which forms its plural by means of the sound of *z—beeves* (pronounced *beevz*).

If we ask the reason of this peculiarity in the formation of the plurals of these words in -*f*, we shall find that it lies with the singular rather than the plural forms. In Anglo-Saxon, *f* at the end of a word was sounded as *v*; and it is highly probable that the original *singulars* were sounded *loav, halv, wive, calv, leav.*

§ 104. *Plural forms in* -ce.—1. The word *penny* should form its plural by means of the sound of *z* in *zeal*. It does so, and consequently, there is the plural form *pennies* (*penniz*). But, besides this, there is the form *pence*.

Now there are two plurals to the word *penny*, because there are two meanings. *Six pennies* means *six separate penny-pieces*. *Six pence*, or *sixpence*, means a *single coin equivalent to six penny-pieces*. This last sense is Collective rather than Plural.

The plural *pence* has a further peculiarity. According to § 102, it ought to end in the sound of *z* in *zeal*, which it does not: it ends in the sound of *s* in *seal*. This serves to distinguish it from the plural of *pen*, which is *penz* (spelt *pens*).

2. *Dice.*—This word ends in the sound of *s* in *seal*, instead of that of *z* in *zeal*. This serves to distinguish *dice* for play from *dies* (*diez*) for coining.

§ 105. *Equivocal forms from Singulars* in s.—The number of the following words has always been a matter of discussion amongst Grammarians.

1. *Alms.*—The -s is no sign of the plural number, but part of the original singular, like the *s* in *goose* or *loss*. The Anglo-Saxon form was *œlmesse*. Notwithstanding this, we cannot say *alms-es* in the same way that we can say *loss-es*. Hence the word *alms* is, in respect to its original form, singular : in respect to its meaning, either singular or plural.

2. *Riches.*—The -s is no sign of the plural number, since there is no such *substantive* as *rich* ; on the contrary, it is part of the original singular, like the *s* in *distress*. The form in the original French, from which language it was derived, is *richesse*. Notwithstanding this, we cannot say *richess-es* in the same way that we *can* say *distresses*. Hence the word *riches* is, in respect to its original form, singular ; in respect to its meaning, either singular or plural : most frequently the latter.

3. *News.*—The -s here is *no* part of the original singular, but the sign of the plural, like the *s* in *trees*. Notwithstanding this, we cannot subtract the *s*, and say *new*, in the same way that we *can* form *tree* from *trees*. Hence the

word *news* is, in respect to its original form, plural; in respect to its meaning, either singular or plural: most frequently the former.

4. *Means.*—The -*s* is no part of the original singular, but the sign of the plural, like the *s* in *trees*. The form in the original French, from which language the word is derived, is *moyen*, singular; *moyens*, plural. If we subtract from the word *means* the letter *s*, we say *mean*. Now, as a singular form of the word *means*, with the sense it has in the phrase *ways and means*, there is, in the current English, no such word as *mean*, any more than there is such a word as *new* from *news*. But, in a different sense, there *is* the singular form *mean*; as in the phrase *the golden mean*, meaning *middle course*. Hence the word *means* is, in respect to its form, plural; in respect to its meaning, either singular or plural.

5. *Pains.*—The form in the original French, from which language the word is derived, is *peine*. The reasoning that has been applied to the word *means* is closely applicable to the word *pains*.

6. The same also applies to the word *amends*. The form in French is *amende*, without the *s*.

7. *Mathematics, Physics, Metaphysics, Optics, Politics, Ethics, Pneumatics, Hydraulics, Hydrostatics, Mechanics, Dynamics, Statics.*—All these words are plural in form; in sense they are either singular or plural.

The words just noticed may be called equivocal forms. In words like *alms* and *riches* the original *s* of the singular is confounded with the *s*, the sign of the plural. In the remainder the *s*, the sign of the plural, is taken for a part of the original singular. This confusion prevents the words in point from having either true singulars, like *new, mean, pain*; or true plurals, like *riches-es, alms-es*.

If the reason of this confusion be inquired into, it will be found,

1. That all the words in question are of foreign origin.

2. That in sense they are partly singular and partly plural. *Alms* means either *a number of separate donations taken severally*, or *a number of separate donations dealt with as a single act of charity*. In the first case the plural, in the second the singular, sense predominates.

§ 106. *Signs of Number not ending in -s.*—Besides the usual plural forms in *s*, there are four other methods in English of expressing a *number* of objects.

§ 107. *Change of vowel.*—This class consists in the present English of the following words:

1. *Man*, singular; *men*, plural. The vowel *a* changed to the vowel *e*.

2. *Foot*, sing.; *feet*, pl. The vowel *oo* (sounded as the *ou* in *could*) changed to the vowel *ee*.

3, 4. *Tooth*, sing.; *teeth*, pl.: *goose*, sing.; *geese*, pl. The vowel *oo* (as in *food*) changed to *ee* as in *feet*.

5, 6. *Mouse*, *louse*, sing.; *mice*, *lice*, pl. The diphthong *ou* changed to the vowel *i* (as in *night*). The combination *ce* used instead of *se*, for the same reason as in *pence* and in *dice*, *i. e.* lest, if written *mise*, *lise*, the words should be pronounced *mize*, *lize*.

§ 108. *Addition of* -en *or* -n.—In the present English the word *oxen* is the only specimen of this form in current use. In the older stages of our language the number of words in -*en* was much greater than at present.

hos-en	= *hose or stockings*		*scher-en*	= *shire-s*
shoo-n	= *shoe-s*		*doghtr-en*	= *daughter-s*
ey-ne	= *eye-s*		*sustr-en*	= *sister-s*
bischop-en	= *bishop-s*		*uncl-en*	= *uncle-s*
eldr-en	= *elder-s*		*tre-en*	= *tree-s*
arw-en	= *arrows*		*souldr-en*	= *soldier-s.*

§ 109. *Childer.*—Here the analysis is child-*er-en*, the *en* being the *en* in ox-*en*, and the *er* or -*r*, that of child-*er*, which is the ordinary Northumbrian form. In A. S. the *r* was followed by an -*u*, the sign of the nominative case in the

declension to which the word belonged. *Æg=egg, lam=*
lamb, cealf=calf were thus declined, the plurals being *ægru,*
lambru, ceafru; eggs, lambs, calfs. From the first we get
the word *eyry* or *eggery*, applied to the nest of the eagle. To
the second we owe the *b* in lam*b*, which is no part of the
original word: for when *lam-*, after becoming *lam-er-u,*
undergoes contraction, the euphonic insertion of *b* between
the *m* and the *r* takes place, and then, because the letter *b*
presents itself in the plural, it passes for a part of the
simpler singular form.

§ 110. *Combination of two of the preceding methods.*—
Three words occur in this class.

1. *Kyne=cows;* a plural formed from a plural by the
addition of *-n;* as *cow, kye, ky-ne. Kye* is found in provincial English, and *cý* in Anglo-Saxon.

2. *Children;* a plural formed from a plural by the addition of *en;* as *child, child-er, child-er-en=children.*

3. *Brethren;* a plural formed from a plural by the addition of *-en;* as *brother, brether* (?) or *brethre, brether-en=*
brethren.

§ 111. When the singular ends in *o*, the plural ends in
oes; as *cargo, cargoes.*

When the singular ends in *y*, preceded by a consonant,
the plural ends in *-ies;* as *lady, ladies; quantity, quantities.*

In *youth, oath, truth,* and *path,* the *th,* though sounded
in the singular as in *thin,* is generally sounded in the plural
as in *thine.* Youth, pronounced you*dh*z, not you*thce.* Tru*th;*
pronounced tru*dh*z, not tru*thce.* Path, pronounced pa*dh*z,
not pa*thce.*

In *house,* the *s,* though sounded in the singular as in *sin,*
is sounded in the plural as *z. Houses* is pronounced *houzez.*

The plural of *woman* is pronounced *wimmen.*

§ 112. *Current and obsolete processes.*

By adding the sound of the *s* in *seal* to the word *father,*
we change it into *father-s.* Hence the addition of the sound
in question is the process by which the word *father* is

changed into *fathers*. The process by which *ox* is changed into *ox-en* is the addition of the sound of the syllable *-en*.

Let us suppose that from the Latin, Greek, French, or some other language, a new word is introduced; that it is a substantive; and that it has to be used in the plural number. The formation will be in *-s*, and not in *-en*—the habit of forming plurals in *-s* being *current* or usual, the habit of forming them in *-en* being *obsolete*.

In all languages there are two sorts of processes, those that are in operation at a certain period, and those that have ceased to operate.

§ 113. *The Possessive Case.*—In the language as it is *spoken*, the possessive case singular is the same as the ordinary nominative plural—both ending in *-s*.

Such is the rule, to which there is only one class of exceptions. Words in *f* form their possessive case in the sound of *s* in *seal*; as *loaf's*, *wife's*, *calf's*, and *leaf's*, &c.; sounded *loafce*, *wifce*, *calfce*, *leafce*, and not *loavz*, *wivz*, *calvz*, *leavz*. We say *the wives are good-tempered*, but *the wife's temper is good; the loaves are well-baked*, but *the loaf's baking is good; the calves are well-fed*, but *the calf's feeding is good; the leaves are changing colour*, but *the leaf's colour is changing.*

§ 114. The possessive case singular is distinguished, in the language as it is *written*, from the nominative (or objective) case plural by the insertion of an ' between the last letter of the original word and the letter *-s*; as *father, father's, fathers; the father's son; the fathers are speaking.* This, however, is merely a point of spelling. It does not affect the spoken language.

Athough at the present time identical, the possessive case singular and the nominative case plural were originally distinct. The first ended in *-es*, as *endes=end's*; the second in *-as*; as *end-as=ends*. The ejection of the vowels (*a* and *e*) reduces the two words to the same form.

The possessive case plural, when it is formed at all,

G

is formed, in the *spoken* language, from the nominative case of the same number, in the same way as the possessive case singular is formed; that is, by the *addition* of the sound of -*s*; as *children, children's; oxen, oxen's: the children's bread; the oxen's horns.*

It is rare, however, that in the *spoken* language the possessive case plural differs at all from the nominative case. As the nominative plural generally ends in -*s*, and as the possessive is also formed in -*s*, there would be too many sounds of *s* accumulated in a single word; *e.g.* the possessive plural of *trees* would be *treeses*, and the possessive plural of *fox* would be *fox-es-es*; as the *foxeses tails.* Hence, in the *spoken* language, the nominative and possessive cases plural are alike whenever the former ends in the sound of -*s*.

In the *written* language the difference between the nominative (or objective) case plural, and the possessive case plural, is expressed by the addition of an ' *after* the letter -*s*; *the trees are in leaf*, but *the trees' leaves are coming out; the ships are in full sail*, but *the ships' sails are spread.*

ADJECTIVES.

§ 115. A word capable, by itself, of forming the predicate, but not capable of forming the subject of a proposition, is called an adjective.

An adjective is not exactly the name of anything, though something akin thereto. In such an expression as *snow is white*, it cannot be said that *white* is a name. That it is a word is certain. It is also certain that it denotes a quality, or attribute. Yet it is not the name of that quality. The name of that quality is *whiteness.* Neither can it be said that *white* is quite equivalent to *white thing.*

White, then, and adjectives like it, are not names. They are, rather, words that suggest names. The true name is the Abstract, *white-ness.*

§ 116. An adjective shows that the substantive with which it is united possesses a certain quality. To say that *glass is smooth, clear, brittle,* and *bright,* is to say that it possesses the qualities of *smoothness, clearness, brittleness,* and *brightness.*

Qualities may be possessed in different degrees. One piece of glass may be *brighter* than another, another may be *brighter* still, and a third the *brightest* of all. English adjectives, therefore, have degrees of comparison, viz. :—

1. The *positive;* which gives the word in its simple form : as *bright :*

2. The *comparative;* formed from the positive by the addition of *-er;* as *bright-er :*

3. The *superlative;* formed from the positive by the addition of *-est;* as *bright-est.*

§ 117. The sign of the comparative degree is equivalent in meaning to the word *more.* In the word *bright-er,* the syllable *-er* is the sign of the comparative degree; and the word *bright-er* is equivalent in meaning to *more bright.*

The sign of the superlative degree is equivalent in meaning to the word *most.* In the word *bright-est,* the syllable *-est* is the sign of the superlative degree, and *bright-est* is equivalent in meaning to the words *most bright.*

§ 118. The comparative degree is formed from the positive by the addition of the syllable *-er :* as *cold, cold-er; rich, rich-er; dry, dry-er; low, low-er.* We have, also, just seen that *brightest* is the superlative of *bright,* or, we might say, of *bright-er.*

The following positives have no comparative, and also no superlative forms :—*good, bad, evil, ill.* There are in the current English no such words as *good-er, badd-er, evill-er, ill-er;* or *good-est, badd-est, evill-est, ill-est.*

The following comparatives (and superlatives) have no positive forms : *worse, worst; better, best.* There are in the current English no such words as *wor* and *bett.*

The comparative form elder.—The positive form *old* has two comparatives; *a) old-er; b) eld-er.* A knowledge of the following facts will account for the latter form. In

G 2

Anglo-Saxon there were several words, which, besides
adding the syllable -*re*, changed the vowel.

A.S. Positive.	A.S. Comparative.	A.S. Superlative.	English.
Lang	Leng-re	Leng-est	*Long*
Strang	Streng-re	Streng-est	*Strong*
Geong	Gyng-re	Gyng-est	*Young*
Sceort	Scyrt-re	Scyrt-est	*Short*
Heah	Hy-rre	Hyh-est	*High*
Eald	*Yld-re*	*Yld-est*	*Old.*

The Anglo-Saxon form *yld-re*, then, explains the English
form *elder*. The word *elder* is often used as a substantive.
We say *the elders of the people*.

§ 119. *Latter.*—The word *late* has two forms for the
comparative degree: (1) *later*, (2) *latter*. In the first the
vowel is the *a* in *fate*; in the second, the *a* in *fat*.

More.—As late as the reign of Queen Elizabeth we find
the positive form *moe*. From this *more* (*mo-er*) is regularly
derived.

Nether.—The positive form *nith* is obsolete. From this,
the comparative form *neth-er* (in A.S. *niðere*) is regularly
derived. In phrases like *the Netherlands, the nether regions*,
the word *nether* means *low*, or *lower*.

Less, lesser.—This form is not satisfactorily accounted for.

Near.—This word, although, in meaning, an adjective
of the positive degree, is, in respect to its form, a comparative. The -*r* is no part of the original word. The Anglo-
Saxon form is *neah* for the positive; *nea-rre*, *nea-r*, and
ny-r for the comparative. Speakers who would be shocked
at calling an *idea* an *idear*, say *near* for *neah* without mis-
giving. Hence,

Nearer is, in respect to its form, a double comparative,
nea-r-er.

Further.—This means *more in front*, or *more forward*. It
is derived from the word *fore*, as found in *foremost*. Besides
the change of the vowel from *o* to *u* (*fore, fur-th-er*), there
is the addition of the sound of *th*. This sound was inserted

in an early stage of language. It occurs in the Old High German forms *vor-d-aro*, *for-d-oro*, *vor-d-ero*, *for-d-ar*, *fur-d-ir*, and in the A.S. *forð*, and English *forth*.

Farther.—This means *more far*, or *more distant*. It is derived from the word *far*, which appears in the following different forms: *fairra*, Mœso-Gothic; *vërro*, *vër*, *fër*, Old High German; *feor*, Anglo-Saxon; *fiarri*, Old Norse. The proper comparative is formed without the *th*; as *vërr-ôr*, *vërr-ôro*, Old High German. In the English word *far-th-er* the *th* is inserted, either because *far-er* is inharmonious, or from the word being confounded with *fur-th-er*.

Former.—A comparative from the original word *fore*. For the insertion of the *m* (*for-m-er*) see § 124.

§ 120. It is necessary to know that in the Mœso-Gothic the comparative degree was formed differently from the comparative degree in Anglo-Saxon, English, and the other allied languages. Instead of being formed by the addition of the sound of -*r*, it was formed by the addition of the sound of -*s* or -*z*.

Positive.	Comparative.	English.
ald	ald-iza	old, old-er
sut	sut-iza	sweet, sweeter
blind	blind-oza	blind, blind-er.

In the latter stages of languages this *s* became *r*.

In the word *worse* we may suppose that there is a remnant of the old comparative in -*s* or -*z*. The Mœso-Gothic form is *váirsiza*, the Anglo-Saxon *vyrsa*.

§ 121. The Superlative degree may be formed from the positive by the addition of the syllable -*est*; as *cold*, *cold-est*; *rich*, *rich-est*; *dry*, *dry-est*; *low*, *low-est*. This is the manner in which the greatest part of the English superlatives are formed.

§ 122. *Best, last.*—By comparing these with the words *bett-er* and *lat-er* (or *lait-er*), we discover that the sound of *t* has been lost. The full forms would be *bett-est* and *lat-est*.

Least.—The nature of this form has not been satisfactorily determined.

First.—A superlative from the original word *fore.*

Worst.—By referring to § 120, we shall see that the comparatives in Mœso-Gothic were formed in -*s* or -*z*. We have also seen that the Mœso-Gothic is supposed to exhibit the oldest forms of the languages allied to the English. Hence it is considered that the oldest process for forming the comparative degree consisted in the addition of -*s* or -*z*; and that it was during some later period that the sound of -*s* or -*z* became changed into that of -*r*.

By referring to § 121 it will be seen that the superlative is formed from the positive by adding -*st*, or *s* followed by *t*. Such is the view that in the present English, and in most of the allied languages, it is necessary to take. It is clear, however, that, if the comparative were formed by adding to the positive *s* instead of *r*, a different view might be taken. If the comparative degrees of words like *sweet* and *blind* were *sweet-es* (or *sweet-ez*) and *blind-es* (or *blind-ez*), just as they really were in Mœso-Gothic, we might then say that the superlative was formed from the *comparative* by adding *t*, instead of saying that it was formed from the *positive* by adding -*st*. Now this is the view really taken by J. Grimm, who, on all these points, is a high authority; in which case the word *worst* is a superlative regularly formed from the old comparative form *worse.*

§ 123. *Most.*—See § 119.

Nearest.—See § 119.

Next.—The superlative of *nigh*, contracted from *nighest.* The Anglo-Saxon forms were *neah, nyh-st, neh-st, nyh-ste.* In A. S. the letter *h* was pronounced strongly, and sounded like *g* or *k*. This fact is still shown in the spelling; as *nigh.* In the word *next* this sound is preserved, slightly changed into that of *k*; *next=nek-st.*

Furthest.—See § 119.

Farthest.—See § 119.

Eldest.—See § 118.

§ 124. *Upmost*, &c.—Words like *upmost* look as if they were compounds formed by the addition of *most*.

The Anglo-Saxon language presents us with the following forms; which show that the *m* has nothing to do with the word *most*.

Anglo-Saxon.	English.
innema (inn-ema)	. inmost
ûtema (ût-ema)	outmost
siðema (sið-ema)	latest
lætema (læt-ema)	latest
niðema (nið-ma)	nethermost
forma (for-ma)	foremost
æftema (aft-ema)	aftermost
yfema (uf-ema)	upmost
hindema (hind-ema)	hindmost
medema (mid-ema)	midmost.

From the words in question there was formed in Anglo-Saxon, a regular superlative form in the usual manner; *viz.* by the addition of -*st*; as *æfte-m-est, fyr-m-est, læte-m-est, sið-m-est, yfe-m-est, ute-m-est, inne-m-est.*

Hence the *m* is the *m* in the words *innema*, &c.; whilst the -*st* is the sign of the superlative. Hence, we should write

mid-m-ost	*not*	mid-most	fore-m-ost	*not*	fore-most
ut-m-ost	„	ut-most	in-m-ost	„	in-most
up-m-ost	„	up-most	hind-m-ost	„	hind-most

In *neth-er-most*, &c., there is a superlative super-added to a comparative.

VERBALS AND VERBS.

§ 125. The Verbals are names of actions and of agents.

Hunt-*ing* is the act performed by a hunt-*er*, or the agent.

The Verbal in -*ing* is identical in form with the Present Participle. But it is this only when we compare the later forms of the two words. The Verbal Abstract

in Anglo-Saxon ended in -*ung*, as clæns-*ung*=cleans-*ing*.
The Participle ended in *ande, ende*, or -*inde*: as clæns-*iande*.

For the present this is nearly all that need be said.
We are passing from one of the chief parts of speech to
another, from the Pronoun, the Substantive, and the
Adjective, to the Verb and Participle. Which class is the
most important is difficult to say. The Verb, by many
grammarians, is looked upon as the primary part of speech,
and from this view it derives its name. The Latin *verbum*
means *word*, and the Verb has been held to be pre-eminently *the word* in language. Whether this doctrine be
right or wrong need not now be asked. The object of the
present remarks is to show that the difference between the
two great classes is by no means very great; and, in order
to do this, an apparent deviation from the right line of investigation has been resorted to. The Verbal is evidently
derived from the Verb; and the Verb is the basis of the
Verbal. Yet the Verbal, though a secondary and derived
form, has been taken first. However, by thus taking it,
we show more clearly the connection between the Verb and
the Substantive.

§ 126. A Verb can form, by itself, *both* the Predicate
and the Copula of a Proposition; as *I call; he speaks.*

Verbs can be resolved into their elements, and that part
which coincides with the Predicate can be separated from
that which coincides with the Copula. *I call*=*I am calling; he speaks*=*he is speaking.*

That part of the Verb which gives the Predicate is
called a Participle. *Calling, speaking, called,* and *spoken*
are Participles.

The words which give the Copula are *am, art, is, are,
was*, and *were.*

In such propositions as *I am speaking, thou art writing,
he is singing*, the words *am, art, is, are, was*, and *were* connect the subjects *I, thou, he, she, it, we, ye,* &c., with the
predicates *speaking, writing, singing,* &c.

§ 127. Verbs express actions. Actions are either Intransitive or Transitive.

Intransitive actions imply an agent and an act; as *I sleep*, *I walk*, and *I live*.

Transitive actions imply an agent, an act, and an object acted on; as *I strike the ball*; *he loves his parents*; *Brutus killed Cæsar*.

Certain Transitives have Intransitives with which they correspond, and from which they are formed by changing the vowel. Thus *rise, lie, sit, fall, drink*, are Intransitive; *raise, lay, set, fell, drench*, Transitive. To *rise* is to *raise oneself*. To *fell* is to *make to fall*.

§ 128. In respect to their inflection Verbs are (1) related to the Substantive, (2) related to the Adjective, and (3) characterized by peculiarities of their own.

So far as the Verb is related to either the Substantive or the Adjective it is Declined. So far as it is characterized by peculiarities of its own it is Conjugated.

The Declension of the Verb in Anglo-Saxon was fuller than it is in the present English.

In Anglo-Saxon there was a true Infinitive Mood which ended in *-an*, as *bærnan = burn, lufian = love*. When this was preceded by *to*, *-an* became *-enne*; as *to lufienne = to love, to bærnenne = to burn*.

This will perplex no one who has gone through the elements of the Latin grammar, and knows what is meant by an Infinitive Mood or a Gerund. Such a reader will at once compare *lufian = love* with *amare*; and *bærnan = burn* with *urere*; whilst *to lufienne = to love* he will compare with *ad amandum*; and *to bærnenne = to burn* with *ad urendum*.

Verbs, when Conjugated, have Number, Person, Mood, and Tense.

§ 129. *Number.*—When we say *he read-s*, we speak of an action performed by one person. In this case the Verb is Singular. But when we say *they read*, we speak of an action performed by more than one person. In this case the Verb is plural. When there is a positive distinction of form between verbs singular and verbs plural, there is a positive sign of Number. In Latin, *voco*=*I call*; whilst *vocamus*=*we call*.

§ 130. *Person.*—In the words *thou speakest*, the pronoun *thou* is of the Second Person, and the verb *speak*, when taken along with it, has attached to it the syllable *-est*. The syllable *-est* is an ending or termination. It shows that the word is taken with a pronoun of the second person. It is a positive sign of the Second Person. The sign of the Third Person is *-s*; as *he speaks*.

§ 131. *Tense.*—The forms *call* and *call-ed* are different. The presence of the *-d* is one sign, its absence another— the former being positive, the latter negative. A word with the sign of past, present, or future, time, is said to be in a certain *Tense*. The word *call* is in the Present, the word *call-ed* in the Past Tense.

§ 132. *Mood.*—When we say *John walks*, we state something as a fact. We say positively that the action of walk- ing is going on.

When we say *John! walk!* we give orders for something to take place; *viz.* the action of walking. We do not say that the action of walking is positively taking place, or going to take place. We only express a wish, or give a command, that it should do so.

When we say *if John walk fast he will fatigue himself,* we use the word *walk* in a third sense. We do not say that the action of walking is taking place, or has taken place, or will take place. Neither do we deliver an order that it may take place. We say, however, that *if* it do take place, something else will take place also; *viz.* that the person who causes it to take place will fatigue himself. Now in this case there is the idea of conditions and contin- gencies. John's fatigue is contingent upon his walking fast.

In *John begins to walk*, the word *walk* is in a different

sense from any of the preceding; for it depends neither upon *John*, nor upon any conditional conjunctions. It depends upon *begins*. Hence—

In *John walks*, the verb is in the *Indicative Mood*.

In *John! walk!* it is in the *Imperative Mood*.

In *if John walk fast, he will fatigue himself*, the word *walk* is in the *Conjunctive Mood*; in which case the words *he will fatigue himself* form one proposition; *John walks fast*, another. The word *if* connects or conjoins the two, and this connection changes the mood.

In *John begins to walk*, the verb *walk* merely states what the action is that *John begins to perform*. And this is an action without any *direct* agent. That *to walk* is *indirectly* connected with *John* is true. It is also true that the person who *begins to walk* is a *walker*, whilst in such expressions as *John refuses to walk*, or *John ceases to walk*, there is no *walking* at all. All that John does is *to refuse*, or *to cease* to do something; and it is upon the verbs *refuse* or *cease*, *not* upon the substantive *John*, that the *Infinitive to walk* depends.

How slight, however, is the difference between *refusing to walk* and *refusing the action of walking!* Equally slight is the difference between a verb in the Infinitive Mood and a Noun. Slighter still is the difference between *he begins to move*, *he begins a movement*, *he begins motion*.

This makes the Declension of the Infinitive Mood, which was prevalent in Anglo-Saxon, and which is still to be found in a fragmentary form in the present English, intelligible. At the present moment the Infinitives like *to err*, though preceded by a Preposition, and originating in an Oblique Case, are, for all practical purposes, Nominatives. When we say—

To err is human; *to forgive*, divine:

we really use—

To err = error; to forgive = forgiveness.

Signs of Number.—§ 133. In the words *a-m*, *speak-est*, *speak-s*, the sounds of *-m*, *-est*, and *-s* denote a difference of person. They also denote a difference of number, since they are found only in the singular. But this they do in a secondary way. They are truly the signs of *persons*. Hence, the only real sign expressive of a difference of number occurs in the past tense of the indicative mood of the verb substantive.

Singular.	Plural.
I was.	We *were*.
Thou wast.	Ye *were*.
He was.	They *were*.

In Anglo-Saxon there were other Verbs that thus changed their vowel in the Plural.

Ic arn, *I ran*.	We urnon, *we run*.
Ic ongan, *I began*.	We ongunnon, *we begun*.
Ic span, *I span*.	We spunnon, *we spun*.
Ic sang, *I sang*.	We sungon, *we sung*.
Ic swang, *I swang*.	We swungon, *we swung*.
Ic dranc, *I drank*.	We druncon, *we drunk*, &c.

Hence, there were no such forms as *ic*, *swumm*, or as *we swammon*. This distinction of number is not adhered to in the present English. It is the author's opinion that the writers and speakers who say *I sang*, say also *we sang*; whilst those who say *we swum*, say also *I swum*.

Signs of Mood.—§ 134. The only instance in English of a verb in one mood being distinguished from a verb in another by any *positive* sign, occurs in the conjugation of the word *was*.

Indicative.		Subjunctive.	
Singular.	Plural.	Singular.	Plural.
I *was*.	We were.	If I *were*.	If we were.
Thou *wast*.	Ye were.	If thou *wert*.	If ye were.
He *was*.	They were.	If he *were*.	If they were.

Note.—Although in *John walks*, as compared with *if John walk, he will be fatigued*, there is a difference between the two verbs; the difference is only a *negative*, and consequently scarcely constitutes a true distinction in form between the two moods.

Signs of Person.—§ 135. *Sign of the First Person Singular.*—In the word *am* (*a-m*) the *m* is no part of the original word. It is the sign of the first Person Singular Present Indicative. Beyond this, no word in English has, in any mood, tense, or number, any form of termination for the First Person.

§ 136. *Sign of the Second Person Singular.*—The usual sign of the Second Person singular is *-st* (originally *-s*), as *thou call-est.* It occurs both in the present and past tenses; *thou called'st, thou spakest.* Like the pronoun *thou,* it is rarely used except in formal discourse.

§ 137. *Sign of the Third Person Singular.*—The usual sign of the Third Person Singular is the sound of the syllable *-eth*, or of the letters *s, z* (or *es*); as *he call-eth,* or he *call-s.* The first of these two forms is only used in formal discourse. The Third Person is only found in the indicative mood, and in the present tense. We cannot say *if he speaketh,* or *if he speaks*; neither can we say *he called-th,* or *he called-s, he spak-eth,* or *he spake-s.*

Whether the addition be the sound of *s* in *seal* (as *hit-s*), of *z* in *zeal* (as *call-z*), or of the syllable *ez* (as *hiss-ez*), depends upon the same circumstances as the use of the same sounds in the possessive cases, and the nominatives plural.

Throughout the whole of the plural there are no signs of the persons; *i. e.* no changes of form:—*we call, ye call, they call; we called, ye called, they called.*

§ 138. In respect to Person the following peculiarities deserve notice.

Forms sungest and *sangest.*—In Anglo-Saxon, the word *sing,* and a great number of words like it, took in the past tense a different vowel for the second person from the one found in the first and third; *e. g. Ic sang*=*I sang, he sang* =*he sang,* were the forms for the first and third person

singular. But the *second* person singular was þu *sunge*=
thou sungest. In this way were conjugated, amongst others,
the following verbs :—þu *swumme*, þu *on-gunne*, þu *sunge*,
þu *sprunge*, þu *runge*, þu *sunce*, þu *drunne*, þu *runne*=*thou
swummest, thou begunnest, thou sungest, &c.*, &c. ; and on the
other hand, Ic (or *he*) *swam,* Ic (or *he*) *ongann,* Ic (or *he*)
sang, Ic (or *he*) *sprang,* Ic (or *he*) *rang,* Ic (or *he*) *sank,* Ic
(or *he*) *drank,* Ic (or *he*) *rann*=*I* (or *he*) *swam, I* (or *he*)
began, &c., &c. There were no such forms in Anglo-Saxon
as Ic (or *he*) *swumm,* or as þu *swamme.* Now this distinction of person is not adhered to in the present English,
since it is the author's opinion that the writers and speakers
who say *I* (or *he*) *sang,* say also *thou sangest*; whilst those
who say *thou sungest,* say also *I* (or *he*) *sung.*

§ 139. *Second Persons not ending in -st.*—In five words
the sign of the second person singular is not *-est*, but *-t*;
viz. ar-t, was-t, wer-t, shal-t, wil-t. There are no such words
as *ar-est, was-est, wer-est, shall-est*; and the word *will-est*,
when used at all, is different in sense from *wil-t.*

§ 140. Verbs have now been considered in respect to their
mood, their number, and their person, especially with respect
to the last two. This is because it is by its number and
person that the verb in its most characteristic form is distinguished. Where there are no persons and no numbers
the verb begins to be something else. It becomes participial,
and participles are, at least, as closely connected with the
adjective as with the true personal verb. On the other when
the verb is in the infinitive mood, a mood in which there are
no persons, it is very like a substantive.

To err is human; to forgive, divine.

§ 141. As for the forms in-*ing*, they are so thoroughly
substantival, that we shall soon see that the whole class of
the so-called Present Participles is endangered: indeed, it is
for the sake of preparing for this doctrine that I am in the
present remarks drawing attention to the connection. A

Verb is, beyond doubt, a name; and so far as it is this, it is as good a Noun as a substantive or a pronoun, and a better noun than an adjective. Still it is not a substantive, for it is not the name of anything that has a substance, actual or conceivable. It is not a word like *fire, water, stone*, &c., that applies to an object with certain visible or conceivable attributes by which its substantive character is determined. The verb is a word which denotes a *state* or *act* of some such agent. A *horse* may run or a *man* may run. The horse may be in the act of *running* to-day, or the man may have performed the act of *running* yesterday. Or the horse or man may be *about to run* at some future time. But if I wish to have the notion of *running* as an act independent of the person who runs, I get a result of a very abstract character. I treat, however, the word *running* as a name, as the name of an act or state, as so far as it is this it is a noun. Such a noun is '*to err*' (or '*to forgive*)' in the line just quoted. Such nouns preceded by their article, but ending like a verb, are the Greek combinations—τὸ φθονεῖν=*envy* in the nominative case; τοῦ φθονεῖν=of *envy*, or *envy's* in the genitive, and ἐν τῷ φθονεῖν=in *envy* dative. All this we get when we consider any state or act in the abstract or independent of either its object or its agent.

§ 142. And for such states or acts there are names. In English they end in *-ing*, and can be formed, as occasion requires, from the verb: as *hunt, hunt-ing*, &c. These are called Verbals. They are, however, unquestionably substantives.

For the agents in such actions there are also names, which, like the preceding, are derived from the verb. In English these end in *-er;* as *hunt-er*=the person who *performs the act of hunting* or *hunts.*

But what if the name of the agent *coalesce* with that of the action, so that the two together form but a single word? This, at the first sight, looks like a very clumsy and improbable piece of machinery; and if we suppose that it

means that *every* Nominative Case coalesces with its Verb
is absurd. But, it is clear that, countless as are the number
of known and conceivable actions, each one with its agents,
the whole incalculable host of the latter can be reduced to
three classes. Everything that has or will be done, or is
capable of being imagined as a deed, is done by one out of
three doers. It is done by either (1) the speaker, (2) the
person spoken to, or (3) some one of the innumerable
objects spoken about; and if each of these classes has a
short and adaptable name, a coalition with the verb is a
very natural result.

§ 143. Be this as it may—when such a coalition *has*
taken place, the whole character of the verb is changed. It
loses to a great extent its abstract and indefinite character.
It becomes 'invested with circumstances;' for it is no
longer the name of a bare action, but the name of an action
plus that of the actor.

When verbs arrive at this condition, there is a great
tendency to separate them from the noun; and, indeed,
when they thus become *personal*, the difference is a great
one.

As the infinitive and the gerunds are thus *impersonal*,
they retain their abstract character; and may be, as they
sometimes are, called *impersonal*. But the commoner names
are *infinitive* and *finite*.

§ 144. A *finite* verb, then, when it gives us persons, gives
us not only the action, but the agent. Doing this, it does
all that is done by the impersonal verb, and much more
beside. It is a combination of the impersonal verb and
something else, and what this second element is likely to be
has been suggested. That, in some form or other, it was a
personal pronoun has long been the current opinion—an
opinion right in the main, but deficient in preciseness and
speciality. That there was a personal pronoun the world
at large admitted. Whether it was the nominative or any
one of the oblique cases was a question not gone into.

It is chiefly with the name of the late Mr. Garnett, among whose numerous contributions to the higher depart- ments of philology the present doctrine stands, perhaps, the first in value, that it is most especially connected. Mr. Gar- nett, however, with his usual justice towards his predecessors, has indicated a suggestion of the famous Keltic scholar Edward Lhuyd.

The verb, according to Mr. Garnett (who henceforth will speak for himself), is not so much a finite verb as a verbal, i.e. a word like *teaching* or *moving*, rather than one like *teach* or *move;* the pronoun which invests it with personality being not in the nominative case, or in concord with the verb, but in the possessive case, while the verb itself is in a state of regimen or government.

' Grammarians have not been able to divest themselves of the idea that the subject of the verb must necessarily be a *nominative*; and when it was ascertained that the distinctive terminations of the verb are in fact personal pronouns, they persisted in regarding those pro- nouns as *nominatives*, abbreviated indeed from the fuller forms, but still performing the same functions.'

' The personal terminations in Welsh are pronouns; but it is an important fact that they are evidently *in statu regiminis*, not in apposi- tion or concord; in other words, they are not nominatives, but oblique cases, precisely such as are affixed to various prepositions. For ex- ample, the second person plural does not end with the nominative *chwi*, but with *ech, wch, och, ych*, which last three forms are also found coalescing with various prepositions, *iwch*, " to you," *ynoch*, " in you," *wrthych*, " through you."

' Now the roots of Welsh verbs are confessedly nouns, generally of abstract signification; as, for example, *dysg* is both *doctrina*, and the second person imperative *doce*. *Dysg-och*, or *-wch*, is not, therefore, *docetis* or *docebitis vos*; but *doctrina vestrum*, " teaching *of* or *by* you." This leads to the important conclusion that a verb is nothing but a *noun* combined with an oblique case of a personal pronoun, virtually including in it a connecting preposition. This is what constitutes the real *copula* between the subject and the attribute. *Doctrina ego* is a logical absurdity; but *doctrina mei*, " teaching of me," necessarily in- cludes in it the proposition *ego doceo*, enunciated in a strictly logical and unequivocal form.'

The Syntax of the Prepositions greatly strengthens the

argument ; and hence the following table improves the evidence on this point.

Prepositional Forms.			Verbal Forms.		
er-ov	.	. 'for me.'	*car-ov*	.	. 'I will love.'
er-ot	.	. 'for thee.'	*car-ot*	.	. 'thou wilt love.'
er-o	.	. 'for him.'	*car-o*	.	. 'he will love.'
er-om	.	. 'for us.'	*car-om*	.	. 'we will love.'
er-och	.	. 'for you.'	*car-och*	.	. 'you will love.'
er-ynt	.	. 'for them.'	*car-ont* or *car-wynt*		. 'they will love.'

'No one capable of divesting his mind of preconceived systems, who compares the Welsh prepositional forms with the verbal forms, will deny the absolute formal identity of the respective sets of endings, or refuse to admit that the exhibition of parallel phenomena of languages of all classes, and in all parts of the world, furnishes a strong *primâ facie* ground for the belief of a general principle of analogy running through all.'—*Philological Essays*, pp. 289–342.

Such is Garnett's doctrine; and it is given in his own words.

§ 145. *Tense.*—The question of Tense now presents itself; and of this I must say explicitly what, I hope, shows itself in almost every page of my chapters on Etymology and Syntax, viz., that by Tense I mean an Inflection.

Collections of *different* words, like *I am speaking*, are *not* true Tenses.

Collections, like *I shall go*, are *not* true Tenses.

Collections, like *I have slept*, are *not* true Tenses.

They are combinations of certain words which serve in the place of true Tenses; just as combinations like *of a man, to a man, from a man*, &c., are combinations that take the place of true cases.

They are not Tenses like γέγραφα=*I have written*, in Greek; nor Tenses like *monui, I advised* (or *have advised*), in Latin. They are rather like such combinations as *amatus sum*=*I have been loved*, in Latin; or γράψας ἔχω=*I have written*, in Greek.

They are *combinations* of more words than one; and not one single, separate word in a changed, modified, or deter- • minate state; so that they belong to Syntax rather than to Etymology.

What, then, is the number of the Tenses in English, and what are they? There is, certainly, a Present Tense; and there is, certainly, *not* a Future Tense. Whether there be one or two Tenses of *Past* Time depends upon what we mean by the term.

If Tense mean the Time, and the Time only, to which the action or state conveyed by the verb is assigned, the Past Tense in English is one and indivisible; and words as different as *moved*, and *spoke*, inasmuch as they denote the same period of Time, are both in the same Tense.

On the other hand, however, if fundamental differences of Form are considered to make different Tenses, the Past Tenses in English amount to two.

§ 146. Upon this point the *History* of the forms may guide us; for it may tell us that the antagonism between the difference of form, and the identity of meaning, is not irreconcileable. It may tell us that the identity of meaning is due to the modern, recent, or advanced stage of the language in which it occurs, rather than to the language in its older form. And this certainly tells us something.

In words like *moved* from *move*, the Tense is indicated by the addition of the sound of *d*, *ed*, or *t*. In words like *spoke*, there is no addition of anything; but there is a change of the vowel. The great majority of existing Tenses belongs to the first class, a majority so overwhelming that, for the practical purposes of teaching, it may be excusable to call the exceptions *Irregular*. Still it is well to know wherein the irregularity lies. It manifestly lies not in words like *spoke*, *swam*, *drank*, &c., being irregular forms of a single Tense, of which words like *moved*, &c. are the regular ones; but in the fact of two different Tenses having merged their two distinctive imports into one.

H 2

One element in this distinction we can see with great clearness. We can see how there are two sorts of Past Time. We can see, within the limits of our own language, the difference between *I wrote a letter* and *I have written a letter.* The former makes the writing simply a past action. The latter connects it with the time at which the sentence is uttered. It means *I have written the letter you are asking about;* or the *letter which I promised to write;* or the *letter which I am now ready to forward you.* These and other similar illustrations show that the letter is by no means done-with at the time of speaking; but that something is still connected with it. This is called *Past Time continued up to the Present.* Sometimes, when the combination is treated as a Tense, it is called the *Perfect* Past, or the Preterit ; *Perfect,* or, simply, the *Perfect.*

§ 147. The Greek language helps us to the next step. It gives us for the Perfect *Time,* a definite, separate, and truly inflectional Tense ; and, as it has, also, an equally true one for the more indefinite Past Time, it shows us how the two Tenses may co-exist in the same language. Thus γέγραφα=*I have written* ; ἔγραψα (ἔ-γραπ-σα)=*I wrote.*

The Latin carries us a step farther. Like the Greek, it has not only two forms, but two forms of the same construction—e.g., *mo-mordi,* from *mordeo,* where, as in γέγραφα, from γράφω, the form is attained by doubling the initial vowel of the root, and *rexi* (*rec-si*), which, like ἔ-γραπ-σα, is formed by the addition of -*s.* The two Latin forms, however, like the English, have only one meaning. The identity not only of the two meanings, but of the two modes of expressing them, must be borne in mind. *Mo-mordi* not only means *I have bitten,* but it expresses its meaning by the same process ; viz., the reduplication of the first letter of the root. Between the two forms, the conclusion that, so far as the *process of formation goes,* the Greek and Latin Reduplicate Perfects belong to the same Tense is legitimate. With *scrip-si,* and ἔ-γραπ-σα, there is

a difference of another kind; but it is only a matter of
detail. The Greek prefixes ε; the Latin ignores it. Yet
both agree in the use of *s* as the distinctive sign of the two
Tenses of Past Time. Surely the two Tenses of the same.

Such would be the case if the Latin and Greek were
identified, or separated from one another in the way of
Tense, on one principle only. But such is not the case. In
Greek, a word like γράφ-ω has, as a matter of course, *two*
Tenses of Past Time; and, as such, γέ-γραφ-α, and ἔ-γραπ-σ-α,
are classified in Greek grammars. Each has its proper
form, and each has its appropriate meaning; and no one
thinks of their being the same Tense in a different Conjugation, still less of one being an irregular or exceptional
form of the other. There are, simply, two forms with two
corresponding meanings. But in Latin (and here begins
the antagonism) there are *two* forms, but only *one* meaning;
which, so long as we hold that difference of Tense implies
difference of Time, suggests that there is but *one* Tense.

§ 148. It may be replied, that two meanings in the
way of Time, if they are sufficiently near one another, may
be treated as one, and that they will, then, meet the real
or apparent difficulty.

But this is not all. As a general (though not an
universal) rule, the words in Latin which have a Past
Tense in -*s*, have no Tense at all formed by a reduplication;
and *vice versâ*. There are a few exceptions. *Mordeo* has
the so-called double form *mor-si*, and *mo-mordi*. *Pango*
has, in like manner, *pang-s-i* (*panxi*) and *pe-pig-i*. But,
generally speaking, the exception confirms the rule, *i.e.*, it
shows that, in Latin, some words had both forms.

Be this, however, as it may be. It is easily intelligible
that, when two forms were invested with the same meaning, one would predominate and exclude the other in some
words, while some would do the same in other; and this
explains the difference between the Latin and the Greek
grammars. The Greek found two forms with two different

meanings to match; and treated the forms as two different Tenses. The Latin found two forms, but only *one* import; and treated the two as belonging to the same Tense.

§ 149. *The Mœsogothic Reduplication.*—What the Greeks and Romans did in the way of Reduplication, the Germans did also. That the Mœsogothic gives us the earliest form of the languages in general of the German family has already been stated : but, upon this peculiar point, it gives us the most valuable point of its information. It gives us the Greek Reduplicate Perfect.

Sometimes it gives it after the manner of *curro*=*I run,* and *cu-curr-i*=*I have run* (or *ran*); or *mord-e-o*=*I bite,* and *mo-mord-i*=*I have bitten* (or *I bit*); *e.g.*—

MŒSOGOTHIC.

·Present and Past.

Salt-a, sái-salt =I leap, I leapt.

Háit-a; hái-háit = I bear the name; I bore the name,

without a change of vowel.

Elsewhere it gives us the same Reduplication *with a change of vowel; e.g.*—

Slêp-a, sái-slêp = I sleep; I slept, or have slept.

Thirdly, it gives us the form which presents itself in *spoke, swam, sang, rose,* and the like, as opposed to the forms in *-d* or *-t,* or the forms like *mov-ed* and *wep-t*: forms in which the Reduplication has disappeared.

In English, as in Latin, the verbs which have forms like *spoke* have, as a general rule, no forms like *moved,* and *vice versâ*; and in English, as in Latin, the two forms are assigned to the same tense. But in English, as in Latin, these are, as far as *history* and *structure* go, *two* distinct tenses.

§ 150. Historically, and in the way of structure, the forms like *spoke,* &c., belong to the same tense as the Greek τέ-τυφα. This tense is the Greek *Perfect.*

In the way of meaning, or import, the English forms

like *moved* belong to the same tense as the Greek ἔ-γραπ-σ-α; though not identical in the details of their structure. This tense is called, in Greek, the *Aorist*, in Latin the *Preterit*. This latter word is the better suited for the English.

If so, it is easy to see what the two forms belong to. Forms like *spoke* are Perfects : forms like *mov-ed* Preterits. They are two tenses of the same Conjugation.

But it is better to fix our attention on what they are *not*. They are *not* different forms of the same tense, in different Conjugations ; least of all are they what is called *Irregular*.

Such is the real character of a class of verbs which, until lately, have been treated in a very summary manner. Their historical identity with such true and genuine Perfects as τέ-τυφα and γέ-γραφα is undoubted. Whether, however, the recognition of them as two Past Tenses, each limited to certain words, and both conveying the same meaning, in our ordinary Grammars is practicable, is another question.

§ 151. That the class is a natural one is beyond doubt.

a. The same words, as a general rule, that appear in our own language as Perfects appear as Perfects in all the languages of the German family ; in other words, the list of the so-called Irregulars is nearly the same in Dutch, German, Mœsogothic, Frisian, Danish, Swedish, and Icelandic. Some languages have more than others ; but more than half of the list, in any one of the above-named languages, will be found in all the others.

b. With very few exceptions they are of German, and none of foreign, origin.

c. No new word ever takes the Perfect as its tense for past time, but always the Preterit.

d. Derived verbs form their Past tense as Preterits, even when the words from whence they are derived have a Perfect—*lie, lay ; lay, laid—rise, rose ; raise, raised—drink, drank—drench, drenched.*

e. In the few cases where we find *both* tenses, the Perfect is Intransitive, the Preterit Transitive—though this, by some, may be considered a refinement : 'It *hung* till it fell to pieces '—' It *swoll* till it burst '—' He *hanged* the offender '—' He *swelled* it by blowing air into it.'

f. Verbs which, in the earlier stages of English, took the Perfect form, change it in the course of time for the Preterit : *sowed, mowed, rowed, leapt, slept, helped, melt, sheared, shaped, squeezed. wash,* and others, were originally *sew, mew, rew, lep, slep, holp, molt, shore, shope, squoze,* and *wesh.* The converse change rarely takes place. Hence, the number of Perfects is gradually decreasing. Many, however, of the tenses which are Preterit in the Literary English are current in our Provincial dialects as Perfects : the old form being there retained longest.

That they were ' native and home-born words ' is the remark of so old a writer as Ben Jonson. The great Ben, however, despairs of ' beating them into proportion.' He does his part ' in tolling this bell to draw others to a deeper consideration of the matter.'

Wallis writes that ' *Anomaly* scarcely touches introduced (*Exotica*) words, but only those that are native— which are all Monosyllables, or derived from Monosyllables, and, for the most, allowing for a slight change, common to us with the Germans, Flemings (*Belgæ*), and Danes.' He does, however, venture to classify them.

§ 152. ' *Strong* ' *and* ' *Weak* ' *as terms.*—At present I think it safe to say that (except so far as *Defect* is Irregularity) the belief that the words in question are Irregular has died away, and that it has been doing so for the last forty years. That the recognition of them as words of different Tenses, is delayed for no very distant period is what I hope. Unless such a recognition be accomplished sooner or later the great principle of historical examination, which has thrown so much light upon the darker regions of Philology, will have done less than we expect from it. Meanwhile, the opinion of the present time is that of a period of transition and compromise.

. In the exposition and illustration of this opinion the two terms which have recommended themselves are ' *Strong*' and ' *Weak*.' Forms like τέτυφα, *momordi*, and *spoke* are constructed out of the original verb itself, by the process of changing the vowel and doubling the consonant. Forms like ἔτυπσα, *scripsi*, and *moved* are constructed by *adding* to the fundamental word something from a wholly different source. The former are called *Strong*, or self-supporting; the latter are called *Weak*, or constituted by additions extraneous to the theme or the fundamental word. As applied to such forms as *spoke* and *moved*, &c., except that they are somewhat fanciful, and (a graver objection) are used in another sense in the Declension of the Nouns, they are good terms. But except when we limit them to the *form* of the particular words to which they apply, and that in respect to the process from which it results, and the materials out of which it is made, they suggest something either more or less than the bare facts of the case, which are simple in character and two only in number.

1. A system of Inflection which is manifest and recognised in the Greek was originally common to the languages of the German family, and the Latin; not to mention the fact of its being as manifest in the Sanskrit as in the Greek. This gave each verb *two* Tenses of Past Time.

2. The loss of the distinction between these two sorts of Time, and the result of some words retaining the form of the Perfect and some that of the Preterit Tense.

The closer we keep these two forms to their old names of *Perfect* and *Preterit*, the more clearly do they carry with them their history.

§ 153. *The Perfect Tense.*—The characters that in the first instance determine the divisions of this class, are (1) the quantity of the Vowel, and (2) the number and nature of the consonants which follow it.

After this the numbers of times that the vowel is changed demands notice, for sometimes it is changed in the Perfect only, sometimes in the Participle as well, and sometimes in the Perfect itself it is (or was) changed with the number, e.g., in Anglo-Saxon.

		Present.	Perfect Singular.	Perfect Plural.	Participle.
A. S.	{	*Bleuwe*	*bleow*	*bleow-on*	*ge-blaw-en*
	{	*Swimme*	*swam*	*swumm-on*	*ge-swumm-en*
English.	{	*Blow*	*blew*	*blew*	*blown*
	{	*Swim*	*swam*	*swam*	*swum*

§ 154.

Vowel Long.

(1.) Here the *sound* in the present English is that of a Vowel, but, according to the *spelling*, the words end in the Semivowel *w*. Change from *o* or *a* to *e*. The vowel in the Participle the same as in the *Present*.

Present.	Perfect.	Participle.
Blow	*blew*	*blown*
Crow	*crew*	*crown*
Grow	*grew*	*grown*
Know	*knew*	*known*
Throw	*threw*	*thrown*
Draw	*drew*	*drawn*
Fly	*flew*	*flown*
Slay	*slew*	*slain.*

In the first five of these words *w* represents *v*. In *fly*, *draw*, it represents *g* softened into *y* or *h*, as in A. S. *ic drage*=I draw; *ic droh*=I drew; *dragen*=drawn.

In *slay* the *w* represents a *g*, softened into *h*; A.S. *ic sleahhe*=I slay; *ic sleóh*=I slew; *slagen*=slain.

(2.) The Vowel (long) and spelt *ea* with two letters followed by *l* or *r* (two of the four liquids) and *k* as a mute: change to *o*. The Vowel in the Participle the same as in the *Perfect*.

Present.	Perfect.	Participle.
Steal	*stole*	*stolen*
Bear	*bore*	*borne*
Swear	*swore*	*sworn*
Tear	*tore*	*torn*
Wear	*wore*	*worn*
Break	*broke*	*broken*
Speak	*spoke*	*spoken*
Weave	*wove*	*woven*

Most of these Perfects have, or have had, a second, obsolete, or obsolescent form, as *bare, stale, sware, tare, ware, brake, spake*. *Borne* when it means *carried* or *supported* is spelt with an *-e ;* when it means *brought into the world* (Latin, *natus*) it simply ends in *-n*, born (Latin, *latus*).

(3.) The vowel (long), the consonant by which it is followed being a Sibilant—*s* or *z*.

Present.	Perfect.	Participle.
Freeze	*froze*	*frozen*
Choose	*chose*	*chosen*

This is rather a sub-section of the previous division than a class by itself. The difference, however, between a Sibilant and an ordinary Mute is important. It has a tendency to change into *r*, sometimes in the Plural alone, sometimes in the Participle alone, and sometimes in both the Participle and the Plural. In the present English the single word *forlorn* represents this class, and that only as a Participle, or perhaps as an Adjective. In form, however, and origin, it is the Perfect Participle of the word *lose*.

Frore, in Anglo-Saxon *gefroren*, is used by Milton.

> The parching air
> Burns *frore*, and cold performs the effect of fire.
> *Par. Lost*, II., 595.

The Anglo-Saxon conjugation of these words was more than usually complex; the Vowel changes being

four, two for the Perfect and two for the *Present* Tense,
with which the Participle agreed. For *was*, which belongs
to this class, see below.

Prsnt. 1st Per.	S. P.	F. P.	Perfect S.	Perfect P.	Participle.
Lese	*lest*	*lest*	*læs*	*læs-on*	*ge-les-en*
(Ge)-nese	*genist*	*genist*	*genæs*	*genæson*	*ge-nes-en*
Ceôse	*cŷst*	*cŷst*	*ceâs*	*cur-on*	*ge-coren*
Dreôse	*drŷst*	*drŷst*	*dreâs*	*drur-on*	*ge-dror-en*
Freôse	*frŷst*	*frŷst*	*freâs*	*frar-on*	*ge-fror-en*
Be-greôse	*begrŷst*	*begrŷst*	*greâs*	*grur-on*	*ge-gror-en*
Hreôse	*hrŷst*	*hrŷst*	*hreâs*	*hrur-on*	*ge-hror-en*
Forleôse	*forlŷst*	*forlŷst*	*forleâs*	*forlur-on*	*for-loren*

(4.) Vowel long, spelt with a single letter, and followed
by a mute. Change from *a* to *v* (spelt *o o*). Vowel on the
Participle the same as on the Present.

Present.	Perfect.	Participle.
(For)sake	*(for)sook*	*(for)saken*
Shake	*shook*	*shaken*
Take	*took*	*taken*
Wake	*woke*	*waken*

(5.) Vowels of the Present spelt with the letter *i*;
but, in sound, a diphthong. Changed into *o* in the Perfect,
in the Participle into *ĭ* (the *i* in pit). The vowel of the
Participle that of the Present, rather than the Perfect.

Present.	Perfect.	Participle.
Bide	*bode*	*bidden*
Bite	*bit*	*bitten*
Drive	*drove*	*driven*
Ride	*rode*	*ridden*
Shrive	*shrove*	*shriven*
Smite	*smote*	*smitten*
Strike	*stroke*	*stricken*
Strive	*strove*	*stridden*
Thrive	*throve*	*thriven*
Write	*wrote*	*written*

Here, in Anglo-Saxon, the vowel was changed in the
Plural, with which the Participle agreed. In both cases,

however, it seems to have been long; or, at any rate, the consonant is not doubled.

Present.	Perfect. 1st Pers.	Perfect. 2nd Pers.	Participle.
Scíne	*scân*	*scin-on*	*ge-scin-en*
Bite	*bât*	*bit-on*	*ge-bit-en*
Smite	*smât*	*smit-on*	*ge-smit-en*
Ride	*râd*	*rid-on*	*ge-rid-en*
Strice	*strâc*	*stric-on*	*ge-stricen*

§ 155.
Vowel Short.

Followed by *m*, *n*, *ng*, or *nk*. Change to *a* for the Perfect in the Singular, to *u* for it in the Plural number. The vowel of the Participle that of the *Plural* of the Perfect.

Present.	Perfect Singular.*	A. S. Plural.	Participle.
Swim	*swam*	(*swumm-on*)	*swum*
Begin	*began*	(*begunn-on*)	*begun*
Run	*ran*	(*runn-on*)	*run*
Spin	*span*	(*spunn-on*)	*spun*
Win	*wan*	(*wunn-on*)	*won*
Cling	*clang*	(*clung-on*)	*clung*
Fling	*flung*	(*flung-an*)	*flung*
Ring	*rang*	(*rung-on*)	*rung*
Sing	*sang*	(*sung-on*)	*sung*
Spring	*sprang*	(*sprung-on*)	*sprung*
Sting	*stung*	(*stung-on*)	*stung*
Wring	*wrang*	(*wrung-on*)	*wrung*
Drink	*drank*	(*drunc-on*)	*drunk*
Shrink	*shrank*	(*scrunc-on*)	*shrunk*
Sink	*sank*	(*sunc-on*)	*sunk*
Stink	*stunk*	(*stunc-on*)	*stunk*

In the following words the *i* and *ou*, now diphthongs, represent the short sounds of *i* in *pin* and the *u* in *full*. Like *swim*, &c., they had *a* and *u* in the Plural. The Scotch retains both the short vowel and double form, the Perfect being regularly in *a*, in the Participle in *u*—as *band*, *fand*, *grand*, *wand*; *bund*, *fund*, *grund*, *wund*.

* The *second* Person *Singular*, also, takes -*u*, as þu *swumme* = *thou swummest*.

Present.	Perfect.	Participle.
Bind	*bound*	*bound*
Find	*found*	*found*
Grind	*ground*	*ground*
Wind	*wound*	*wound*

The loss of the syllabic inflections -*an*, and -*e*, &c., for the Infinitive mood and the Present tense, by shortening the word, would encourage the lengthening of the vowel ; for in *find-an*, *grind-an*, &c., the *i* was doubtless sounded as in *swĭm*. So it would be in *clĭmb-an*, of which the Perfect was *clŏmb* or *clamb* in the Singular, and *clumb-on* in the Plural ; the Participle being *clumb-en*.

§ 156. REDUPLICATION RETAINED.

(1.) *Did*. This word, in the current English of the present time, stands alone ; the solitary instance of the old reduplication after the manner of τέ-τυφα. The Anglo-Saxon form was *di-de*, Old Saxon *dĕ-da*; in which case it is the *first* of the two *d*'s which gives us the sign of tense, and the last of them the one that belongs to the root.

(2.) *Hight*. There is another word in the same condition as *di-d*, i.e. another word wherein the reduplication is preserved. Here the *g* is out of place ; the better spelling being *hiht*; in Anglo-Saxon *hēht*, Mœsogothic *hái-háit*. *Hight*, however, scarcely belongs to the current language ; being either obsolete, or obsolescent.

> An ancient fabric raised to inform the sight,
> There stood of yore, and Barbican it *hight*.'
> Dryden, *Mac Flecknoe*.

As *hight* is an Active verb, it is better translated ' *bore the name* ' than ' *was called* ;' for it is *not a Participle*, but a Perfect tense, and it agrees with the Greek κλύω (Latin *cluo*) rather than with *vocor*, *nominor*, or *nuncupor*. In both the German and Norse languages it is still the ordinary

word for '*what is your name ?*'—German, *wie heissen Sie ?*
Danish, *hvad hede De ?* The Anglo-Saxon forms were
hate, hêht, ge-hâten.

Behight = promised. So little was this form understood in the six-
teenth century that we actually find *behighteth* = promiseth, used by
Sackville, as if from a present *behight* : cp. *ought* and *must*, originally
past tenses which have acquired a present meaning.—Morris, *Historical
Outlines of English Accidence*, p. 156.

§ 157. *Did, hight,* and *held.*—We have seen that *did* is
a reduplicate form current in the present language, and by
no means likely to become obsolete. It gives us two *d*'s,
the import of each being undoubted. The first *d* is the
sign of the tense, the second the consonant of the root.
The opposite notion, to the effect that the second *d* was the
d in *loved*, and the first the *d* of the word *do*, is exploded.
The first *d* represents the reduplication.

§ 158. *Hight* differs from *did* in being obsolescent. It
differs, too, in having *h* for its initial; for *h* is a breathing
rather than a true articulate sound, and is by no means
a very stable element at any time, especially between two
vowels. In sound, then, *hight* (*hiht* best represents the old
orthography *hêht* and *háiháit*) differs from *did*; for it only
gives us what we may call an historical or orthographical
reduplication; in other words, the *h* is only doubled to the
eye : and if it were spelt *hite* it would show no sign of reduplication at all.

§ 159. *Held* differs from *hight*, with which it agrees in
having once been a true reduplicate form, in having not
even a second *h* in the spelling ; *i.e.* no second *h* at all. Its
history, however, is that of *hiht*.

Mœsogothic.	Old High German.	Anglo-Saxon.
Hái-háit	*hât*	*hêht* from *hait-an*
Hái-hald	*hi-alt*	— ,, *hald-an*

Let the *gh, g,* or *h*, one or both, drop out of *hiht*, and
held may be looked upon as the result of *hái-hald, i.e.* a

reduplication for which one of the doubled letters is lost. Such is, probably, the case; the result being that in *held* it is *not* the letter of the *root* with which the word begins, but that of the *reduplication*. If so, other words may be in the same predicament; indeed, every Perfect in our language in which there has been a reduplication, and in which, now, only one of the two consonants implied by the term remains, may be like *held, i.e.* may have lost its radical consonant and retain only that of the prefix. How far the present doctrine favours this view is uncertain. It is certain, however, that it favours it to a great extent. The extent to which it does so is a point for which, in a work like the present, the reader can only be prepared to expect.

§ 160. The little that is here written is written mainly with the view of correcting the notion that the verbs under notice are anything like *Irregular*. They are, with few exceptions, *Defective*, inasmuch as they have no Preterit, or no case corresponding with the Greek Aorist. And as the Verbs which *have* such a tense are generally without a Perfect, more than nine-tenths of the English Verbs are Defective. That this as a characteristic is of great importance is beyond doubt. But Defect is an explicable and common phenomenon, whereas Irregularity, when real, is inexplicable and, to say the least, rare. What the English Verbs really give us is a vast number of exceptions to such rules as Grammars of ordinary magnitude can find room for.

§ 161. The two most elaborate attempts in English to throw the class of Perfects into system are those of Professor March and Dr. Morris; and to those the reader is referred. To a great extent they agree. Professor March has five classes, one of which falls into as many sub-classes; Dr. Morris six undivided classes. The American scholar, in my mind, holds closest to the principle of taking the vowel and the consonants by which it is followed as his basis, and subordinating to it the changes between the vowel of the Perfect and the Participle. Dr. Morris, who connects the evidence of reduplication with the difference or likeness between these two vowels, naturally invests them with primary importance. But the two writers should be read together. The consideration of the Perfect Tense has taken precedence of the Preterit; for it has every sign of being the older one of the two. Indeed, provided that the forthcoming view be correct, it will be something more than this. It will be, in a manner, the Tense out of which the Preterit was developed. But even if it be not this, it will still be the older Tense.

§ 162. *The Preterit Tense.* — The fullest form in which the characteristic sign of the Preterit is known is in the Plural of the Mœsogothic; where *nasi-dêd-um=we saved*, from the Infinitive *nasi-an*, and Present *nasi-a*. One of these two *d*'s is certainly the *d* in *moved, called*, &c.

But what is *d* in *nasi-d-a?* It is believed to be the Perfect of the verb *do* (*did*). If so, it had, as a Post-positive affix, incorporated with the main verb, a power akin to its present power as an Auxiliary in combinations like *I did move*.

The Mœsogothic Preterit is found in both the Indicative and the Conjunctive Moods, and also in the Dual, as well as the Singular and Plural, Numbers.

a. *Past Tense of the Indicative Mood.*

Singular.	Dual.	Plural.
1. Nasi-*d*-a	—	nasi-*d*-êdum
2. Nasi-*d*-ês	nasi-*d*-êduts	nasi-*d*-êduþ
3. Nasi-*d*-a	—	nasi-*d*-êdum

b. *Past Tense of the Conjunctive Mood.*

Singular.	Dual.	Plural.
1. Nasi-*d*-êdjau	—	nasi-*d*-êdeima
2. Nasi-*d*-êdeis	nasi-*d*-êduts	nasi-*d*-êdeiþ
3. Nasi-*d*-êdi	—	nasi-*d*-êdeina

From the fact of this double *d* being Dual as well as Plural, the inference that that consonant is a sign of

I

Tense rather than one of Number is held, by the present writer, to be impaired in respect to its validity. The Dual form may have been extended to Plurals, and in the Dual the letter *d* is a very likely element.

Be this, however, as it may, the doctrine that the *-dêd-* in nasi-*dêd-*um is the *d* in *nasida*, the *d* in nasi-*d-*a, the *d* in *move-d*, and the *d* in *did*, is generally admitted. As a matter of philological fact, a small minority may demur to it. As a matter of opinion, it is a fact of a different kind; but still an important one.

§ 163. *The Connecting Vowel.*—The next element is the letter *i*—*nas-*i-*dêdum*. This is the connecting link between the theme and the sign of Tense; for it belongs neither to the Tense nor the main word. The Mœsogothic has three such connectives: *nas-*i-*da*=*I saved*; *salh-*o-*da*=*I healed*; *hab-*ai-*da*=*I had*. The first two are found in the Anglo-Saxon *ner-*e-*de*=*I saved*; *luf-*o-*de*=*I loved*. Here *d*, and *d* only, is the sign of the Tense.

§ 164. Then follow the signs of Person—*lufod-e, lufod-est*; *lufod-e* with *lufod-on* for all the three Persons of the Plural.

Of these the second (*loved-st*), is the only one still in existence, though scarcely common and current.

Of the connecting vowels the *o* has become obsolete, while *-e* is becoming so, or *obsolescent*. So far as we *pronounce* it in the reading of the Bible, or use it for the purposes of metre, it is, in words like *blessed, moved*, &c., a part of the *spoken* language. In *loved, moved, stabbed*, &c., as used in ordinary language, it is a sound to the eye only; in other words, no sound at all.

When, however, the fundamental Verb ends in an Explosive Dental (*d* or *t*), the *e* is *sounded*. This is because two Dentals require to be separated by a vowel before they can be distinctly pronounced; e.g. *mend-ed, augment-ed*, is more easily uttered than *mend'd, augment't*. After *th*, however, the *Continuous* Dental *d* is attached directly to the verb, as *wreath-d*, *breath-d*. Here the *th* is sounded as the *th* in *thine*. With *th* sounded as in *thin* no English verb ends.

If the final sound of the fundamental Verb be a Surd, *p*, *f*, *k*, or *s*, the *d* of the affix becomes *t*; in other words, is accommodated to the original consonant in respect to its sonancy. This is what we have already seen in the *s* (or *z*) of Plural Number and Possessive Case of Substantives. Indeed the change is only a portion of a general Euphonic Law.

§ 165. Subject to these Rules the formation of the English Preterit is comparatively simple. Under the first, or the one concerning the interposition of the *e* between two Explosive Dentals, the most important exception is the rejection of one of the two *d*'s, þ, and, along with it, the connecting vowel *e*. This reduces the Preterit to the same form as the Present.

(1) Verbs ending in *-d*:

Rid	rid	rid
Shed	shed	shed
Shred	shred	shred
Spread	spread	spread

(2) Verbs ending in *-t*:

Burst	burst	burst
Cast	cast	cast
Cost	cost	cost
Cut	cut	cut
Hit	hit	hit
Hurt	hurt	hurt
Knit	knit	knit
Let	let	let
Put	put	put
Set	set	set
Shut	shut	shut
Slit	slit	slit
Split	split	split
Sweat	sweat	sweat
Thrust	thrust	thrust

When the *d* is preceded by *l*, *n*, or *r* (liquids), the *e* is ejected, and, along with it, one of the *d*'s, the other being changed to *t*.

Bend	bent	bent
Build	built	built
Gild	gilt	gilt
Gird	girt	girt
Lend	lent	lent
Rend	rent	rent
Send	sent	sent
Spend	spent	spent

In all these cases the vowel is short. When long, however, it is shortened.

Bleed	bled	bled
Breed	bred	bred
Feed	fed	fed
Lead	led	led
Read	read	read (*pronounced* red)
Speed	sped	sped
Meet	met	met

§ 166. To the second rule, or the one that *t* should follow Surd, I remember no exceptions. As it stands, however, at present it is a *general* rule of Euphony rather than a *particular* rule for the English Verbs, and as such it must be taken. Even as it stands it is not universal. Combinations like *pluckd*, *stopd*, *misd*, &c., must, doubtless, be avoided. But there are two ways of avoiding them. The first letter may be accommodated to the second, when the result would be such combinations as *plugd*, *stobd*, and *mizd*, concerning which all that can be said is that the English Language, though it might, if it chose, adopt them, does not do so.

But, when the Main Verb ends in a Vowel or a Liquid, there is no necessity for any accommodation at all. We can, if we like, say *swelt* or *heart*, *spiet* (pronounced *spite*), or the like, as easily as we say *sweld*, *heard*, or *spied*. It is not, however, the practice of the English Language to do so. *D* is the true sign of the Tense, and to *d* it adheres where it can.

Hence the more special rule is that, in respect to the addition of *d* or *t*, the English * Language treats Vowels and Liquids as if they were Sonant Mutes.

§ 167. But to this rule there *are* exceptions. They are certain words where, after a Liquid, *t*, instead of *d*, presents itself—as *deal, dealt; feel, felt; smell, smelt; burn, burnt*; generally·when the Vowel is *short*. Sometimes, however, after a *long* one—as ·*mean, meant; dream, dreamt*. But here the Vowel is shortened.

And here the spelling is uncertain : for we write *burnt* and *burned; dreamt* and *dreamed; learned* and *learnt*.

This takes us to another division. The great exceptional cases have, hitherto, turned upon the verbs that end in *d* or *t*; or the same sounds as those of the Affix.

In words where the Vowel before a Liquid was changed, or shortened, we begin with a new series.

§ 168. In *bereāve, cleāve, creēp, keēp, leāve, lōse, sleēp, sweēp, weēp*, of which the respective Preterits are *berĕft, clĕft, kĕpt, lĕft, lŏst, slĕpt, swĕpt, wĕpt*, we have the Vowel shortened—but still the same vowel; the Consonant that follows being *not* (as in *burnt*, &c.) a Liquid. Here the Vowel is the same; but it is changed in respect to *Quantity*.

§ 169. In *tĕll, tōld; sĕll, sōld*, it changed not only in respect to Quantity, but to *Quality* as well; and here the

* *English* here means only the English of England. In respect to the Scotch, wherein the connecting vowel is retained where it is not wanted for the purposes of Euphony only, Mr. Murray writes that the termination is *t*. ' In the old Scotch the Past Tense and Participle were formed by adding *it, yt* to all verbs of this class. In the modern dialects this full form undergoes certain euphonic changes in accordance with the character of the preceding letter or syllable.'—p. 199. The whole section shows that in Scotland, *t* was the regular, *d* the exceptional sign of the Tense. This was possible because the Scotch kept the connecting vowel; which the English did not.

Vowel that follows *is* a Liquid.   In Anglo-Saxon the forms
were *telle, tealde; selle, sealde*.

§ 170. The three points upon which the exceptions to
the rules given for the formation of the Preterit are reducible to three cases ; two of which have been already
noticed.

1. Those that refer to Verbs ending in *d* or *t*.

2. Those wherein the Vowel is changed.

3. Those wherein the Consonant is changed.

The first has been considered.   The second has been
indicated.   The third gives us the small, but important,
class of apparent exceptions : which now come under notice.

§ 171. *Verbs in which the final Consonant is* k *or* g.   The
allied sounds of *k* and *g* (as in *gun*) undergo the same, or
nearly the same, changes ; and they are numerous.

a. They pass into the sound of *y*.   The Anglo-Saxon
forms of *lay* and *say* were

Present.	Preterit.	Participle.
Lecge	*lægde*	*ge-lægd*
Secge	*sægde*	*ge-sægd*
Lay	*laid*	*laid* (pronounced *lade*)
Say	*said*	*said* (pronounced *sed*)

b. Also into that of *h*, originally a guttural *g*.   The
Anglo-Saxon forms of *seek* were

	Present.	Preterit.	Participle.
	Sece	*sohte*	*ge-soht*
Hence	*Seek*	*sought*	*sought*

c. Also into that of *ng*.

	Present.	Preterit.	Participle.
Anglo-Saxon	*Bringe*	*brohte*	*ge-broht*
Modern English	*Bring*	*brought*	*brought*

d. Also into that of *ngk*.

	Infinitive.	Preterit.	Participle.
Anglo-Saxon {	*þencan*	*þôhte*	*ge-þôht* = *think*
{	*þincan*	*þuhte*	*ge-þuht* = *seem*

Compare the German *Ich denke=I think*; *mich dünkt= meseems*.

e. Also into that of *tsh*.

	Present.	Preterit.	Participle.
Anglo-Saxon	*Tæce*	*tæhte*	*ge-tæht*
Modern-English	*Teach*	*taught*	*taught* ·

Here the Preterit is like that of the preceding instances. The *Present*, however, is changed : the *k* becoming *tsh*.

Catch, caught, caught does not occur in the oldest English. In Layamon we find *caeche, cahte, caht*. This verb has conformed to the Past Tense of *teach*, &c.—Morris, *Historical Outlines*, &c., p. 171.

Buy. In A. S. *bycge, bohte, ge-boht*.

Work. In Ac. *wyrce=*I work: *worh-te=I worked*; *ge-worht=worked*. In addition to the change in the consonant, *r* is transposed. *Beseech.*—The main Verb is *séc-e =I seek*. In English *be-seech, be-sought*. The simple Verb *seek* preserves the *k*. The compound changes it after the manner of *teach*, &c.

Owe—for this see § 179.

PARTICIPLES.

§ 172. *Voice in connection with the Participles.*—Considered from one point of view the Participle is a Noun : considered from another it is a Verb. Now, although so far as Moods, Tenses, and Persons are concerned, we have, in English, no *Voices*, we have them in respect to the Participles. The form in -*ing*, as in *moving*, &c., is a Present Participle in point of Time, but it is Active in the way of *Voice*. The forms in -*en* and -*ed*, as *taken* and *moved*, are Passive in the way of Voice, but Past in their character of Participles. There is nothing in the nature of Language that makes this necessary. The Greek Language has its Active and Passive Participle for each Tense ; as τύπτω=*I beat*, τύπτων=*one in the act of beating*; τυπτόμενος=*one who is being beaten* ; and, for the Passive Voice, it has τύπτομαι=*I am being beaten* ; τι-τυμμένος=*one who has been beaten*. In English, however,

there is only one form for each. Hence, though we have
no Passive Voice for the Verb Proper, we have both an
Active and a Passive Participle—the Active Participle
being Present, and the Present Participle Active; whilst
the Passive Participle is Past, and *vice versâ*. As it is universally agreed that, whether Perfect or Preterit, the Participles of Past Time are Passive, *Passive* will be the name
under which they will be considered. The Active will be
considered first. As far as its form goes, this is the most
regular one in the English Language; and the rule for it
has the merit of being absolutely without an exception.
It is not even affected by the laws of Euphony. The sign
of the Active, or Present, Participle is *-ing*, which can be
added without alteration to every Verb in the language,
with the exception of *is, was*.

§ 173. Though all this is clear and simple, the form in
-ing is one of the most difficult in our language; for it has
been, and is at present, doubted whether it be a Participle at all.

There are *four* Parts of Speech with which the termination *-ing* may be connected: the Substantive, the Adjective,
the Adverb, and the Participle.

Let us consider, in the first place, its attachment to the
Substantive. In expressions like the *blessings of a poor
man*; *the wanderings of a traveller*; *the risings* (*insurrec-
tions*) *of the North*, and others like them, it has a Plural
Number.

In *I was going a-hunting, I was a-saying,* &c., the *a*
stands for *on*, and the word *hunting* is in that particular
Oblique Case which the Preposition *on* governed. That
these combinations are now condemned as provincial, old-
fashioned, or colloquial, does not make them bad English.
They had, then, when the preposition *on* was prefixed, an
Oblique Case; and this, along with its Plural Number,
makes the termination Substantival.

As for the word *morn-ing*, it is at the present moment a

Substantive, and nothing else. The Verb *morn*, if it exist at all, is a scarce one.

The original Vowel of these Substantives was *-u—clæns-ung=cleans-ing*; *hwistlung=whistling*. The sign of its oblique case, which was governed by *on*, was *-e*. Hence *Ic was on cleansunge*, &c., *Ic was on hwist-lunge*, was the original of I was *a-cleansing* and *I was a-whistling*; and these were the older forms of *I was whistling* and *I was cleansing*. But these are now called Present Participles.

Taking such a combination as *a-cleansing, a-whistling, a-hunting*, by itself, and looking at the parsing of it, we may say that in its *Syntax* it is *Adverbial*. It is not, in its origin, an Adverb; but its place in a proposition is that of one.

Such is the history of the old Verbal, or Verbal Abstract, in *-ung*.

If no other word had changed in the same direction, it is probable that nothing would have to be said about it. But the Present Participle in the existing English also ends in *-ing*; as *I am moving*. Moreover the Participle is used as an Adjective; as *a moving (emotional) scene*. Then we have phrases like *a dying day*, which, though it sometimes means *a day that is dying (passing away)*, generally means *a day on which some one dies*; or *a death-bed day*. The construction here is substantival; and still more so is that of *a wedding day*; which certainly very seldom means *a day that is being wedded*.

This brings us round to the previous series, that of the changes of the Verbal Abstracts in *-ung*, to which few would hesitate to assign the word *morning* exclusively, and the words *wedding* and *dying* particularly.

Finally, as the Verbal Abstract in *-ing* began in *-ung,* so did the Participial *-ing* begin in something different from its present form. The older and oldest forms of the Verbs of the Anglo-Saxon middle periods of our language ended in *-nd*.

If this is nothing else, it is the history of two forms originally distinct becoming confluent, interchangeable, or identical; and, what is more, their meanings, however different at first, do the same.

So long as English Grammar is studied on the principles of the Grammars of the Latin and Greek languages only, this complication or parallelism commands but little attention. We know, however, what will happen when it is studied critically. If the combination *I am hunting* be reducible to *I am on hunting*, other so-called Participial constructions may be reduced in the same way—other, and perhaps all.

This view of the nature of the Present Participle, with special reference to its identity (in form) with the Verbal Abstract, was taken by the grammarians of the last generation and their predecessors almost exclusively in reference to its bearing upon our *Syntax:* when the parsing of such a sentence as *what is the meaning of the lady holding up her fan?* was a question of which grammar-reading students might read a good deal. Which was the better English— *lady holding*, or *lady's holding*? And then if we say *lady's holding*, should we not also say *holding up of her fan?* Answer as we may, there are always authorities on the other side. The one point, however, which is certain is that the question, when thus put, is one of *Syntax*.

Within the last forty years, however, its character has changed. It has become mainly a question of Etymology. It has borne less upon the Government and Concord of words like *holding* and *fan* in certain combinations than upon the history of the terminations *-ing* as a form of *-ung*, and *-nd* as the old sign of the Participle. Which does the present form come from? Does it come from one exclusively, or does it sometimes come from the one and sometimes from the other? This suggests a very complicated investigation.

§ 174. *What are the forms ending in -ing ?*—Are they Participles or are they Verbal Substantives? A few are certainly Verbal Substantives: e.g. *morning*. But words of this kind are not numerous. Every Verb, whether old or new, can be the basis of a form in -*ing*; some of them, as *waltzing*, of such late origin that they have come into our language since the prefix *a-* (as *a-hunting*) became obsolete. But these, again, are only a fraction of the whole. What is the rule for the inordinately vast majority wherein the Verbs are from two to nine hundred years old, and which are known to have had undoubted Participles ending in -*nd*, and, in many cases, to have corresponding Verbal Abstracts in -*ung*? What is the general rule for these? Or is there a general rule at all? Are forms of this kind *always* Participles, or are they *never* Participles? The extreme opinions, as is natural, are most in favour of the -*ing* denoting a Verbal. And this is what we expect. A new doctrine is adopted, if adopted at all, with a tendency to extend, rather than to limit, its application. Hence, there is a fair amount of influential authority which goes to the length of implicitly abolishing the Present Participle. But this is an extreme one; for it is clear that, though such combinations as *I am going hunting* may be reduced to *I am a-going a-hunting*, combinations like *a growing tree*, or *a moving crowd*, cannot so be reduced. Still, they may be combinations like *wedding morn* or *dying day*. Now, it is difficult to deny that every one of the so-called Present, or Active, Participles can be so explained. On the other hand, combinations like *early rising is good for the health*, though not inexplicable, are not so easily reduced to Participles.

Presuming then that the rule must be general, we may easily see that a case may be made out strongly in favour of the Participle, as such, having become displaced and superseded by the Verbal Substantive; and the doctrine that it is more likely that the Verbal Substantive should, as a Part of Speech, have displaced the Present Participle, rather than that the termination -*nd* should have been changed into *ng*, becomes, to say the least, plausible.

This shows the real gist of the question. Is it, as a matter of history, a case of forms in *ing*, into which the Participle of the older English has transmuted forms in *-nd*, in the way of letter-change; or is it, as a matter of history, one of the Verbal Substantive in *-ng*, as a Part of Speech displacing, or superseding, the Participle in *-nd*?

It is difficult to form an opinion on this point; so difficult that we must decide that it is one for which *no general rule can be laid down*. And such is the case. We cannot well, even in the most formal and theoretical grammar, abolish the Present, or Active, Participle; whilst to enter upon the individual history of each word, and every difference of meaning with which it may be invested, is impracticable. Few, too, even as a matter of letter-change, now hold that the change from the *-nd* of the Participle to the *-ng* of the Verbal Participle is improbable. On the other hand, the doctrine that the two forms have become what we may call Confluent is recognised; and that Confluence is not an exceptional process in language is, also, recognised. Still, this undoubted Confluence of the Participle and the Verbal is Confluence on a very large scale. Instances of it on a smaller one may be seen elsewhere. (See § 184.)

The Passive Participles in *en*.

§ 175. The Passive Participles are two in number, both indicating Past time. There is no *Present* Participle for the Passive, and there was no *Past* Participle for the Active, Voice; though there is no reason, beyond the practice of the English Language, why there should not be both. The Greeks have τετυφώς=*one who has beaten*, as well as τύπτων=*one who is in the act of beating*. They have also τυπτόμενος=*one who is being beaten*, as well as τετύμμενος and τυφθείς=*one who has been beaten*.

§ 176. *The Perfect Passive Participle.*—The sign of the Perfect Passive Participle is *-n* or *-en*. Sometimes the vowel is that of the Present Tense, as *take*, *taken*. Sometimes it is that of the Perfect, as *stole*, *stolen*. When the Perfect had one vowel for the Singular and another for the Plural, as *Ic swam*, *Wi swummon*, the one which the Participle takes is (as has been already indicated) that of the Plural.

The chief points connected with the Participle that are not involved in the history of the Perfect are—

a. Omission of the final -n or -en.—Sometimes this is wholly obsolete; as in *swum*, *found*, *run*, &c. Sometimes it is obsolescent, or archaic; as *shapen*, *graven*, *gotten* (commonest in compounds, as *forgotten*, *begotten*), *bidden*, *trodden*, &c. Sometimes both forms are equally current, but with a difference of meaning; as *drunk* and *drunken*, *bound* and *bounden*; *he had drunk too much*; *a drunken man*; *we are bound to do it*; *it is our bounden duty*. The *e* in *borne* is a mere artificial expedient for indicating a difference of this kind—*born=natus*, *borne=latus* in Latin.

b. When the *-n*, or *-en*, is thus dropped, the difference between the Participle and the Perfect is reduced; and when the vowel of the two forms is the same it is entirely abolished; in other words the two forms become confluent. The result of this is a great deal of very exceptionable English in admirable and influential writers:

> The widows of Ashur are loud in their wail;
> And the idols are *broke* in the Temple of Baal;
> And the might of the Gentile, *unsmote* by the sword,
> Hath melted like snow in the glance of the Lord.
> > Byron, *Hebrew Melodies, The Destruction of the Army of Sennacherib.*

This is, perhaps, to be excused on the score of its being found in poetry. There is, however, full as much of it in prose.

c. Upon the extent to which the Preterit, as a Tense, has superseded and displaced the Perfect, so much has already been said that it need only be added that the prin-

ciple which applies to the two Tenses applies to the two
Participles also; indeed, their histories have been considered together.

When one changes the other generally changes also,
though not necessarily at the same time; and it is the
Participle which, as a rule, retains its form the longest.

Present.	Perfect.	Participle.
Hew	*hewed*	*hewn*
Mow	*mowed*	*mown*
Show	*showed*	*shown*
Sow	*sowed*	*sown*
Melt	*melted*	*molten*
Swell	*swelled*	*swollen*

d. In A.S., as in the present Dutch and German, the
syllable *ge-* was prefixed to both the Participles of Past—
as *ge-boren, ge-lufod*=*borne, loved.* The archaic word
y-clept=*called*, from the A.S. *clepean*=*call*, still retains it.

§ 177. *Clad*—the Participle of *clothe.*

In the oldest English *clôthian* = *to clothe*; perf. *clâthode*, p. p. *clôthod*.
In the thirteenth and following centuries we find *clothien, clethen, to
clothe*; perf. *clethed, clothed*, and *clad, cled*, p. p. *clôthed, clad*.

Clad seems to have arisen out of analogy with such O. E. forms as
ladde = *led, radde* = *read, cleth-de* = *cledde* = *clad-de* = *clad.*—Morris, *Historical Outlines*, &c., p. 171.

§ 178. *Sodden.* Two words ending in *th* in A.S.
changed it, in the Participle, into *d.*

Cwethe	*cwæth*	*ge-cweden*
Seothe	*seâth*	*ge-soden*

Seothe changed its vowel in the Plural of the Perfect belonging to the same class as *choose, freeze,* and *lose.*

In *writhe* the *th* was retained.

Present.	Perfect S.	Perfect Pl.	Participle.
Writhe	*wrâth*	*writhon*	*writhen*

See list in March; Grammar, &c., p. 104.

In *scathe* the consonant was changed in Tense, but retained in the Participle.

Present.	Perfect S.	Perfect Pl.	Participle.
Sceathe	sceôd	sceôdon	sceathen

See list in *March; Grammar*, &c., p. 107.

§ 179. PRESENT PERFECTS.

A state or an action which, at the time of speaking, is a matter spoken about, is of course *Present*. So far, however, as it has to be done, it is *Future*, and so far as the motive for doing, or the power to do it depends upon antecedent conditions, it is *Past*. Hence, Perfects may become invested with the power of Presents. In Greek we see this in words like *οἶδα*＝*I have experienced* or *learned* which＝*I know*. In Latin *memini, I have called to mind*＝ *I remember*.

In the German languages, words of this kind are something more than mere logical Presents. They serve as formal and fundamental Presents upon which a fresh Past Tense can be founded. This is always a *Preterit*, i.e. never a *Perfect*. *Can, shall,* and *may* are the most notable words of this class. So far as form and origin go, they are Perfects after the manner of *οἶδα* and *memini*. But they are, also, the bases of such Preterits as *could, should,* and *might*; just as if they were Present Tenses, Infinitive Moods, or the word in its original form. There are others beside : though the class is a small one. It falls, however, into two divisions.

I. *Shall.*—Second Person Singular *shal-t* : in Mœso-gothic *skal-t*. Preterit *shoul-d*.

May.—Second Person Singular in Anglo-Saxon, *meaht* : Preterit *meahte—meght*. Mœsogothic *mag-t*.

Can.—Second Person Singular *canst*, in Anglo-Saxon and Modern English. Preterit *cuthe* in Anglo-Saxon, *cou(l-)d* in Modern English, Mœsogothic *kan-t*.

II. *Owe.*—Anglo-Saxon form *áh*, where the *h* represents

the *g* in the Infinitive *ágan* and the Participle *ágen*. Preterit *áhte*, *ought*.

Dare and *Durst.*—The *s* is part of the root, Greek θαῤῥεῖν and θαρσεῖν. In Mœsogothic it appears in all the persons except the second. 1. *dars*, 2. *dar-t*, 3. *dars*. Pl. *daurs-um*. In A.S. it is 1. *dear*, 2. *dearst*, 3. *dear*. Plural *durr-on*—Preterit *dors-te*—Infinitive *durr-an*.

Must.—In M. G. Pr. Ind. Sing. *môt*, *môst*, *môt*—Pl. *motum*—Pr. *môsta*. *Mote*, when used, had the sense of *may*.

Mind.—In A.S. *ge-man*, *ge-munde*—Inf. *ge-munan*.

§ 180. In these Verbs we have seen a Perfect comport itself, in its character as the theme or basis for a secondary or derivative Tense, like a Present. All the secondary forms we have hitherto seen have been Preterits; or forms by the addition of *t* or *d*. But have we any assurance that they might not have changed their vowel and formed Perfects as well? or have we any assurance that other Verbs might not do so? If so, obsolete Perfects may be revived, though not exactly in the same form. Upon this point I can only quote the following extract. Other Verbs (writes Dr. Murray)

Develop a new strong form, as English *let*, *let*, *let*; Scotch *lœt*, *luit*, *luiten*; so *sœt*, *suit*, *suiten*; *pyt*, *pàt*, *putten*. . . .

This is as old, at least, as the 16th century:—

Thay *lute* the leiges pray to stocks and stanes.
                    Alexander Scot, *New Year's Gift to Queen Mary.*

Witht in the quilk he *pat* five thousand fut men and horsemen.—*Complaynt of Scotland*, fol. 133, (138) *b*.

I met Gude Counsail be the way,
Quha *pat* me in ane fellon fray.
                              Lyndsay's *Satyre*, 1. 686.

AUXILIARY VERBS.

§ 181. *The root in -s.*—In the inflection of this Verb, which is the same as the Latin *sum*, the forms *am*, *art*, *is*, and *are* are the only ones that have to be considered: the chief question concerning them being the extent to which they are all forms of the same word, and, when they are shown to be so, how the differences are explained.

The radical letter is *s*; so that the Third Person is the one which in English alone represents the original form. In *ar-t* and *are* it is changed into *r*. In *a-m* it is dropped altogether. *M* and *t* are signs of the first and second persons respectively.

The form, *is* is exceptional: for though it is found in the *Anglo*-Saxon, the *Old* Saxon form is *is-t*, as it, also, is in the present Dutch and German, and as it *is* in the Mœsogothic. In the Scandinavian languages the *s* becomes *r*. In Greek the form is ἐστὶ (also εἰ).

It is in the Present Tense that this root is most especially found; and in the Past Tenses—whether Perfect or Preterit—that it is most conspicuously absent. It is found in the Infinitive Mood and in the Active, but never in the Passive, Participle. In the Present Indicative it is *always* found, though not always throughout, e.g. in German:—

Ic bin	= *I am*	*Wir sind*	= *We are*
Du bist	= *Thou art*	*Ihr seyd*	= *Ye are*
Er ist	= *He is*	*Sie sind*	= *They are.*

Here a second root (*be*) presents itself. In the Imperative and Present Subjunctive this *be* is common.

Like the Personal and Demonstrative Pronouns, the Auxiliary Verbs *am* and *be* are among the oldest words of our languages, indeed of the Indo-European class, in which they are found throughout. This being the case, we are prepared to find that they have undergone more than an ordinary amount of change. That such is the fact we find by an inspection of the Present Tense, where *am*, *is*, and *are* are undoubted forms from the same root. In West-Saxon, however, and in German, the Plural runs *wi*, *ge*, *hi sind* or *sindon*—*wir sind*, *ihr seyd*, *sie sind*; yet these we may hold (truly) are, word for word, the present Plural *are* under another form. Then there are words as unlike as *es*, *sunt*, and *sim* (*sis sit*), and *eram*, &c., all from the same root.

K

This root is *s* preceded by a Vowel, *i. e. as* or *es,* and all the changes it undergoes may be reduced to the four following processes :—

1. The retention or omission of the vowel before *s*— Latin *sum,* for *e-sum.*

2. The changes of *s-* itself—

a. Before the sign of a Person—as *ahmi* in *Zend,* εἰμί in Greek=*asm-i* in Sanskrit.

b. Int. *r-* ; as in *art* and *are* in English, and *ert* and *er* in Scandinavian.

In Greek εἰμί=*sum*=*am* has its *maximum* of Conjugation, and its *minimum* use as an Auxiliary. Indeed, the Persons and the Tenses in that language are so numerous that Auxiliaries can scarcely be said to form a class. Where in Latin it is necessary to say *verberatus sum, es, est,* &c., we can say in Greek τέτυμμαι, τέτυψαι, τέτυπται, &c. The σ in Greek, though sometimes rejected, always retains its character as a sibilant, *i. e.,* never becomes *r.*

In Latin, where the Inflections are fewer than in the Greek, the Auxiliary character of *sum, es, eram, esse,* &c. is more decided, and the Conjugation is more defective; inasmuch as in Latin, the root *fu-* plays a conspicuous part. In Latin the *s* becomes *r* in *ero, eram,* &c. In Sanskrit, as in Latin, it is defective; the parts which are wanting being made up from the inflection of the root *bh-, i.e.* the German *be,* and the Latin *fui.*

In Lithuanic, as in Sanskrit and Latin, the two roots *s-* and *bu,* each in itself defective, are complementary to one another, *i. e.* the inflection of one makes up for what is wanting in that of the other.

The same is the case in the Slavonic.

In German or Gothic, both roots are defective. The extent, however, to which they are complementary to one another is modified by the use, throughout all the languages of the family, of a third auxiliary, viz.—*was.*

§ 182. *Was.*—Of this Verb there are in the present

English four forms : two current, *was* and *were* ; and two obsolete or obsolescent, *was-t* and *wer-t*.

Of the three auxiliaries, *was* is the only one which is limited to the languages of the Gothic family.

Like the other two, it is defective ; the Present *Indicative* being the Tense from which it is the most conspicuously absent.   Professor March gives for this Tense the forms *wese, wesest, wesep,* adding that they are rare.   Dr. Morris gives no instances at all.   In the Present Imperative we find *wes* and *wesath.*   *Wesan* Infinitive ; *wesende* Present Participle ;   and *ge-wesen,* Perfect, are ordinary forms. Hence the Past Tense then *was,* and the Conjunctive Mood *were,* are the parts to which at present this word is limited in English.

a.

I was	We were
Thou wast	Ye were
He was	They were

b.

If I were	If we were
If thou were	If ye were
If he were	If they were

In Frisian and Dutch we find the Preterit Participle *ge-weest.*

We have seen that all strong verbs in the oldest English had the suffix *-e* for the second person singular.   In the Gothic *was-t* we have an older suffix *t* (suffix of the second person, as in *ar-t*), altogether lost in O. E. (Old English).   But *wast* is not found in the oldest English it is quite a late form, not older than the fourteenth century.   The O. E. form was *were* (that is *wese*), from which we have formed, after the analogy of *shall* and *will, wer-t,* which is sometimes, but wrongly, used for the subjunctive *were* (second person singular), as ' *thou wert grim* ' (*King John,* ii. 3).—*Morris, Outlines, &c.,* p. 183.

In Mœsogothic the *s* of the Singular and Indicative is retained in the Plural and Subjunctive—as *was, was-t, was ; wês-um, wês-uth, wês-un=was, wast, was, were,* &c. ; *wês-ja-u (if I) were ; wês-ei-ma (if we) were.*

As a Tense *was* is like *can*, and a Perfect rather than a true Present. As such it belongs to that small and peculiar class wherein the vowel is long, the succeeding consonant is a Sibilant, and the *s* or *z* is changed into *r*. Nevertheless, the Gothic, German, Dutch, and English Participles are all formed in *s*. M.G. *wis-ans*, A.S. and German *ge-wes-en*; Dutch *ge-wees-t*.

In the Scandinavian languages, however, the *r* has wholly superseded the *s*.

It is, also, in the Scandinavian languages that *var-* has its greatest importance as an Auxiliary: being used both in the Infinitive and the Participle to the exclusion of *bĕ*. Still it is excluded from the Present.

§ 183. *Be, being, been,* are the present forms of the word : in Anglo-Saxon *be, beonde, yben*—besides which there were two forms for the *Second* Persons Singular, *bist, beest* (used by Milton); and Plural *beoth*. No special form for the Third Person present Indicative, which is always some form of *is*. It is this even in the literary German, where the First and Second Persons are *bin* (*bim, beom*) and *bist*—the third being *ist*.

Be, with its *maximum* of inflection, in the German family of languages, has the following forms :—

Infinitive; *beon, ben, be.*
Present Participle; *beonde, being.*
Perfect Participle; *yben, been.*
Indicative Present { Singular; 1. *beom, bin*; 2. *bist*; 3. *bith.* / Plural; 1. *beoth*; 2. *beoth*; 3. *beoth.*
Imperative Present { Singular; 2. *beo, be.* / Plural; 2. *beoth, be.*
Conjunctive Present { Singular; 1, 2, 3. *be, beo.* / Plural; 1, 2, 3. *beon.*

This tells us that, like *ami, sum, εἰμὶ*, &c., it formed its First Person Singular in -*m*; so corresponding to the Greek Verbs in -*μι*; also, that it changed the *m* into *n* (German *bin*).

Forms of the Latin *sum = esum*.

Sanskrit.	Latin.	Lithuanic.	Bohemian.	Servian.
Asmi	*sum*	*esmi*	*gsem*	*yesam*
Asi	*es*	*esu*	*gey*	*yesi*
Asti	*est*	*esi*	*gest*	*yest*
Smas	*sumus*	*esme*	*gsme*	*yesme*
Stha	*estis*	*este*	*gste*	*yeste*
Sánti	*sunt*	—	*gsau*	*yesy*

Forms of the Greek φῦμι.

Sanskrit.	Latin.	Lithuanic.	Bohemian.	Servian.
Bhaváme	*fui*	*buvao*	*budu*	*budem*
Bavasi	*fuisti*	*buvac*	*budeš*	*budesh*
Bhavati	*fuit*	*buvo*	*bude*	*bude*
Bhavamas	*fuimus*	*buvome*	*budeme*	*budemo*
Bhavate	*fuistis*	*buvots*	*budete*	*budete*
Bhavants	*fuerunt*	—	*budau*	*buti*

The Greek is the language in which the root *be* plays the smallest part as an Auxiliary. On the other hand it is the Greek where its character as an independent word is the most manifest. Both as a Verb in μι and as a Baryton, with a regular Conjugation, the word denotes *coming into being, birth, passage from one state to another, development* rather than a Present state of anything that is not going on, or a Past state of any thing that is over and done. Φύω is the Latin *nascor*, and φύσις=*natura;* and with Nature we connect the notion of *growth* or the progress of *becoming something.* The Past Tense, then, in which the root presents itself is the Perfect rather than the Preterit. In the Slavonic it is the Future with which it is most specially connected. It is the Slavonic, too, in which it has its most peculiar functions as an auxiliary.

§ 184. *Defective Verbs.—Quoth.*—The sections upon the two Tenses of Past Time, the Perfect and the Preterit, have shown that in some degree almost every Verb in English is defective. Those that have a Perfect Tense are, as a rule, destitute of a Preterit, and *vice versâ.* This is *defect* on a great scale; and there is defect in many intervening degrees throughout our language. The present section, however, omits these intermediate instances, and deals with it in the opposite extreme, viz., defect limited to a single Verb; and this is either obsolete or obsolescent.

The Verb, however, is *quoth*. We sometimes say *quoth I.* We never say *quoth thou.* We rarely if ever say *quoth we, quoth ye,* or *quoth they.* The Infinitive and Participial forms are unknown. No one living has ever said—*to quoth* or *quothing.*

On the other hand, however, the compound *bequeath* is perfectly regular. To *bequeath; bequeathed, I bequeathed,* &c. are ordinary Verbs with the usual inflection.

The word *quoth,* then, so far as it is not obsolete, is a signal, typical, or representative instance of Defect iu its most limited form.

Nor is it this as a single word only. It impresses its character on the Syntax. We rarely, if ever, say *he quoth,* but *quoth he*; in other words, it is *followed* by its Pronoun, which in other Verbs, as a rule, comes first.

Add to this that the Pronoun itself is, from a comparatively late period, not given in full, but abbreviated (*quoth-a*), and, to a great extent, incorporated with the main word as a Postpositive Affix.

§ 185. *Confluent Forms.*—In words like the Anglo-Saxon Participle in *-nd* on the one side, and the Abstract Substantives in *-ung* on the other, we had in § 173 forms originally distinct, but which (as the language advanced) were merged into the single form *-ing.* Hence undoubted Participles, like *clænsi-and,* and undoubted substantives, like *clæns-ung,* are, at present, represented by the single termination which gives us *clæns-ing* for both. How ambiguous this form is, we have seen.

When words originally different thus merge into a third form, they may be called *Confluent*; and *Confluence* is a phenomenon which becomes common as languages become recent, or modern. There is not a little of it in the present English. In considering the forms in *-ing* we treated of

Confluence on a large scale. On a smaller scale we have it in certain individual verbs :

(1) *Do, did, done.*—These forms have two meanings, each of which was originally conveyed by a different verb.

Do, in the sense of *perform an act*=the Latin *facio,* had as its Past Tense the reduplicate Perfect *dede.*

Do, in the sense of *be sufficient or suitable*=the Latin *valeo,* had as its Past Tense the Preterit *dohte.*

The root was *dug-* ; Infinitive *dug-an* ; Present *duge* (?) ; Perfect *dedh* ; plural *dugon.*

In German *do*=*facio,* is *thun, thue, thut, ge-than* : while *do*=*valeo* is *taugen, taugede, ge-taught.* From this there is the Substantive *Tugend*=*efficiency, virtue,* and the like. In English we have *doughty*=*strenuous, efficient.*

(2) *Become.*—When this word corresponded with the Latin *fio,* as it does in such expressions as *he became powerful,* the Present was *becommen,* the Perfect *becam,* the Participle *becuman.*

When it corresponded with the Latin *decet,* as it does in *that dress becomes you,* the Present was *becwœmen,* the Preterit *becwœmede,* the Participle *becwœmed.* In the present German they have both the Verb *bequemen*=*to suit, befit,* and the Adjective *bequem*=*suitable, fitting, convenient.*

(3) *Think, thought, thought.*—In the sense of *consider,* &c. =the Latin word *puto* and the A. S. forms were—

> Þencan, þôhte, ge-þôht.

In the sense of *seem,* as in *me-seems*=*mihi videtur,* and the A. S. forms were

> Þincan, þûhte, ge-þuht.

The first of these words corresponds with the German *denken* ; as *Ich denke*=I think ; the second *dünken* ; as *mich dünkt*—(it) seems to me. So far as being limited to the third Person constitutes an Impersonal Verb *thinks,* when it corresponds to the German *dünkt,* is Impersonal ; for it is only in the third person that it is found in either language. But it does more than in the way of Impersonality. It has no Nominative Case by which it is preceded. The word *me-thinks*, when analysed and parsed, is *me=mihi* in an oblique case ; while *thinks* (*it*) *seems*, the Pronoun of the Person being omitted.

§ 186. *Comparison of Adverbs.*—Adverbs form their Degrees of Comparison like Adjectives ; so that when we say *the sun shines* brighter *to-day than it did yesterday*—the word *brighter=more brightly* may be the Comparative Degree of either the Adverb or the Adjective ; and, as Adjectives may be used Adverbially, there is no proof in the numerous words like *bright, soft*, and the whole list of Adjectives, that Adverbs have any *proper* Comparative or Superlative Degrees.

In words, however, like *often-er* and *seldom-er*, there is no doubt as to *often* and *seldom* being Adverbs.

In Anglo-Saxon this Adverbial system of Comparison, in detail, though not in principle, varied with the Part of Speech. The Adjectival forms were *-re* and *-est*, or *-este* ; the Adverbial *-or* and *-ost*.

Heard,	heardre,	heardest or heardeste.
Hard,	harder,	hardest.
Heard,	heardor,	heardost, i.e.
Hardly,	more hardly,	most hardly.

§ 187. *Adverbs originating in Cases.*—Of these, *then* and *when, then* and *there*, along with *here*, have been already noticed.

Needs—as *I needs must go.*

Else—for *elles*=otherwise.

Once, twice, thrice=*ones, twics, threes* ; from Genitives or Possessives.

Seldom, whilom ; archaic, from *while*=*time, pause* ; from Datives.

Some adverbs thus formed are still in common use, such as *needs* = *of necessity.* Compare the expression in our Prayer Book:
Any ways afflicted or distressed.

Others explain this as a corruption of *wise.*

> 'Days' is similarly used:
> 'Tis but early days.—
>
> *Troilus and Cressida,* iv. 5, 12.

i.e. 'in the day,' as the Germans use '*morgens.*' Compare *now-a-days.*
—*Abbott, Shakesperian Grammar,* p. 35, 1870.

§ 188. *Forms in -ing.*—In such an expression as—

> The candle went out and we were left *darkling.*—*King Lear.*

the last word is no participle of the verb *darkle,* even if such a one exist.

Again, in Cowper—

> Dick heard; and tweedling, ogling, brideling,
> Turning short round, strutting and *sideling.*

the word *sideling* by no means implies the verb *sidle,* though such a verb might easily grow out of it.

That the verb *grovel* has actually grown out of the supposed participle is shown in a masterly monograph by Dr. Morris, to which the reader is referred.

This Adverbial form in *-ling* or *-lung* is common throughout the German family.

Genitive forms—*blindlings*=*blindly,* German, &c.

Dative forms—*darnungo*=*secretly,* Old Saxon; *backlinga*=*backwards*; *nichtinge*=*by night,* Dutch.

In modern English they are rare, and disguised in form—*headlong, middling,* and a few others being formations of the same kind as *darkling* and *groveling.*

In Scotch they are common, chiefly with the form *-ins*—*blindlins, backlins, darklins, middlins, scantlins, stridelins, stowlins.* This *-s* extends even to the adverbs in *-ly.*

The Adverbs of Manner, which in English are formed by the termination *-ly,* Ags. *-lice,* O. E. *-liche,* are in Scotch as in most of the Teutonic dialects, identical with the Adjective; thus *a lood synger, hey syngs lood; nerr duin,* nearly done; *schui can eisie dui'd,* she can easily do it. *Guid* is an adjective only, the adverb being *weill.* From adjectives in -*lie* we sometimes find adverbs in -*lies*, as if genitive forms, like *once, thrice, needs*; thus *leyklie, leyklies, rædilies*, probably; compare *stridlings*, astride, *gruvelings* (also *a-gruif*), prone, *eäblins, eäbles* perhaps, *mæbey, mæbeys*, mayhap.—Murray, *Dialect of the Southern Counties of Scotland*, p. 226.

In these formations, though the Case is an Oblique one, it must not be supposed to imply a corresponding Nominative. In most of the terminations, -*ng* is like the -*ly* in such words as *man-ly*, Adverbial, or at least Adjectival.

§ 189. This Adverbial use of the Cases of certain Nouns explains those words which, like *toward* and *towards*, *backward* and *backwards*, present them under two forms—one a Genitive; the other either an Accusative or the Dative that has dropped the final -*e*.

PART IV.

SYNTAX.

§ 190. The word *Syntax* is derived from the Greek words *syn* (*with* or *together*) and *taxis* (*arrangement*). It relates to the arrangement or putting together of words. Etymology deals with the forms of single words; Syntax, with the combination of more words than one.

§ 191. The notice of the Compounds of a language leads from Etymology to Syntax; for it is clear that in expressions like *hot-headed* and *horn-blower*, &c., we have something more than an individual word, and, consequently, something which, in some sense, belongs to Syntax. We have *two* words at least. In some cases, as in *midshipman*, &c., we have *three*. We also have them in a state of combination. The combination, however, constitutes but a single word.

It is not always an easy matter to distinguish between two separate words and a Compound; a fact which has already been suggested. A crow is a *black bird*. It is not, however, a *bláckbird*. The best criterion is the accent. When the two words are equally accented, the result is a pair of separate words, connected with one another, according to the rules of Syntax: *the crow is a bláck bírd*. When the two words are *un*equally accented the result is a Compound, as *the bláckbird is akin to the thrush*.

§ 192. In etymology we *decline* and *conjugate*; in syntax we *parse*. Parsing is of two kinds; logical and etymological. Logical parsing gives the analysis of sentences according to their terms and copulas, telling us which is the subject and which the predicate, which the chief, and which the secondary, parts of each. Etymological parsing gives the analysis of sentences according to the parts of speech of which they are composed. It tells us which is the noun, and which the verb, &c. It separates adjectives from substantives, pronouns from adverbs, and the like. It deals with numbers, cases, persons, &c.

§ 193. Speech chiefly consists of (1) commands, (2) questions, and (3) statements. The combination of words by which these are effected is called a proposition. There are, at least, three kinds of propositions; one to express commands, one questions, and one statements.

Propositions which convey commands are called imperative, as *do this, do not delay, walk.*

Propositions which convey questions are called interrogative, as—*what is this? who are you? Is it here?*

Propositions which convey statements are called declaratory,—as *summer is coming, I am here, this is he.*

Sentences like *may you be happy* are called optative, from the Latin word *opto=I wish.* By more than one good authority, they are placed in a class by themselves as a fourth species of proposition. And it cannot be denied that they are expressions of a peculiar character. *Would I could* is also optative, meaning *I wish I could,* or more fully,

> *I wish*
> *that*
> *I could.*

Such being the case, we have two propositions conveyed by three words. There is the omission of the conjunction *that;* and (more remarkable) that of the personal pronoun as well.

Sentences like *how well you look!* convey an exclamation of surprise, and have been called exclamatory. Optative propositions are, to a certain extent, imperative, and to a certain extent declaratory. In *may you be happy*, change the place of *may* and *you*, and the result is an ordinary assertion, *you may be happy*. On the other hand, *you be happy* is a command. There is no command, however, without a real or supposed wish on the part of the speaker.

Exclamatory propositions are, to a certain extent, interrogative, and to a certain extent declaratory. In *how well you look!* change the place of the essential parts, and the result is an ordinary assertion, *you look well.* 'Meanwhile, *how* indicates the degree or extent of your well-looking. But it only *indicates* it. The degree itself is undefined; and (as such) the possible object of a question. *How do you look?* is an actual interrogation. These belong to that part of general syntax which is called Collocation.

Besides being imperative, interrogative, or declaratory, propositions are either affirmative or negative—*Summer is early—summer is not early.*

§ 194. In respect to their structure, propositions consist of terms and copulas.

Terms are of two kinds, subjects and predicates.

The subject is the term by which we indicate the person or thing concerning which the statement is made or the question asked. In imperative propositions it denotes the person to whom the command is given. Thus :—*summer is coming—what is this?—make* [*thou*] *haste.*

The predicate is the term by which we express what we declare, ask, or command. There is no subject without its corresponding predicate; no predicate without its corresponding subject; and without both a subject and predicate there is no such thing as a proposition. Without propositions there are no questions, commands, or declarations; and without these, there would scarcely be such a thing as language. The little which there would be would consist merely of exclamations like *oh! ah! pish*, &c.

§ 195. The simplest sentences are those which consist of single simple propositions; as

The sun is shining.
The moon is shining.
The sun is red.
The sun is bright.

Sentences like

The sun and moon are shining;
· The sun and moon are shining bright,

are anything but simple; for although, when we consider them merely as sentences, they are both short and clear, they each consist of *two* propositions, as will be stated again.

§ 196. The simplest propositions are those that consist of the simplest terms; as

Fire is burning,
Summer is coming,
Man is mortal,
I am glad,

and the like; wherein the number of words is three—three and no more; one for the subject, one for the predicate, and one for the copula.

§ 197. The shortest propositions are not always the simplest. When each word represents either a term or a copula, their grammatical elements coincide accurately with their logical, as was the case with the preceding examples. When, however, these contain fewer than three words, it is clear that either something must be supplied or that a term and copula are combined in the same word; as is the case with such expressions as

Fire burns,
Summer comes,

where *comes* and *burns* are both predicate and copula at once.

§ 198. The simplest propositions, then, are those that consist of what are called *single-worded* terms. Most terms, however, are *many-worded.* If it were not so, what would become of those words which, though incapable by them-selves of forming a name, are still used for forming a *part* of one—words like *the*, *of*, and the like? Very simple pro-positions can easily be converted into their opposite; as may be seen by the following operations upon the words

Fire is burning.

1. Prefix the definite article.—*The fire.*
2. Insert an adjective.—*The bright fire.*
3. Add an adverb.—*The very bright fire.*
4. Add a participle, and convert *bright* into its corresponding adverb. —*The very brightly-burning fire.*
5. Introduce a second substantive, showing its relations to the word *fire* by means of a preposition.—*The very brightly-burning fire of wood.*
6. Insert *which* after *fire*, followed by a secondary proposition.— *The very brightly-burning fire which was made this morning of wood.*
7. Add another secondary *proposition* relating to *wood*.—*The very brightly-burning fire which was made this morning out of the wood which was brought from the country.*
8. Add another secondary proposition by means of a conjunction.— *The very brightly-blazing fire which was made this morning out of the wood which was brought from the country, because there was a sale.*

It is clear that processes like this may be carried on *ad infinitum*, so that a sentence of any amount of complexity will be the result. Meanwhile, the predicate may be made as many-worded as the subject. Notwithstanding all this, the primary and fundamental portion of the term is mani-festly the word *fire.* To this all the others are subordinate. In like manner, the following lines from the opening of the Paradise Lost give us but a single term, of which the word *fruit* is the fundamental element.

The *fruit*

> Of that forbidden tree, whose mortal taste
> Brought death into the world, and all our woe,
> With loss of Eden; till one greater Man
> Restore us, and regain the blissful seat, &c.

§ 199. In declaratory propositions the subject precedes the predicate. We say *fire is hot*, rather than *hot is fire.*

§ 200. In interrogative propositions the predicate

precedes the subject; as *what is this?* rather than *this is what?*

§' 201. In imperative propositions the name of the subject is usually suppressed; *e. g.* we say, *shut the door*, instead of *shut thou the door.*

PROPOSITIONS IN LOGIC AND IN GRAMMAR.

§ 202. Considerable prominence has been given to the word *Proposition*. Propositions do not form the *whole* of either written or spoken language. Nevertheless, they form the greatest and the most important part of it. Nine hundred and ninety-nine thousandths, at the very least, of the ordinary discourse of Mankind consists in them. Every complete sentence contains one at least; many contain more. Indeed, it is scarcely too much to say that where there is no proposition there is no sentence. A few combinations of words, no doubt, are to be found, which fail to deliver a proposition. They are, however, very few. In the so-called Interjections, words like *oh, ah, pish,* &c., there is no proposition: neither is there a sentence. In broken and incomplete utterances, there is neither a full sentence nor a proposition; and in the case of the Conjunctions, there is and there is not a proposition. But upon this more will appear in the sequel. At present, it is enough to say, that combinations of words which fail to deliver a proposition are extremely rare. As a general rule, discourse consists of propositions, and of nothing but propositions. *Man is mortal; Summer is pleasant; Winter is cold; Life is short; Art is long; Fire is hot; Iron is useful; Bread is cheap*; to which may be added innumerable others, are all propositions. And it may be added, that they are all propositions of one sort, and that of the simplest. They all contain three words, neither more nor less. They all, too, contain a statement or assertion. In the first, for instance, it is asserted of *man* that he is *mortal*; in the second, it is asserted of *summer* that it is *pleasant*, and so on throughout.

§ 203. Propositions are,* *at least*, of three kinds, (1) Declaratory, (2) Interrogative, and (3) Imperative. Such, indeed, is the view that is taken by the *grammarian*. In treatises, however, upon *Logic*, Declaratory Propositions are the only ones recognized; it being expressly stated that Questions and Commands are incapable of constituting Propositions.

§ 204. However much this may be the case in the Art and Science of Reasoning, it is not the case in the Art and Science of Language. Grammar, as has just been stated, not only recognizes, but peremptorily requires three kinds of Propositions. It should be added, however, that the Declaratory ones are of much the most importance; for which reason they will be taken as the type and sample of the others, and be described in full. The structure of these being understood, that of the others is easy: the parts being the same in all.

§ 205. Propositions are divided according to their *Quality*; as may be seen by adding to the ones under notice the word *not*, and writing *man is not mortal, summer is not pleasant*, and so on. This gives us the two classes; one of Affirmatives and one of Negatives. Hence, a Declaratory Proposition is often described as a sentence, in which something is either affirmed or denied.

To say *man——mortal, summer——pleasant, winter—— cold, life——short*, &c., is to combine words to no purpose. They form only *parts* of propositions.

Again to say,——*is mortal,——is pleasant,——is cold, ——is short,——is long*, &c., is to combine words to no purpose. They form only parts of propositions; conveying no meaning, and requiring the addition of something else in order to complete the sense. If a person use them, we ask the questions *what is mortal? what is pleasant? what is cold?* &c. Something or other must be *mortal*, or *pleasant*,

---

* Optative and Exclamatory Propositions will but rarely be noticed in the present work.

or *cold*. What this *something* is we wish to know. We wish to know the *something* to which the words *mortal*, *cold*, *warm*, apply.

Again; if we say, *man is*—, *summer is*—, *winter is*—, *life is*—, *art is*—, *fire is*—, &c.; or if we say, *man is not*—, *summer is not*—, *winter is not*—, *life is not*—, &c., we combine words to no purpose. They form only parts, fragments, or rudiments of propositions. We speak, indeed, of *man*, *summer*, &c., but we state nothing concerning them : we say nothing about them. As to whether they are *mortal* or *not mortal*, *cold* or *not cold*, we make no assertion.

§ 206. The object concerning which we make an assertion is called the *Subject*. *Man*, *summer*, *winter*, &c., are Subjects ; and we can assert of them that they are *mortal*, or *warm*, or *cold*, &c. ; or the contrary.

The assertion made concerning any object, or concerning the subject of our discourse, is called the *Predicate*. *Mortal*, *warm*, *cold*, &c., are Predicates : and we can speak of certain things as *mortal*, *warm*, *cold*, or the contrary.

That part of a proposition which connects the Subject and Predicate is called the *Copula*. If the word *is* stand by itself, the proposition is Affirmative ; if it be accompanied by the word *not*, it is Negative.

§ 207. The following words, amongst many others, are capable of forming, by themselves, Subjects :—

man	bow	wealth	ox	pen	atmosphere
mother	fishing-rod	length	ass	ink	firmament
daughter	hunter	fire	bird	virtue	sky
horse	shooter	water	egg	vice	essence
dog	book	soul	winter	apple	truth.

The following words, amongst many others, are capable of forming, by themselves, Predicates :—

good	deep	shooting	hot	fatherlike	moved
great	happy	laughing	cold	bodily	beaten
red	womanly	conquered	strong	essential	sifted
weak	atmospheric	drifted	weak	important	buried.

There are, *at least*, three sorts, or classes of words : (1) those that can, by themselves, form *either* subjects or predicates ; (2) those that can, by themselves, form predicates *only* ; (3) those that can, by themselves, form copulas. To these must be added a fourth class, consisting of words like *not*, that can convert an affirmative copula into a negative one.

§ 208. The form of proposition which is at once the simplest and the most regular, is that where the number of words and the number of parts coincide ; that *is*, where an affirmative proposition consists of *three* words, and a negative one of *four*. In this case, each part consists of a single word ; *e. g.* the subject of one, the predicate of one, the affirmative copula of one, the negative copula of two ;— *man is mortal, man is not mortal.*

It is not, however, the usage of language for propositions to take always the simple and regular form exhibited above. Language may be so constructed as to admit of two of the parts of a proposition being included in a single word ; and, in reality, most languages are so constructed. Thus—

The copula and predicate may be expressed by a single word. To say *men die*, or *fires burn*, is to make an assertion concerning *men* and *fires*. This assertion is that they *are dying*, or that they *are not dying* ; that they *are burning*, or that they *are not burning*. Instead, however, of saying *are dying*, or *are burning*, we say *die*, and *burn*.

The following words, amongst others, are capable of forming, by themselves, both a predicate and a copula, at once :—

eat	teach	shoot	see	sigh	murmur
die	petrify	laugh	hear	hunt	astonish
hunger	impeach	beat	speak	fish	pine.

§ 209. Inasmuch as the copula connects the subject and predicate, it comes between them : *man is mortal.* Hence the copula forms the middle part of a proposition. Consequently, the subject and the predicate form the two limits, boundaries, or extremities of a proposition. Now the Latin word for a *limit, boundary*, or *extremity*, is *terminus*. Hence the subject and predicate of a proposition are called, in logical and grammatical language, the *terms* of a proposition. The subject is one *term*, the predicate another.

§ 210. The following list of words indicates a fresh series of facts :—

wisely	then	in	once	for	near
justly	to-morrow	over	twice	by	on
slowly	of	through	thrice	with	about, &c.

Not one of these words can form a term by itself; that is, not one of them can be either subject, predicate, or copula, so long as it stands alone. No one says *wisely is good, from is black, man is wisely*.

This, for the present, is sufficient. As we proceed we shall hear of Nouns, Pronouns, Verbs, Adverbs, Prepositions, Conjunctions and Interjections, &c., and the so-called Parts of Speech. When we do this it will be most especially necessary to remember that, in the present English, the Part of Speech to which a word belongs *is determined by the place it takes in the Structure of a Proposition.*

§ 211. *Names and Nouns.*—The word for Noun is, in French, *nom*. It is the Latin *nomen*; which means *name*. Hence, the two words are the same in respect to their derivation. But the word *Name* is a current English word; used by every Englishman who has a name, which means by everybody. *Noun*, on the other hand, is a word used in a limited sense; or mainly, if not exclusively, in Grammar only. This suggests that the two forms may not, in all cases, bear the same meaning; and such is the case. As words of the same origin they are the same. As words of *similar* meaning they are also the same. But, whether they are words of the *same* meaning has now to be considered.

A great deal depends upon this, because the ordinary division of the English and other Grammars runs thus—

Substantives and Adjectives are Nouns; the former a Noun Substantive, the latter a Noun Adjective; a classification which implies that they are both *Names*—one as good a name as the other. Then come the *Pronouns.* These are considered not true Names, but substitutes for them. If so, the Adjective is more of a true Noun, and a better *Name,* than the Pronoun.

Again, between the Verb and the Noun, whether Substantive, Adjective, or Pronoun, there is, always, drawn a wide difference.

As for the Participle, it is a Verb in one respect and Adjective in another. But, if so, how comes the difference between the Verb and Noun to be so decided? for, surely, the Participle graduates into both.

This is manifestly a preface to an objection against this use of the terms.

§ 212. *Names.*—There is more than a million of persons in London, and each of these has a name. There are more than ten thousand towns and villages in England, and each of these has one also. There are more than fifty racehorses at Newmarket, no one of which is without its name.

Of the persons, then, in London, of towns and villages in England, and of the racehorses at Newmarket, every individual has its own designation: *John—Hammersmith— Eclipse,* &c., &c. And as the number of other persons, other towns and villages, and other racehorses, is great, the number of names, in England only, becomes enormous. There is more than a million for the Londoners only. Yet London and Newmarket are only parts of England, and England is only a part of the world in general. Persons, too, and towns, villages, and racehorses are mere fractions of the whole collection of the innumerable somethings, real or imaginary, of the universe. Have all these names? They have and they have not. They have not names in the way that the persons of London, the towns and

villages of England, and the racehorses of Newmarket
have. They have not names like *Thomas*, *Hammersmith*,
or *Eclipse*. Nevertheless they have all names. The thousands
of *Johns*, *Thomases*, *Janes*, and *Marys*, that occupy London,
are all *persons*, *men*, *women*, *boys*, *girls*, *children*, as the case
may be. The numerous *Hammersmiths*, *Londons*, *New-
markets*, &c., are all *places*, *towns*, *villages*, *hamlets*, &c., as
the case may be. The fifty *Eclipses*, &c., at Newmarket,
are all *horses*, *mares*, &c., as the case may be. The
Hammersmiths, &c., constitute part of an indefinite collection of individual places, towns, or villages; the word
place, *town*, *village*, being names for the class or collection
thus constituted. The *Eclipses*, &c., of Newmarket constitute part of an indefinite collection of individual horses, the
word *horse* being a name for the classes to which these
Eclipses, &c., belong. This leads us to a great twofold
division of all names whatsoever; names being either *Individual* or *Common*.

§ 213. An *Individual* name is one which denotes a single
object and no more. A *Common* name is one which denotes
a whole class of objects.

Thomas is a single and particular individual of the class
called *man*: *Julius Cæsar*, a single or particular individual
of the class called *conquerors*. Or it may be that we look
upon him rather as a *hero*. In that case he is an individual
of the class of *heroes*. Whether, however, he be a *conqueror*,
a *hero*, or a *man*, he is still *Julius Cæsar*; for this is what
he is as an individual, irrespective of the particular class
under which it may please the speaker to place him, and
independent of any class at all.

Examples of this sort may be given *ad infinitum*. The
main point, however, to be remarked, remembered, and
reflected on, is the following: *Common* names apply to
things of which there may be more than one. *Individual*
names apply to things of which there is one and no
more.

There are many *towns*, but there is only one *London*;
many *men*, but only one *Thomas*; many *conquerors*, but
only one *Julius Cæsar*.

§ 214. Individual names are also *proper* names, and there
are many good writers who habitually call them so, pre-
ferring the term *proper* to either *singular* or *individual*.
The reason for this lies in the fact of individual names
being *appropriated* or made *proper* to certain single individual objects to which they are exclusively attached.

§ 215. Common names are also called *general*; and
there is no objection to the term. It is possible, indeed,
that it may be the better one of the two.

§ 216. Individual names are essentially *singular*, and it
is a common as well as true statement, that no *individual
name can be plural*. A grammarian would say that *no
proper name can be plural*. How, then, can we use such
expressions as *both the Bostons are important sea-ports*, or,
*as long as Mæcœnases abound Maros will be plentiful—Sint
Mæcœnates non deerunt, Flacce, Marones?*

The *Boston* in Lincolnshire is a different town from the
Boston in Massachusetts; so, though the same combination
of sounds or letters applies to both, it cannot be said that
the same *name* is so applied. The same name is one thing;
the same word applied to different objects is another. A
name is only so far individual as it applies to some individual object. The two Bostons, however, are different
objects.

The case of *Mæcœnas* and *Virgil* is different. Here there
are but two individuals; one Mæcænas, and one Virgil. But
the famous Mæcænas is something more than the particular
patron of Virgil. He is the sample, type, or representative
of *patrons in general*. Virgil, in like manner, is something
more than the particular poet patronized by Mæcænas. He
stands for *poets in general*. Hence, the meaning of the
Latin line, and of the English sentence that preceded it, is
this :—*As long as there are men like Mæcœnas, there will also*

be men like Virgil. But a man like Mæcænas is a patron, and a man like Virgil a poet. Hence—*As long as there are patrons there will be poets also.*

§ 217. We now come to four new terms, that mutually illustrate each other. They run in pairs: (1 and 2), *Substance* and *Attribute*; (3 and 4), *Abstract* and *Concrete*.

Take (for instance) an orange. It strikes our senses. We see with our *eyes* that it is more or less round, *i. e.* that it is endowed with the *property or quality of roundness.* We see, too, that it is more or less *yellow, i. e.* that it is endowed with the *property or quality of yellowness.* We see that it is more or less *smooth, i. e.* endowed with the *property or quality of smoothness.* Our eyes tell us all this; the sight being the sense by which our belief as to the properties in question is conveyed to us. They tell a great deal more; but this it is unnecessary to enlarge on.

Then comes the evidence of our other senses.

By our *ears*, we detect a sound if we rub the skin with our fingers.

We *smell* it and find a peculiar and not unpleasant aroma.

We *taste* it and are gratified with a not unpleasant flavour.

We *feel* that it is elastic, or endowed with the attribute of elasticity. We feel, too, that it has a certain figure and size. We feel, too, that it has a certain weight.

On the strength of all this we say that an orange is *round, yellow, smooth, capable of exciting sounds, fragrant, sapid, elastic,* &c.

When we say that an orange is this, we *attribute* to it certain properties, or qualities. What are they? The qualities, or properties, of *roundness, yellowness, smoothness, sonorousness, fragrancy, sapidity.*

And how do we speak when we say that we do so? It is convenient to begin with saying how we do *not* speak. We do *not* say that an *orange has the property of round,*

yellow, smooth, &c. On the contrary, we say that it has the
property of *round-ness, yellow-ness, smooth-ness,* &c.

So much for the attributes of an *orange*; at least, for
some of them. The attributes of a *guinea,* a *loaf,* a *man,* a
fish, or anything else, may be considered in the same way.
They are, of course, when taken altogether, different from
those of an orange. The principle, however, of considering
them is the same.

Let us now suppose that all these attributes are, one by
one, taken away, *and replaced by others;* that instead of an
orange striking our eyes and sense of touch as round, it
strikes them as square, or rhomboid; that it loses its fra-
grance and becomes fetid; that it sounds like a bell, and
tastes like a loaf of bread. Would the object still be an
orange? Would it not be something else? This leads to
the question of the *essential* attributes or *essences* of things.
We need not mind them for the present; but may turn
our thoughts in a somewhat different direction.

Divest the orange of all its attributes *without supplying
it with new ones.* What will it be then? Take away its
original colour without replacing it by any fresh one. Let
it lose its softness without becoming hard, its roundness
without becoming of any other form. Annihilate its weight,
taste, and smell. Let it have no means of appealing to eye,
ear, taste, smell, or touch, so that it become, at one and the
same time, impalpable, invisible, imperceptible. What will
it be then? Will it be anything at all?

What becomes of the attributes? We have seen that
they were taken away. What was done with them? They
were taken away *separately,* and it is separately that they
are put aside. *Roundness and yellowness* no longer go
together. Each is in its own place; and that is a place by
itself. No link now unites them; the orange in which they
met being no more.

But we may unite them afresh; say in the idea of a
golden ball, a guinea, a full moon, &c. And we may, also,

separate them, again and again. United, they give the
idea of an object clear, palpable, sensible. Separated, or
abstracted from those objects, they do nothing of the kind.
Yet the mind takes cognizance of them. The idea of the
particular attribute of yellowness, abstracted from an
orange, is not much more difficult than the idea of the
orange *minus* the attribute of yellowness. It is merely a
case of difference and remainder; the additions and sub-
tractions being made unconsciously and instinctively.

What becomes of the orange? Is it annihilated by the
abstraction of its attributes, one and all? Few are prepared to say *yes* to that question. Few divest themselves
of the notion that sensible, and material, objects are
nothing more than the combination of certain properties,
qualities, and attributes, each and all of which may be
removed in such a way as to leave an absolute nothing.
We rather imagine that, where there are certain attributes
in union, there is a certain link which connects them; a
basis, or foundation, which supports them; a basis or foundation different from the attributes themselves, but upon
which they rest.

This *something supports* them. This something stands
under them. This something is the *sub-stance*, or *understanding*, of objects opposed to, and contrasted with, their
attributes. Now Concrete terms are the names of Sub-
stances; whilst Abstract terms are the names of Attributes; *e. g.* :—

ABSTRACT.		CONCRETE.
Brightness,		*Sun.*
Heat,		*Fire.*
Light, &c.		*Spark.*
Mortality,	are Attributes of the	*Animal.*
Vitality,	Substances	*Man.*
Animality,		*Horse.*
Solidity,		*Wood.*
Resistance, &c.		*Stone.*
Fluidity, &c.		*Water.*

Vice Versâ.

CONCRETE.		ABSTRACT.
The Sun,		Brightness.
Moon,	are Substances with the	Heat.
Stars, &c.	Attributes	Warmth.
Man,		Mortality.
Horse, &c.		Animality.

§ 218. *Variable and Invariable Names.*—Besides being either Proper or Common, and Abstract or Concrete, names are Invariable or Variable.

Words like *stone, tree, man,* &c., denote certain objects which constitute a class including an indefinite number of individuals. To any of these the name may apply; but we cannot apply it to an object belonging to a different class. It is nonsense to call a *tree* a *stone,* or a *stone* a *tree.* Each name applies to the individuals of a certain group, and, as it cannot be applied otherwise, it is an *invariable* name.

All names, however, are not invariable. The word *I,* for instance, is *variable.* It changes its meaning with the person speaking. When William says *I,* it means William; when John says *I,* it means John. So, again, with *you*—it denotes the person to whom I happen to be speaking at the moment; but the next moment I may alter its meaning by speaking to some one else. The same applies to *that, this, these,* and several other words.

If a *mother* say *I,* it means a *mother* and a *female*; if a *father* say *I,* it means a *father* and a *male.* Even if an inanimate object be personified and be supposed to speak about itself and to say *I,* it means that inanimate object. It denotes the speaker, whoever he may be; but it is not the invariable name of any speaker whatever. Or, it denotes the object spoken of, whatever it may be; but it is not the invariable name of any object whatever. The word *this* means a *table,* when the speaker is talking of *tables*; a *dog,* when he is talking of *dogs,* &c.

§ 219. *Relational and Notional Names.*—Why are Pro-

nouns *Variable?* The answer to this lies in the meaning
of the word *Attribute.* An Attribute, as we have seen, is
some property that we separate, or *abstract,* from a sub-
stance. It may be a permanent or inherent one, like the
weight, colour, or form of a material object; or it may
be a fundamental or characteristic one, like the power of
growth in a vegetable or an animal. But it may, also, be
one which has no fixed or permanent character whatever;
and may apply to an object only so far as it is in a certain
relation to the speaker, or to something spoken about.
Thus the word *I,* by which Thomas calls himself when he
is speaking to John, means Thomas only so long as Thomas
speaks of himself. When he is addressed by John, he is
addressed as *thou* or *you;* and, so long as John addresses
him, that is his name. It is, of course, his name only so
long as John uses it; but it is his name *for the time being.*
When Thomas addresses John, the two names change their
application, and *I* means Thomas, *thou* John. Again, when,
with two oranges lying before me at different distances, I
call one *this* and the other *that,* the meaning, import, or
application of the two words is reversed when I change
their places. Still, they are names *for the time being.*

Now names of this kind depend on the *Relations* of the
objects to which they apply; and as *Relations* change, the
import of the name changes with them. Hence, they are
Variable in respect to their application, and *Pronominal* as
Parts of Speech.

The permanent *Attributes* of an object are called its
Qualities. As names they are called *Notional,* as Parts of
Speech they are *Substantival.*

Number is a Relation rather than a Quality; and hence
the Numerals are Pronouns.

The Pronouns of which the Relations are the most
direct and definite are those of the First and Second Person—*I, thou; we, ye.*

The next in order are the Demonstratives, *this* and *that;*

of which the Pronoun of the *Third* Person is merely an
applied variety. When we get into the class of the Adjectival Pronouns, the direct character of the Relation is
greatly reduced. The word *same* denotes identity; but the
name of the object with which the identity is connected
may, itself, require explanation : e.g. A. *This is the same as
the other.* B. *But what is the other ?* A. *The same as that*
(or *this*). Still the fundamental attribute is a Relation.

§ 220. PARTS OF SPEECH.

The Syntax of a language is always regulated by its
Etymology; so that in those languages where the etymological details are numerous, the rules of syntax are also
numerous. On the other hand, where the etymology is
simple, the syntax is of moderate dimensions.

In English, as has been seen, our etymological forms are
few. The adjective is wholly destitute of them : yet it is a
part of speech which, in many languages, has at least two
genders—often three. In French, for instance, we say *le
bon père*=*the good father;* but *la bonne mère*=*the good
mother.* In Latin *bonus pater*=*good father; bona mater*=
good mother; bonum telum=*good weapon.* Meanwhile, the
plural runs *boni patres, bonæ matres, bona tela.* The French-
man who said *bon mère* or *bonne père* might be accused of
making a false concord; inasmuch as he would join an
adjective in one gender to a substantive in another. No
Englishman can possibly commit an error of this kind ; because in the word *good* there is no change at all, and because, in English, we say *good father, good mother, good
thing, good fathers, good mothers,* and *good things* indifferently.

The same applies to the articles. In French there are
the forms *un* and *une*=*a* (or *an*) ; along with *le, la, les,*
meaning *the.* Meanwhile, the German says *der, die, das,
einer, eine, eines,* where the Englishman says simply *the* and
a (or *an*). Of course, then, the details of the syntax of the
article must be simpler in English than in German.

This, however, will be shown in detail as we proceed; since the points which the previous remarks suggest are that, as the outward and visible signs of concord, government, &c., are, to a great extent, wanting, the place that a word takes in the structure of propositions is of more than ordinary importance.

Some parts of speech can form terms by themselves. Others can only form *parts* of terms. This distinction should be attended to.

§ 221. *Details.*—The pronoun and the substantive.

The pronoun and the substantive can, *by themselves*, form *either* the subject or the predicate. They are both *names*. But the pronoun is a *convertible*, the substantive an *inconvertible* one.

The adjective and the participle can, *by themselves*, form the predicate of a proposition. The participle differs from the adjective in implying a corresponding verb.

The *finite* verb (for the verb in the infinitive mood is a noun rather than a verb) can form *both* the predicate and the copula.

The adverb can form no term by itself, but can, when associated with a verb, a participle, or an adjective, form *part of one*.

The preposition can form no term by itself; neither can it without *two* terms capable of doing so. It connects the two by *government*.

The conjunction can form no term by itself, neither can it (with a few exceptions) enter *into* a proposition at all. Its presence implies two propositions *between* which it finds place, and which it either connects or disconnects.

The affirmative and negative words *yes* and *no* can, *by themselves*, constitute a proposition. But they always imply, and depend upon, a previous one.

> Have you done this ? *Yes.*
> Have you done this ? *No.*

The interjection neither forms nor enters into a proposition.

The article, in respect to its *origin*, is a pronoun; a *numeral* in the case of *an* or *a;* a *demonstrative* in the case of *the*. As an element in the structure of a proposition it must be looked upon as a part of its noun rather than as an independent word. In some languages it actually coalesces with it and forms part of its declension; and in others it coalesces with the proposition which precedes the noun.

§ 222. *The concords.*—Concord is derived from the Latin word *concordia*, and signifies *agreement*.

The word *man* is the name of a male, and, in respect to its gender, is masculine. The word *she* relates to a female, and, in respect to its gender, is feminine. We do not, when speaking of the same person, say I saw the man and *she* saw me; or I saw *him* and *she* saw me. If we do, there is a *discordance* in the matter of gender. On the other,

> I saw him and he saw me,
> I saw her and she saw me,

are concords; and, as there are more kinds of concords than one, this is called the concord of *gender*.

The other concords will be noticed in their details as we proceed. But a general view of their nature and numbers may be given now.

If I say *I saw* these *man*, or *I saw* this *men*, there is a discord. *This man* and these *men* are the true combinations. This gives us a concord of *number*.

If I say *he is* him, there is a discord of case. The true combination is *he* is *he*. This gives us a concord of *case*.

If I say *I speaks*, there is a discord. What I ought to say is *I speak*. This gives us a concord of *person*. This is peculiar to the verb. So is *we speaks*, which gives us a discord of number; but this has been already noticed under the noun.

If I say *I do this that I* might *gain by it*, or I *did this that I* might *gain by* it, this is a *discord*. The right expression is either *I* did *this* that I *might gain by it*, or *I* do *this that* I may gain by it. This gives us a concord of tense. This is not generally recognized as a concord; but it

evidently is one.   The recognized concords are four in
number; *the* four concords—*i.e.* those of gender, number,
case, and person; the latter being limited to the verb, which,
on the other hand, has no concord of gender.

There is another kind of concord, which, from having a
special and conspicuous name of its own, has not been
classed among THE FOUR recognized concords—viz. Apposition—which see under Compound Sentences.

§ 223. *Apposition.*—In expressions like *George, King of
England,* we must notice—

1. That the words *King* and *George* are in the same case.

2. That they denote the same object.   The word *George*
applied to that particular monarch means the same person
as the *King* of England; and the words King of England
applied to the same monarch mean the same person as
George.

3. That they explain each other.   If we say simply the
King of England, we do not sufficiently explain ourselves;
since we may mean a *Henry,* an *Edward,* or a *William.*
And if we say simply *George,* we do not sufficiently explain
ourselves; since we may mean any person in the world
whose name is *George.*   But if we say *George, King of England,* we explain what *king* and what *George* is meant.

Words that thus explain each other, mean the same
thing, and are in the same case, may be said to be *placed
alongside of each other,* or to be in *apposition.*   The Latin
word *appositio* means *putting by the side of.*   The following
are specimens of apposition :—*Solomon, the son of David.—
Crœsus, King of Lydia.—Content, the source of happiness.—
John's the farmer's wife.—Oliver's the spy's evidence.—Cœsar,
the Roman emperor, invades Britain.*—Here the words *Roman
emperor* explain, or define, the word *Cœsar ;* and the
sentence, filled up, might stand, *Cœsar, that is, the Roman
emperor,* &c.   Again, the words *Roman emperor* might be
wholly ejected; or, if not ejected, they might be thrown into
a parenthesis. The practical bearing of this fact is exhibited

by changing the form of the sentence, and inserting the conjunction *and*. In this case, instead of one person, two are spoken of, and the verb *invades* must be changed from the singular to the plural. Now the words *Roman emperor* are said to be in apposition to *Cæsar*. They constitute, not an additional idea, but an explanation of the original one. They are, as it were, *laid alongside (appositi) of* the word *Cæsar*. Cases of doubtful number, wherein two substantives precede a verb, and wherein it is uncertain whether the verb should be singular or plural, are decided by determining whether the substantives be in apposition or the contrary. No matter how many nouns there may be, so long as it can be shown that they are in apposition, the verb is in the singular number, provided that the main noun is also singular. There is still another concord; but it must be put into logical rather than grammatical phraseology. It is that the *predicate must agree in case* with its subject. It was noticed in § 219.

§ 224. *Government.*—So much for the concords, or for concord in general. It means what its name denotes, *agreement* in certain points between any two words of which number, gender, &c., have been the chief. The effect of all concords is to keep such words in the same grammatical place as they were.

The opposite to concord is *government*, or *regimen*. This puts each word out of two in a *different* place. Thus in *I strike him*, while *I* is in the nominative case, and *strike* in the corresponding person, *him* is in the objective case, and, so being, agrees with neither of them.

The chief forms of government are:

1. Government of a noun by a noun, as the *father's son*.

2. Government of a noun by a verb, as *I strike him*.

3. Government of a noun by a preposition, as *the father of the son; speak to me*.

4. Government of a verb by a conjunction or a relative pronoun, *e.g.* :

He strikes me; as opposed to *if he strike me, I shall strike again.*

The man who did this shall die, whoever *he be.* This is generally considered more correct grammar than *the man who did this shall die,* whosoever he *is.*

§ 225. *Caution.*—A great deal of government in the way of grammar is done by the *verb ;* and as a general rule, the verb *governs* an objective case. But it is only the *transitive* verb that does so. Still, the transitive verbs are the chief members of their class. Hence the ordinary government of the transitive verb has been identified with that of the verbs in general; and as the transitive verbs govern their noun in the objective case, any instance of any other case being governed by a verb has been treated as exceptional. Whether it is so or not is a matter, *practically*, of small importance, because, in English, all the cases of *substantives*, except the possessive, end alike. Hence, the rule that verbs govern an objective case has been made to imply more than is legitimate. It puts all the cases with the exception of the nominative on the same level. Yet we know that even the possessive case had originally certain verbs that governed it—*he weold middangeardes=dominatus est terræ.*

There is confusion here, but it is not this particular form of confusion we are guarding against. The notion that the verb *governs* has unduly extended itself. The verbs *be* and *am* are known as substantive verbs; and it has not only been admitted, but it has been specially taught, that the verbs substantive *govern* a nominative case. Sometimes it is stated in a more general way, that they are followed by the case by which they were preceded. The fact is true enough, but what the reader is especially cautioned against is that the result is not a case of *government* at all. When Milton wrote

If thou beest *he*, &c. &c.,

he would have been wrong in writing

If thou beest *him.*

But the rule which (had he done so) would have been violated is a rule of concord, *not* of government. It is a rule of concord, and a very general one. It is the rule that the *Predicate agrees in case with the Subject.*

§ 226. *Collocation.*

The order or arrangement of the words of a sentence is in English a matter of more than ordinary importance; and it is easy to see why it should be so. In languages, like the Latin, where the inflections are numerous, words like *bonus dominus* or *pulchra filia* may be placed far apart from one another, and so may words like *milites pugnant*, or *pueri ludite*, and thousands of others in similar circumstances. This is because in the terminations *-us, -a,* we have certain outward and visible signs of gender, and these show that the words in which they occur agree with one another in that respect. And the same is the case with *-es, -i, -nt,* and *-ite,* except that the agreement here is in the way of number, and it is number of which these syllables are the signs. But in English, where the adjectives have no signs of anything at all, or, in other words, no inflection, while the remaining parts of speech have but few, no such latitude is admissible. Hence, words which agree with one another must, as a general rule, be kept in one another's neighbourhood.

§ 227. Such are the three chief heads under which the great majority of the rules of syntax may be arranged. There are none of them of an abstruse character; indeed, the class of concords is so thoroughly a matter of common sense that, at the first view, it seems scarcely worth explanation; for it is clear enough that in the concords of number, gender, case, and person, the two words in agreement are really two names of the same object, and such being the case, *must*, in both cases, be of the same gender, number, and the like. This is so simple a matter, that, at the first view, it appears that we want no grammarian to enlarge upon it.

§ 228. Such would, doubtless, be the case if the concords, &c., stood alone, *i.e.* if there was nothing to disturb them.

But this is not the case. The following is a notice, not of all, but only of some of these disturbing influences. They are well known and generally recognised. They have been, to some extent, classified, and some of them have names—old names dating back to the classical time of Greek language; and thus showing that they have belonged to grammar ever since it was first cultivated.

§ 229. *Ellipsis.*—Such a name is *Ellipsis*, signifying 'omission,' 'deficiency,' or ' falling short,' or ' short coming.'

This was bought at *Rundell and Bridge's*, i.e. shop, warehouse, or place of business. I am going *to St. Paul's*, i.e. cathedral.

§ 230. *Pleonasm.*—Such a name is *Pleonasm*, signifying excess.

The king *he* is just.	I saw *her*, the queen.
The men *they* were there.	The king *his* crown.

In the comparative degree we occasionally find, even in good writers, besides the syllable *-er*, the word *more; as, the more serener spirit.* Expressions like these are pleonastic, since the word *more* is a superfluity.

In the superlative degree we occasionally find, even in good writers, besides the syllable *-est*, the word *most; as, the most straitest sect.* Expressions like these are pleonastic, since the word *most* is a superfluity.

§ 231. *Personification.*—Such a name is Personification, of which the following are instances:

> *Gold, whose touch seductive leads to crime.*
> *The cities who aspired to liberty.*

The unexceptionable forms for these two texts are: 1. gold, the touch *of which*, &c. ; 2. the cities *which* aspired, &c.

Still the exceptionable texts can be explained, perhaps excused. We may say that *a city* is what it is on the strength of human individuals that constitute it; and we say *Gold* is treated as a personal agent, like Sin, Death, Virtue and Vice, &c.

§ 232. *Violations (real or apparent) of the concord of number.—I have not travelled this twenty years.—As this is*

singular, and *twenty years* plural, there is an apparent violation of the concord of number. Still, it is only apparent.
The words *twenty years* may be considered to mean, not
twenty separate years taken severally, but *a number of years
amounting to twenty dealt with as a single period*. In this
latter case the words *twenty years*, though plural in form,
are singular in sense.

These sort of people.—Here *these* is plural, and sort is
singular; so that there is a violation (real or apparent) of
the concord of number. Still, as the word *sort* implies the
existence of more persons than one, the expression is open
to the same kind of explanation as the preceding one.

The reason of this confusion of number is clear. There
are in all languages certain substantives called Collectives.
Of these collectives the word *sixpence* is a good example. It
involves two notions: (1) that of *six separate pennies*; (2)
that of *six pennies dealt with as a single sum*. In the first
case it is plural; since in talking of *six separate pennies* we
contemplate a plurality of parts. In the second case it is
singular, since in talking of *a single sum* we lose sight of
the plurality of parts, and contemplate only the unity of
sum that results from them. In all collective substantives
there is a mixture of two notions. *Army, parliament, people,
mob, gang, set, family*, &c. are collectives.

By remembering that in all languages there is a tendency
to *personify*, we can explain many apparent violations of the
concord of gender.

By remembering that in all languages there is a certain
number of *collective* substantives, we can explain many
apparent violations of the concord of * gender.

§ 233. The special details of English syntax now come
under notice. They will be arranged according to the several
parts of speech. As has been already stated, the place which
a word takes in a proposition will determine its place as a

---

* For *Attraction*, which belongs to the Syntax of Compound Sentences, see § 280, *note*.

part of speech. As a preliminary, however, we must divide propositions into two classes: (1) simple propositions; (2) complex, or compound, propositions.

SIMPLE PROPOSITIONS.

ARTICLES.

§ 234. In the generality of grammars, the definite article *the*, and the indefinite article *an*, are usually the very first parts of speech that are considered. This is exceptionable. So far are they from being essential to language, that, in many dialects, they are wholly wanting. In Latin the words *filius patris* mean equally *the son of the father*, *a son of a father*, *a son of the father*, or *the son of a father*. But, though the Latin language has no article, each and all of the languages derived from it have one. The French has the article *le=the*, and *un=one*. So have the Italian, the Spanish, &c. But the Wallachian is the most remarkable. In Wallachian, or Moldavian, the article *follows* the noun to which it belongs. It also coalesces with it, so that the two form one word. Thus if *om=man*, the combination *om-ul= the man*. In this case it is *post*-positive, or placed after the substantive. This post-position is, by no means, rare. Neither is its amalgamation with the substantive. What occurs in the Wallachian occurs in the Icelandic also. So it does in the Danish, Swedish, Norwegian, and Feroic, derived from it. All this suggests the likelihood of the article being one of those parts of speech which originate during the later rather than the earlier stages of language. It also suggests a manner in which a part of speech, originally non-existent in a language, may be developed. If the Latin be the mother-tongue of the French, &c., and these contain articles, how came those articles there? Though wanting in the old Roman, the materials out of which they might be developed were present. The Latin had the word *unus=one*. It had also the words *ille*, *illa=he* and *she*. Now the French *un*

$=a=unus$; the indefinite article having grown out of the numeral. And the French $le=ille$; the definite article having grown out of the demonstrative pronoun. Neither was the French process of evolution or development peculiar. The articles of *all* the allied languages arose out of *unus* and *ille*; and, *mutatis mutandis*, the origin of the articles in the languages allied to our own is the same. What is *the* but a word of the same origin with the demonstrative *th-is* or *tha-t?* What is *a* but *an;* and *an* but *án* or *ane*, and *án* or *ane* but *one?* The article, then, in respect to its *history* is a pronoun, but, in respect to its syntax, it is a part of speech by itself. This is because it cannot, like the pronoun, form a term. The article is *incapable of existing, except in conjunction with either a substantive or some other pronoun.*

§ 235. The articles in English are *the, an, no,* and *every.* More than one competent writer has already suggested that *no* is an article. If so, it must, of course, be considered as different in its construction from the ordinary negative. It has no independent existence. It *has* an existence when coupled with a substantive or another pronoun. It$=not one$, and *none*, in power. The construction of *every* is exactly the construction of *no.* We can say *every man* as we can say *no man*, and *every one* as we can say *no one;* but we cannot say *every* and *no* alone.

§ 236. When two or more substantives, following each other, denote the same object, the article precedes the first only. Thus—we say, *the secretary and treasurer*, when the two offices are held by one person. When two or more substantives following each other denote different objects, the article is repeated, and precedes each. We say *the* (or *a*) *secretary and the* (or *a*) *treasurer*, when the two offices are held by different persons. This rule is much neglected.

§ 237. Before a consonant, *an* becomes *a;* as *an axe, a man.* In *adder*, which is properly *nadder*, and in *nag*, which is properly *ag*, there is a *misdivision* (*a nag* for *an ag, an adder* for *a nadder*). So, also, in the old glossaries.

Hec auris	a *nere*	*i. e.* an ear.
hec aquila	a *neggle*	— an eagle.
hic anguilla	a *nele*	— an eel.
hec erinaceus	a *nurchon*	— an urchin.
hic comes	a *nerle*	— an earl.
hic senior	a *nald man*	— an old man.
hic exul	a *nowtlay*	— an outlaw.
hic lutricius	a *notyre*	— an otter.
hec alba	a *nawbe*	— an aube.
hec amictus	a *namyt*	— an amice.
hec securis	a *nax*	— an axe.
hec axis	a *naxyltre*	— an axletree.
hec ancora	a *nankyre*	— an anchor.

NUMERALS.

§ 238. The numeral *one* is naturally singular. All the rest are naturally plural. Nevertheless such expressions— *one two* (=*one collection of two*), *two threes* (=*two collections of three*), are legitimate. They are so because the sense of the word is changed. We may talk of several *ones* just as we may talk of several *aces; and of *one two* just as of *one pair*.

§ 239. Expressions like the *thousandth-and-first* are incorrect. They mean neither one thing nor another : 1001st being expressed by *the thousand-and-first*, and 1000th + 1st being expressed by *the thousandth and the first*. In words of this kind the construction is that of *the king-of-Saxony's army*.

§ 240. It is by no means a matter of indifference whether we say the *two first* or the *first two*. The captains of two different classes at school should be called the *two first boys*. The first and second boys of the same class should be called the *first two boys*.

PRONOUNS.

§ 241. A Pronoun is a convertible name which can, by itself, form either the subject or the predicate of a proposition. It agrees with the substantive in this respect, but differs from it in being convertible.

> *I* am he.
> *This* is the man.
> *What* is *that?*

We have seen that as the Pronouns have the fuller inflection, they preceded both the substantive and the adjective when we treated of their etymology. For the same reason they come before them in syntax. Whether we say *feed the horse* or the *horse feeds* is indifferent; inasmuch as, in *substantives* like *horse*, there is no difference between the objective and nominative. Whether we say *a good book* or *good books* is indifferent; inasmuch as, in *adjectives* like *good*, there is no difference between the plural and the singular. Whether we say *feed he* or *feed him* is by no means indifferent; inasmuch as, in *pronouns* like *he*, &c., the objective and the nominative cases differ in form.

Whether we say *this book* or *these books* is by no means indifferent, inasmuch as in *pronouns* like *this*, &c., the plural and the singular numbers differ in form.

§ 242. *You and ye.*—As far as the present English is concerned *you* is a nominative form and *ye* is obsolete. The following passages show that, at one time, the two forms were nearly changing place.

> As I have made *ye* one, Lords, one remain,
> So I go stronger, *you* more honour gain.—*Henry VIII.* 2.

> What gain *you* by forbidding it to teaze *ye?*
> It now can neither trouble you nor please *ye.*—*Dryden.*

§ 243. *Pronomen reverentiæ.*—When we say *you* instead of *thou*, it is doubtful whether, in strict language, this is a point of grammar. I imagine that instead of addressing the person we speak to as a single individual, and applying to him a plural pronoun, we treat him as a collection of persons. If so, the practice is other than grammatical. We treat one person as more than one. There is, evidently, some courtesy in this; inasmuch as the practice is very general. The Germans change, not only the number, but the person, and say (*e. g.*) *sprechen sie Deutsch*=*speak they German?* rather than either *sprichst du* (*speakest thou*), or *sprechet Ihr* (*speak ye*).

§ 244. *Dativus ethicus.*—In the phrase

> Rob me the exchequer.—*Henry IV.*

the *me* is expletive, and is equivalent to *for me*. This is conveniently called the *dativus ethicus*. It occurs more frequently in the Latin than in the English, and more frequently in the Greek than in the Latin.

§ 245. *The reflected personal pronoun.*—In the English language there is no equivalent to the Latin *se*, the German *sich*, and the Scandinavian *sik*, or *sig;* from which it follows that the word *self* is used to a 'greater extent than would otherwise be the case. *I strike me* is awkward, but not ambiguous. *Thou strikest thee* is awkward, but not ambiguous. *He strikes him* is ambiguous; inasmuch as *him* may mean either the *person who strikes* or some one else. In order to be clear we add the word *self* when the idea is reflective. *He strikes himself* is, at once, idiomatic, and unequivocal. So it is with the plural persons. *We strike us* is awkward, but not ambiguous. *Ye strike you* is the same. *They strike them* is ambiguous. Hence, as a general rule, whenever we use a verb reflectively, we use the word *self* also. The exceptions to this rule are either poetical expressions or imperative moods.

> He sat *him* down at a pillar's base.
> Sit *thee* down.

§ 246. *Reflective neuters.*—In *I strike me*, the verb *strike* is transitive. In *I fear me*, the verb *fear* is intransitive or neuter; unless indeed *fear* mean *terrify*—which it does not. Here, after a neuter or intransitive verb, the reflective pronoun appears out of place, or as an expletive.

The system of the syntax of the Reflective Pronouns thus formed is developed in different degrees in the different Gothic languages; but in all more than in the English.

Sometimes the construction is equivocal. The place of the reflective is *after* the verb. The place of the governing pronoun is, in the indicative or subjunctive moods, *before* the verb. Hence in expressions like the preceding there is no doubt as to the power of the pronoun. The imperative mood, however, sometimes presents a complication. Here the governing person may *follow* the verb; so that *mount ye*=either *be mounted* or *mount yourselves.* In phrases, then, like this, and in phrases

> *Busk ye, busk ye,* my bonny, bonny bride,
> *Busk ye, busk ye,* my winsome marrow,

the construction is ambiguous. *Ye* may either be a nominative case governing the verb *busk,* or an accusative case governed by it=*yourself.*

The words *his* and *her* are possessive cases, and *not* adjectives; being equivalent to

> Mater *ejus,* not mater *sua.*
> Pater *ejus,* not pater *suus.*

§ 247. In expressions like *they say,* &c., *they* means *the world at large* or *people in general.* This is the indeterminate use of the pronoun. *One says* is also an indeterminate expression.

It is also indeterminate. It stands for an unexpressed, but understood, *subject.*

Closely connected with the indeterminate sense of *it* is that of *there,* in such expressions as *there is something wrong —there is no one here—there are thieves in the house.* In such expressions *there* stands for an unexpressed, but understood, *predicate.*

In such phrases as *it rains, it snows, it freezes,* it would be hard to say, in express terms, what *it* stands for. Suppose we are asked *what rains? what snows? what freezes?*

—the answer is difficult. We might say *the rain, the weather, the sky*, or what not? Yet, none of these answers are satisfactory. To say the *rain rains, the sky rains*, &c., sounds strange. Yet we all know the meaning of the expression—obscure as it may be in its details. We all know that the word *it* is essential to the sentence; and that if we omitted it and simply said *rains*, the grammar would be faulty. We also know that it is the subject of the proposition.

A curious way of giving precision to this indefinite power of the word *it* is seen in the following list:—

Pluit . .	raynes . .	Deus meus.
Gelat . .	freses . .	„ tuus.
Degelat . .	thowes . .	„ suus.
Ningit . .	snawes. . .	„ ipsius.
Tonat . .	thoners . .	„ sanctus.
Grandinat . .	hayles . .	„ omnipotens.
Fulgurat . .	lownes . .	„ Creator.

Instead of the true nominative *ye*, we use (with few exceptions) the objective case *you; as you speak, you two are speaking*. In this case we substitute one case for another.

Instead of the true pronoun of the second person singular, *thou*, we use (with few exceptions) the pronoun of the second person plural, *ye*; and that in the objective rather than the nominative case, *you speak = thou speakest*.

There are very few languages where the pronoun of the second person singular is used, except in solemn discourse. Sometimes that of the second person plural, sometimes that of the third person plural, serves as its substitute.

§ 248. The words *my, thy, his, her, its, our, your, their*, in respect to their syntax or construction *to a great extent*, are *cases*, in the same way that the word *father's* is a case. They are this to a great extent, but not wholly.

The words *mine, thine, ours, yours, hers, theirs*, are adjectives, in the same way that *good* is an adjective.

If the words *his, her*, and *its* were not *cases*, such expressions as *his mother, her father*, would violate the concord of gender; since *his* is masculine, whilst *mother* is feminine; *her* feminine, whilst *father* is masculine.

This is a discovery of Sir Isaac Newton's is different in sense from *this is a discovery of Sir Isaac Newton.* The latter means *this is how Sir Isaac Newton was discovered:* the former means *of Sir Isaac Newton's discoveries this is one.*

In all such sentences there are *two* substantives: one with which the article agrees, and which is expressed; and one by which the possessive case *s* is governed, and which is omitted, as being understood.

The pronominal possessive cases, *my, thy,* &c., are not in *all* respects like the possessive cases of the substantives (*father's, mother's,* &c.)

We cannot say *an enemy of my* —, *a notion of thy* —, &c. Yet—

We *can* say *these are good books,* but we cannot, *now,* say *these are mine books.* Hence—

Rule 1.—The adjectival pronouns like *mine, thine, ours,* &c., are only used when the substantive is *understood;* as *this book is mine, i. e. my book.*

Rule 2.—The possessive cases are only used when the substantive is *expressed;* as *this is my book* (not *this is mine book,* nor yet *this book is my*).

§ 249. '*Construction of the word* self *in composition with pronouns.*—1. In the words *my-self, thy-self, our-selves, your-selves,* the word *self* (or *selves*) governs the words *my, thy, our, your,* just as in the expression *John's hat* the word *hat* governs the word *John's;* so that *my, thy,* are possessive cases.

2. This is not the case with the words *him-self* and *them-selves.* Here the words *self* and *selves* are in apposition with the words *him* and *them* respectively.

3. The word *her-self* is ambiguous; since it is doubtful whether *her* be a possessive or an objective case.

4. The word *it-self* is also, sometimes, ambiguous; since it is doubtful whether it originated in *it-self* or *its-self*.

This inconsistency in the use of the word *self* in composition dates from the earliest stage of our language.

§ 250. The indeterminate pronouns are admirably illustrated by researches into the history of the language. The word *one* in the expression *one says* has nothing to do with the numeral *one*. The numeral *one* was, in Anglo-Saxon, *áne*, and in Latin *unus*. But the indeterminate *one* had no existence in Anglo-Saxon at all; and it was foreign to the soil of England until the battle of Hastings. Hence, common as it is, it is of French origin. The older forms in French were *om* and *homme*, which are neither more nor less than the Latin *homo=man*. So that *one says=man says* or *men say*. Now this is what our Anglo-Saxon ancestors actually said. Before *on* was introduced from France we said *man* or *men*. At the present time the German for *one says* (*on dit*) is *man sagt*. In West-Saxon we find *me*.

SUBSTANTIVES.

§ 251. A substantive is an *inconvertible* name, which can, by *itself*, form either the subject or the predicate of a proposition.

> *Summer* is coming.
> This is *gold*.
> *Gold* is *metal*.

It differs from the pronoun in its *inconvertibility*.

It differs, too, from the pronoun in its declension, which is simpler. The substantive has only *three* signs of case and number; and, besides this, all the three signs that it has are identical in form—to the *ear*, though not to the *eye*.

> The ship's sail.
> The ships are sailing.
> The ships' sails.

Its syntax from the want of cases is simple. For phrases like *Rundell and Bridge's*, *St. Paul's*, see § 229.

Government of the substantive.—When one governs, or determines the case of another, the noun which is governed is in the possessive case—as the *man's hat, the father's son, the master's house.*

The *order* of the words thus governing and governed by each other gives us almost the only rule without an exception in the English language. The possessive case or the case of the noun governed always precedes, and never follows, the case that governs it. Attention is called to this not only on account of the generality of the rule, but because in the allied language of Germany no such regularity exists. The Germans say *Geschichte Roms* = *History of Rome.*

The meanings of *a man's hat,* &c., and the *hat of a man,* are so closely allied that the preposition *of* has been called the *sign* of a genitive case. It is not the *sign* of a case at all; but the *substitute* for one.

§ 252. *The Case Absolute.*—It is only from the possessive case that the nominative is distinguishable. It is the same in form as the objective, at least for the *substantive.* In the pronoun there is a difference.

This leads to a question often raised, and perhaps even now not finally answered. In sentences like the following,

> The *door* being *open,* the steed was stolen.
> The *sun* having *arisen,* the labourers began to work.

In what case are *door* and *sun, open* and *arisen* ?

To answer this we must frame a similar sentence, and in it substitute a pronoun for the substantive; for, as the pronoun has *two* cases, it will help us to decide the question.

1. *He made the best proverbs of any one,* him *only excepted.*

2. *He made the best proverbs of any one,* he *only excepted.*

Which of these two expressions is correct? This we can decide only by determining in what case nouns standing absolutely in the way that *door, sun,* and *him,* (or *he*) now stand, were found in that stage of our language when the nominative and objective cases were distinguished by separate forms.

In Anglo-Saxon this case was the *dative;* as *up-a-sprungenre sunnan=the sun having arisen.*

In A. S., also, *him* was a dative case, so that the case out of which expressions like the ones in question originated, was dative. Hence of the two phrases, *him excepted,* and *he excepted,* the former is the one which is *historically* correct.

It is also the form which is *logically* correct. Almost all absolute expressions of this kind have reference, more or less direct, to the *cause* of the action denoted. In sentences like *the stable door being open, the horse was stolen,—the sun having arisen, the labourers got up to work,* this idea of either a cause, or a coincidence like a cause, is pretty clear.

Now the practice of language in general teaches us this, *viz.* that where there is no proper instrumental case expressive of cause or agency, the ablative is the case that generally supplies its place, and where there is no ablative, the dative. Hence the Latins had their ablative, the Anglo-Saxons their dative absolute. The genitive absolute in Greek is explicable upon other principles.

In spite, however, both of history and logic, the so-called authorities are in favour of the use of the nominative case in the absolute construction.

The Adjective.

§ 253. An Adjective is a word which can, *by itself,* form the Predicate of a Proposition, but not the Subject.

> Fire is *warm,*
> but not
> Warm is *fire.*

When such an arrangement as the latter occurs (and it does occur in the well-known text, *Great is Diana of the Ephesians*), we have not only the formation of a Subject by the

Adjective, but a transposition of the Predicate. The Adjective is wholly destitute of Inflections ; so that its Syntax is simple in proportion to their paucity.

§ 254. The Adjective generally precedes the Substantive; as a *good man*, not a *man good*. In many other languages the order is reversed. Even in English we may use such expressions as *a man just and good, a woman wise and fair, a hero devoted to his country.*

§ 255. When two objects are compared, the Comparative, when more than two, the Superlative Degree, should be used—*this is the better of the two, but this is the best of all.*

§ 256. The Positive preceded by the word *more* may stand instead of the Comparative. We may say *more wise*, instead of *wiser*.

The Positive preceded by the word *most* may stand instead of the Superlative. We may say *most wise* instead of *wisest*.

§ 257. That they can be used is universally known. Neither is there anything remarkable in their syntax. Common sense tells us what they mean. When, however, do we use the one form, when the other? This depends upon the nature of the Adjective. In general terms, we may say that the object of the circumlocution is to keep the length of the word within certain limits. It is, *probably*, better to say *more fruitful* than *fruitfuller*. It is *certainly* better to say *more pusillanimous* than *pusillanimouser*. But it is doubtful whether this is the only rule to go by. A great many Adjectives (*fruitful* amongst the number) are Compounds, in which case the addition of an *extra* syllable presents an accumulation of subordinate parts, which, to some speakers, may be inconvenient or disagreeable. Thirdly, there is a large number of Adjectives which are of foreign origin. To some of these an English affix -*er* or -*est* would be exceptionable.

§ 258. Thus much, however, may safely be said—

1. That when the word is, at one and the same time,

monosyllabic and English in origin, the forms in -*er* and -*est* are preferable.

2. That when the word is trisyllabic, compound, and of foreign origin, the combinations in *nure* and *most* are to be resorted to.

For intermediate cases the writer may consult his own taste. Of dissyllables, the words that end in -*y* are those that, next to our native monosyllables, have the best claim to be inflected—as *holy, holier, holiest*—*manly, manlier, manliest*; upon which we may remark, by the way, that they are all Anglo-Saxon.

§ 259. The adjective *like* governs a case, and it is, at present, the only adjective that does so. When we say this is *good for John;* the government proceeds not from the adjective *good*, but from the preposition *for*. The word *like*, however, really governs a case.

VERBS (*Finite*).

§ 260. A *Finite* Verb is a word which can form, by itself, both the Predicate and the Copula of a Proposition, as *Fire burns.*

The Concords of the Finite Verb are those of Number and Person, in Simple Propositions. In Complex Propositions there is a third Concord; that of Mood.

§ 261. *Persons.*—In Latin, and certain other languages, the Pronoun is omitted, it being enough to say—

Voco,	*I call.*	*Vocamus,*	*We call.*
Vocas,	*Thou callest.*	*Vocatis,*	*Ye call.*
Vocat,	*He calls.*	*Vocant,*	*They call.*

In English, however, except in three small classes of words, the subject is always expressed. We cannot say *speakest*, however much the termination -*est* may suffice to show that the word is in the second person. On the contrary, *thou speakest* is the form that must be used.

The three cases where the subject may be omitted are

(1) that of the Imperative Mood, (2) that of the Optative Preterit, and (3) that of the three Impersonals.

In Imperative Propositions, the subject, being the name of the person spoken to, is suppressed without either ambiguity or inconvenience. We may say, *walk thou—hold thou thy tongue :* but we may also say, *walk — hold thy tongue.*

The Preterit *would,* when Optative, or expressive of a wish, can stand by itself, *i.e.* without any personal pronoun to precede it. We may say, *I would I could :* but we may also say, *would I could.*

The three Impersonals are (1) Methinks, (2) Meseems, (3) Me listeth.

In Anglo-Saxon *þincan* signified *think,* whilst *þencan* meant *seem.* Hence, *methinks* and *meseems* mean the same, viz. *it seems,* or *appears, to me.* Here *me* is in the condition of the Dative Case, and *it* is suppressed or understood. *Me listeth* means *it pleases me.*

The Personal Pronoun generally precedes the Verb. Expressions like *said I,* or *says he,* instead of, *I said,* or *he said,* are only admitted in very familiar discourse. One verb, however, *always* precedes its pronoun, viz. *quoth*—we always say *quoth he :* never *he quoth.*

The Pronoun of the Second Person is only used in solemn discourse, and by members of the Society of Friends. Instead of *thou speak-est,* we say *you speak.*

§ 262. *Government of Verbs.* — Verbs are of two sorts : (1) Transitive, (2) Intransitive.

In saying *I strike the iron,* the verb *strike* denotes an action. It also does something more: it denotes an action that has an effect upon an object; since the word *iron* is the name of an object, and the word *strike* is the name of an action that affects that object. In this case the *action* may be said to *pass off* from the agent (i.e. *the person who strikes*) to the object (i.e. *the iron*). Verbs expressing action capable of affecting objects are called Transitive Verbs, from the Latin word *transire*=*to pass over.*

In saying *I walk*, the verb *walk* denotes an action. It does not, however, denote an action that has any effect upon any object whatever. The action alone, in its simplest form, is stated to take place. Verbs like *walk* are called *Intransitive*, because *no* action can be said to pass off from them to any object.

Respecting the Government of these two sorts of verbs, there are the two following rules : —

1. Transitive verbs always govern the substantive in the objective case; as *I strike him, he strikes me, they teach us, the man leads the horse*, &c.

2. Intransitive verbs govern no case at all; as *I sleep, I walk, I think*, &c.

The same word has often two meanings, one of which is transitive, and the other intransitive ; as, 1. *I move,*— where the verb is intransitive, and denotes the mere act of motion. 2. *I move my limbs,*—where the verb is transitive, and where the action affects a certain object (*my limbs*) ; or, 1. *I walk,*- where the verb is intransitive, and denotes the mere act of walking. 2. *I walk the horse,* – where the words *I walk* are equivalent to *I cause to walk*, and are also transitive, denoting an action affecting a certain object (*the horse*).

Unless this fact of the same verb having transitive and intransitive meanings be borne in mind, transitive verbs will appear to be without an objective case, and intransitive verbs to govern one.

SYNTAX OF THE PARTICIPLE.

§ 263. This follows that of the *Adjective* and *Verb* ; for the Participle partakes of the character of both.

A Participle, like an Adjective, is wholly destitute of actual inflection.

A Participle, however, like an Adjective, must be considered in respect to its *virtual* Cases, *virtual* Numbers, and *virtual* Genders.

The Past Participle combines with both *am* and *have*, as *I am called, I have spoken*.

§ 264. When preceded by *have*, the Participle is in the Accusative Case and the Neuter Gender. This is explained by what follows.

In phrases like *I have spoken, I have slept, I have moved, I have written*, the verb *have* is in the present tense, whilst *spoken, slept, moved, written*, are past passive participles. Here *have* indicates past time. It indicates past time, even although it be itself in the present tense.

As, however, the natural meaning of the word denotes *possession*, it may naturally be asked how it comes to mean *past time*. To say *I own written a letter, I possess written a letter, I hold written a letter*, sounds as nonsense; at any rate, it gives no such a meaning as is given by the words *I have written a letter*. Nevertheless, it is very evident that, in order for a person to possess an object, the object must be in existence. We cannot say that a man *owns, possesses*, or *holds, a written letter*, without also implying that a *letter has been written.*

Now comes the notice of the construction. The participle *written* has the same form for all cases, genders, and numbers; and this conceals the fact of its following the case, gender, and number of the substantive with which it is connected. Add to this the circumstance that the participle has in the present English a peculiar position in the sentence. If we said, *I have a horse ridden*, we should connect the fact of past time with the idea of *possession*, much more clearly than we do in the current phrase, *I have ridden a horse*. The proofs that the view above is the true one are as follows : —

1. In certain languages we find other words besides *have*, expressive of possession, used for the sake of denoting past time : *e. g.* in Spanish the word *tengo*=*I hold*, and in Old High German and Old Saxon the word *eigan*=*to own*. In these tongues, phrases like *I hold ridden, I own ridden*= *I have ridden*, are actually existing.

2. In Old High German, Old Saxon, and Anglo-Saxon, we have the order of the participle and substantive occasionally reversed; *e. g.* instead of saying *I have forgotten it, I have chosen him, I have made one*; the phrases run, *I have it forgotten, I have him chosen, I have one made.*

3. In languages where there is a sufficient amount of inflection to exhibit the participle as agreeing in case, number, and gender with the substantive to which it applies, such agreement is exhibited. In the Latin of the Middle Ages we find expressions like *literam scriptam habeo*=*I have a written letter*, or *I have written a letter.*

§ 265. In *I have ridden a horse*, and *I have ridden a mare*, the word *ridden*, although *horse* is masculine, and *mare* is feminine, is in the same gender. Moreover, the word *ridden* is in the *neuter* gender, and, as such, equally different in gender from the two substantives *horse* and *mare*.

Apparently this violates the statement made above, *viz.*, that the participle agrees with the noun in case, number, and *gender*. In reality it does not. Sentences like the one in question are elliptical, the word *thing* being understood: so that *I have written a letter* is equivalent to *I possess a letter as a written thing*. *I have ridden a horse* is equivalent to *I possess a horse as a ridden thing*. *I have ridden a mare* is equivalent to *I possess a mare as a ridden thing.*

Hence it is not with the substantive that appears in the sentence, but with the substantive *thing* understood, that the participle agrees. As such it is in the neuter gender.

§ 266. *Syntax of the Verb Substantive in the Present Tense with the Past Participle.*—The Participles *moved, beaten, struck, given*, are Participles of a *past* tense. Hence, *I am moved* should mean, not *I am in the act of being moved*, but *I am a person who has been moved;*—*he is beaten* should mean, not *he is a person who is in the act of suffering a beating*, but *one who has suffered a beating*: in other words the sense of the combination should be *past*, and not *present*. By a comparison between the English and Latin languages this anomaly becomes very apparent. The Latin word *motus* is exactly equivalent to the English word *moved*. Each is a Participle of the passive voice, and of the past tense. Besides this, *sum* in Latin equals *I am* in English. Yet, the Latin phrase *motus sum* is equivalent, not to the English combination *I am moved*, but to the combination *I have been moved;* i. e. it has a past and not a present sense. In Greek the difference is plainer still, because in Greek there are two Participles Passive, one for the present, and another for the past tense ; e. g. τυπτόμενος εἰμι (*typtomenos eimi*)=*I am one in the act of undergoing a beating*; τετυμ- μένος εἰμὶ=*I am one who has undergone a beating*. The reason for this confusion in English lies in the absence of a passive form for the *present*. In Mœso-Gothic there existed the forms *slahada=he is beaten* (*percutitur*, τύπτεται) and *slahanda=they are beaten* (*percutiuntur*, τύπτονται), &c. Now, as long as there was a proper form for the present, like those in Mœso-Gothic, the combinations of the present tense of the Verb Substantive with the Participle Past Passive had the same sense as in Latin and Greek ; that is, it indicated past time : e. g. *ga-bundan-s im*=*I have been bound* (not *I am bound*), *gibans ist=he has been given* (not *is given*), &c. When the passive form, however, was lost, the combination took the sense of a present tense.

Adverbs.—§ 267. Take three words, *e. g. summer is pleasant*. Prefix any such word as *cheerfully, warmly, brightly, mildly*. Ask what sort of sense is made by the combination. The answer will be, that, whether we say *cheerfully summer is pleasant*, or *summer cheerfully is pleasant*, we can only get a meaning by taking the word *cheerfully* along with the word *pleasant* ; in other words, that, although we may talk of *cheerful summer*, we cannot talk of *cheerfully summer*.

1. In the first place, they cannot form by themselves the subjects of propositions ; since we cannot say, *cheerfully is pleasant*, or *cheerfully is summer*.

2. Neither can they form by themselves the predicates of propositions; since we cannot say *summer is cheerfully*.

3. Nor yet can they form the copulas of propositions: since we cannot say *summer cheerfully pleasant*.

4. Nor yet can they form the copula and predicate at once: we cannot say *summer cheerfully* in the way we say *summer cheers*.

Speaking generally, they cannot constitute *by themselves* any of the parts of a proposition.

Although, however, they cannot do this, they can combine with certain words which *can* constitute some of the parts of a proposition, and so form subordinate parts of subjects and predicates.

The class of words with which words like *cheerfully* combine are the Adjectives. We can say *summer is* cheerfully *pleasant, summer is* ardently *hot, man is* certainly *mortal, John is* tolerably *good, James is* exceedingly *bad, this is* enormously *big, that is* contemptibly *little*, &c.

They also combine with the Participles; as *he is hunting* eagerly, *we are fishing* earnestly, *they are shooting* continually, *the sun is shining* brightly, *the wife is weeping* immoderately, &c.

Every verb contains a Participle. Now, words like *cheerfully* can combine with Verbs. This they do on the strength of the Participle involved—*John eats* heartily, *James drinks* deeply, *he speaks* loudly, *she breathes* difficultly, *he lives* piously, *he died* calmly, *he fears* exceedingly, &c. As it is generally with the Verb that words like *cheerfully* are combined, they are called *Adverbs*.

An Adverb, then, is a word that can enter into the proposition only when combined with an Adjective, a Participle, or a Verb; as—*Man is* certainly *mortal, John is* certainly *riding, John* certainly *rides*. The following words, along with many others, are Adverbs :—

once	never	badly
now	yet	much
then	here	brightly, &c.

§ 268. In expressions like *the sun shines bright*, the word *bright*, an Adjective, is equivalent in meaning to the Adverb *brightly*. In English there is, with Adjectives, no distinction of gender; if there were, *bright*, and words like it (used adverbially), would be neuters.

Adjectives in the Neuter Gender are, above all other parts of speech, used in an adverbial sense, and that not only in English, but in most other languages.

§ 269. Adverbs are susceptible of the degrees of comparison. This takes place in three manners:—

1. By adding -*er*, or -*est*, to the Adverb; as *bright-ly, bright-li-er, bright-li-est; tight-ly, tight-li-er, tight-li-est.*

2. By taking the comparative or superlative form of an Adjective, and using it adverbially; as *the sun shines brighter to-day than it did yesterday, and probably it will shine brightest to-morrow.*

3. By prefixing the word *more*; as *the sun shines more brightly than it did yesterday, and will probably shine most brightly to-morrow.*

Of these three methods of denoting the degrees of comparison of Adverbs, the last is most used by the best authorities.

Prepositions.—§ 270. Besides the Adverbs, there is another class of words that can enter into the construction of a proposition only when combined with others. Take the word *to* or *from*, and deal with it in the way that the Adverb *cheerfully* was dealt with.

We cannot make it the subject of a proposition. We cannot say *to is summer*, or *from is summer*.

Neither can we make it the predicate of a proposition. We cannot say *summer is to* or *summer is from*.

Nor yet can it become a copula. We cannot say *summer to pleasant, summer from pleasant.*

Just as little can either *to* or *from* form copula and predicate at once. We cannot say *summer to, summer from*, in the same way that we say *summer cheers*.

In order to admit words like *to* or *from* into a proposition, we must combine them with other words.

Now, words like *to* and *from* will not combine with the same parts of speech as words like *cheerfully* combine with.

1. They will not combine with Adjectives. We cannot say, *summer is from pleasant, summer is to hot.*

2. They will not combine with Participles. We cannot say, *he is hunting from, they are shooting to.*

3. They will not combine with Verbs. We cannot say, *he comes from, he drinks to.*

The class of words with which words like *to* and *from* will combine are the Substantives and Pronouns. We can say, *he comes from London, he comes from the country, he drinks to me, she drinks to him*, &c.

All words like *to* and *from* require a Substantive or a Pronoun to be combined with them.

§ 271. In many languages, where a word like *to* and *from* is combined with a Substantive or Pronoun, the word like *to* and *from* comes first; whilst the Substantive or Pronoun follows after; as *he comes from London*, not *he comes London from.*

Owing to the fact of words like *to* and *from*, when combined with a substantive or pronoun, coming, in many languages, first, they are called *Prepositions*, from the Latin words *præ* (*before*) and *positus* (*placed*), or words *placed first.* In languages where they *follow* the substantive or pronoun, the term preposition is somewhat inapplicable.

A preposition is a word that can enter into a proposition only when combined with a substantive or pronoun; as

John is going to London.
James is coming from London.

The following words, along with several others, are prepositions—*in, on, of, at, up, by, to, for, from, till, with, through.*

§ 272. Every preposition governs a case; that is, every preposition is followed by a substantive or a pronoun in some case or other.

COMPLEX SENTENCES.

§ 273. *Syntax of Complex Sentences.*—Sentences consisting of two propositions are called complex. They always contain either a relative pronoun or a conjunction—(1) *The sun* which *shines to-day will shine to-morrow*, (2) *the sun shines, and therefore the day will be fine.*

§ 274. *Relative Pronouns.*—Sometimes the structure of complex sentences is simple. This is the case when the second proposition follows the first, and the two stand apart from each other, in such a way as to be easily separated. If I say the *man is coming who brings the letters*, we know exactly where one proposition ends, and where the other begins. We find, too, that the analysis of the expression is of the easiest. We see that *the man is coming* constitutes one proposition ; *who brings the letters*, another. We see that the two actions are denoted, (1) the act of *coming ;* (2) the act of *letter-carrying.* We see, too, that, although there are two actions, there is but one agent; for the man *who comes* and the man who *carries the letters* are the same person. Such being the case, the word *who* means *the man*, and *relates* to it; whilst the word *man* explains what is meant by *who*, and *goes before it* as an *antecedent;* for in Latin, *ante=before*, and *cedo=go;* so that *ante-cedent* is *that which goes before.* All this is clear, and may be made clearer by writing the two propositions separately : as

> The man is coming;
> Who brings the letters.

Here, the separation of the two propositions is complete ; so complete, that we may, if we choose, consider that they form two distinct sentences.

To show that *who* means *the man*, we may, if we please, write

> The man is coming,
> He brings the letters.

Or,

> The man is coming,
> The man brings the letters.

The result is the same. There are two actions and one agent. Instead, however, of naming the agent twice, we use a word that *relates* to him.

All this is clear. Nevertheless, it is well known that although complex sentences, like the one just given, are easily constructed, they are, by no means, very common in the actual course of language; wherein few persons keep the two propositions separate. On the contrary, they blend them together, and say *the man who brings the letters is coming.* This, although it adds a little to the complexity, ought not to create a difficulty. A little consideration tells us that we may say

1. The man is coming; the man brings the letters; *or,*
2. The man is coming; he brings the letters; *or,*
3. The man is coming; who brings the letters; *or,*
4. The man [who brings the letters] is coming.

The Relative here means the same as the Antecedent, and is only the Antecedent under another form.

§ 275. The Relative and the Antecedent are, of necessity, in the same Gender.

The Relative and Antecedent are, of necessity, in the same Number.

These rules are universal; for they apply not only to the English language, but to all others. Such being the case, their importance becomes manifest. Such, too, being the case, it may be well to devote some time and attention to obtaining a clear view of them. Every Relative · has its Antecedent, and every Antecedent its Relative. A Relative without an Antecedent, or an Antecedent without a Relative, is impossible. The one, indeed, is necessary to the other; so that the words belong to the same class as *father* and *son*, *husband* and *wife*, *ruler* and *subject*, and the like. There would be no such thing as *husbands* if it were not for the *wives*. There would be no such things as *rulers* if it were not for the *subjects over whom they rule*, and *vice versâ*. In like manner, an Antecedent without a Relative is no Antecedent at all, and a Relative without an Antecedent is a contradiction in terms.

As the Relative is the Antecedent in another form, it follows that the Gender and Number must be the same; so that the principle of the second and third general rules is explained.

On the other hand, the Relative is *not* necessarily in the same *case* as the Antecedent; *e. g.*

1. John [*who* trusts me] comes here;
2. John [*whom* I trust] comes here;
3. John [*whose* trust is in me] comes here;
4. I trust John [*who* trusts me].

§ 276. The Antecedent may appear in either the Subject or the Predicate.

He steals trash
Who steals my purse.

I punished him
Who stole my purse.

Who steals my purse steals trash.

Contrast with this—

He who fights and runs away
May live to fight another day;
But *he* who is in battle slain
Will never live to fight again.

If it were not, however, for the metre, *he* might be omitted; and the sentence run *who fights and runs away may live*, &c.

§ 277. The Relative is occasionally omitted; *i. e.* we may say *the books I sent for are come*, instead of *the books which I sent for*, &c.

§ 278. The construction of the Relative is by no means easy, and some well-known inaccuracies connected with it are to be found even in our best writers. For instance—each of the following passages is inaccurate.

> —— *him* I accuse
> The city gates by this has entered.
>
> *Coriolanus.*

> Better leave undone, than by our deeds acquire
> Too high a fame when *him* we serve's away.
>
> *Antony and Cleopatra.*

Here, instead of *him* we should have *he*.

The explanation, however, of the error is, by no means, difficult. There is an Ellipsis. The full forms would be *he whom I accuse has entered the city gates*—*he whom we serve is away*.

Now Rule 276 has shown that the Antecedent may be omitted; so that we may, if we choose, write *whom I accuse has entered the city gates*, or *whom we serve is away*.

And Rule 277 has shown that the Relative may be omitted; so that we may, if we choose, write *he I accuse has entered*, &c., or, *he we serve is away*.

No rule, however, says that *both* can be dispensed with. Hence, we find that in the instances before us there is a confusion. It is the Relative, which is omitted, whilst, as if by way of compensation, the Antecedent is put in the Relative's case.

§ 279. The following instance is also exceptionable.

> —— Satan, than *whom*
> None higher sat, thus spake.
>
> *Paradise Lost.*

Whom ought to be *who*.

By writing sentences like these in full we easily ascertain the true construction.

> Satan spake:
> None higher sat than Satan * sat.

§ 280. The Syntax of Conjunctions is closely allied, specially to that of Adverbs, Prepositions, Verbs, and Relative Pronouns.   In these relations consists a great part of its difficulty ; a difficulty of which the general character is easily understood. Whilst other words connect only the parts of the same proposition, Conjunctions connect different propositions.   In order to understand how many different kinds of Conjunctions can exist, we must know all the ways in which one proposition may be connected with another.   Many propositions are wholly unconnected. Propositions delivered at long intervals, or by different persons, have, for the most part, no relation to each other. In consecutive conversation, however, one statement is connected with another.   Thus—

> I am pleased,
> *because*
> This has happened ;
> *but*
> I should have been disappointed,
> *if*
> It had fallen out otherwise,
> *and*
> I think
> *that*
> My friends will be more surprised
> *than*
> Satisfied with the arrangement.

§ 281. Conjunctions which connect two or more Terms are called Copulative ; as *and*.

Conjunctions which connect one of two Terms, but disconnect the other, are called Disjunctive ; as *or*.

---

* This figure of speech is called *Attraction*. There are two names for one object. But they differ in their relation to the context. This difference, however, is merged in their identity of import; and one *attracts* the other.

Disjunctives are either true Disjunctives or Subdisjunctives.

A true Disjunctive separates *things*. When we say *the sun, or the moon is shining*, we separate two different objects, one of which shines by day, the other by night.

Subdisjunctives separate *names*. When we say *Victoria, or the Queen of England, is our sovereign*, we speak of the same object, under different names.

The idea expressed by a Copulative may be strengthened and made clearer by the addition of the words *each*, *both*, *all three*, or the like. We may say *both sun and moon are shining*. *All three, Venus, Jupiter, and the Dogstar, are visible*. We may also say *sun and moon are both shining —Venus, &c., are, all three, visible.*

The idea expressed by a Disjunctive may be strengthened and made clearer by the addition of *either*. We may say, *either the sun or the moon is shining.*

The idea expressed by a Subdisjunctive may be strengthened and made clearer by the phrase, *in other words*. We may say, *Queen Victoria, in other words, the Queen of England, &c.*

In all these cases the words *both*, &c., *either*, &c., and *in other words*, &c., are no true Conjunctions. They strengthen the Conjunction. The Conjunction, however, exists without them; for the operation of the strengthening words is generally Adverbial.

§ 282. *Or* and *either* have their corresponding Negatives—*nor* and *neither*. *I will either come or send* is right. So is *I will neither come nor send*. But *I will neither come or send* is wrong.

§ 283. When a question is either asked or implied, *whether* takes the place of *either*.

§ 284. Words like *either*, &c., are generally treated as Conjunctions. This, however, they are not. The most that can be said of them is that they form part of certain Conjunctional expressions. They never stand alone.

Meanwhile, the words with which they correspond can, as a general rule, do without them. We say *this or that, mine or his*, quite as correctly as *either this or that, neither mine nor his. Both, neither* and *whether*, seem to be both Pronouns and Adverbs. When *either* means *one out of two*, it is a Pronoun. When it means *in the way of an alternative*, it is an Adverb.

§ 285. Conjunctions which denote the dependence of one act on another are Causal, Illative, Final, and Conditional.

Causals give the cause of a given effect.

> *The day is warm*
> *because*
> *The sun shines.*

Illatives give the inference from a given premise.

> *The sun shines,*
> *therefore*
> *The day is warm.*

Finals give the object for which a given action is effected.

> *I do this*
> *that*
> *You may follow my example.*

Conditionals give the conditions on which a given event depends. *The night will be fine if the stars shine.*

§ 286. Copulatives, Disjunctives, and Subdisjunctive Conjunctions must be considered in respect to the *Number* of the Verb with which they come in contact.

Copulatives require the Plural, Disjunctives and Subdisjunctives the Singular, Number.

The concord of persons.—A difficulty that occurs frequently in the Latin language is rare in English. In expressions like *ego et ille*, followed by a verb, there arises a question as to the person in which that verb shall be used. Is it to be in the first person in order to agree with *ego*, or in the *third* in order to agree with *ille* ? For the sake of laying down a rule upon these and similar points, the classical grammarians arrange the persons (as they do the genders) according to their *dignity*, making the verb agree with the most *worthy*. In respect to persons, the first is more worthy than the second, and the second more worthy than the third. Hence, they said—

> *Ego et Balbus sustulimus* manus.
> *Tu et Balbus sustulistis* manus.

Now in English, the plural form is the same for all three persons. Hence we say *I and you are friends, you and I are friends, I and he are friends*, &c.; so that, for the practice of language, the question as to the relative dignity of the three persons is a matter of indifference. Nevertheless, it *may* occur even in English. Whenever two or more pronouns of different persons, and of the *singular* number, follow each other *disjunctively*, the question of concord arises. *I or you,—you or he,—he or I.* 1 believe that, in these cases, the rule is as follows :—

1. Whenever the word *either* or *neither* precedes the pronouns, the verb is in the third person. *Either you or I is in the wrong—neither you nor I is in the wrong.* In this case *either* is a pronoun, and means *one of us two*.

2. Whenever the disjunctive is simple, *i. e.* unaccompanied with the word *either* or *neither*, the verb agrees with the *first* of the two pronouns.

> *I or he am* in the wrong.
> *He or I is* in the wrong.
> *Thou or he art* in the wrong.
> *He or thou is* in the wrong.

§ 287. *Conditional Conjunctions.*—Conditional Conjunctions govern the Subjunctive Mood. The chief Conditional is *if*. To say *if the sun shines the day will be clear* is considered inaccurate. The proper expression is, *if the sun shine*, &c.

Although the word *if* is the type and specimen of the Conditional Conjunction, there are several others so closely related to it in meaning as to agree with it in requiring a Subjunctive Mood to follow them.

> 1. *Except* I be by Silvia in the night,
> There is no music in the nightingale.

2. Let us go and sacrifice to the Lord our God *lest* he *fall* upon us with pestilence.

3. Let him not go *lest* he die.

4. He shall not eat of the holy thing *unless* he *wash* his flesh with water.

5. *Although* my house *be* not so with God.

6. — revenge back on itself recoils.

> Let it. I reck not *so* it *light* well aimed.

7. Seek out his wickedness *till* thou *find* none.

And so on with *before, ere, as long as.*

§ 288. On the other hand, *if* itself is not always conditional, being occasionally equivalent to *since*; in which case it may be followed by an Indicative Mood.

§ 289. *As* follows Adjectives or Adverbs of the Positive Degree, preceded by *so*. *Be so kind as to come here.*

§ 290. *Than* follows Adjectives and Adverbs of the Comparative Degree. *This is sharper than that. I see better to-day than yesterday.*

Than, in respect to its etymology, is neither more nor less than *then*. It is not difficult to see the connection in sense between such sentences as *I like this better than I like that*, and *I like this—then (afterwards or next in order) I like that.*

Than is sometimes treated as a preposition when it seems to govern a case.

> Thou art a girl as much brighter than *her*,
> As he is a poet sublimer than *me*.—PRIOR.
>
> You are a much greater loser than *me*.—SWIFT.

It is better, however, to treat it as a Conjunction, in which case the Noun which follows it depends upon the

Verb of the antecedent clause. 1. *I like you better than he*=*I like you better than he likes you.* 2. *I like you better than him*=*I like you better than I like him.*

§ 291. *But*, in respect to its etymology, is *be-utan*= *by out.* It is not difficult to see the connection in sense between such sentences as *all but one*, and *all without* (or *except*) *one.*

But, then, is a Preposition and an Adverb, as well as a Conjunction. Prepositional Construction.—*They all ran away but me*, i. e. *except me.* Conjunctional Construction.— *They all ran away but I*, i. e. *but I did not run away.*

No Conjunction can govern a Case. A word that governs a Case, be it ever so like a Conjunction, is no Conjunction but a Preposition.

§ 292. *Yes* and *No* are, perhaps, words sufficiently peculiar to justify us in treating them as a separate Part of Speech; for it may be observed that, unlike any word hitherto noticed, they constitute a whole Proposition by themselves. *Yes*=*it is*, while *no*=*it is not.* At the same time, they depend upon what has preceded, for unless a question has been asked how is an answer to be given ? There is nothing to reply to.

§ 293. The Negative follows the Verb unless it be in the Infinitive Mood; in which case it precedes it;—*He spoke not, he moved not, he did not, he could not* ; but *not to advance is to retreat* ; *he did not speak, he could not move.*

Two Negatives make an Affirmative. *I have not not seen him*=*I have seen him.*

A question to which no answer can be given is much the same as a Negative. A person who, in extreme perplexity, says *what am I to do ?* really means *I know not what to do.* These are called Questions of Appeal.

§ 294. In all questions there is a transposition of the Terms. In *what is this ?* the word *what* is the Predicate. Yet it begins the sentence. In *are you at home ?* the word *are*, though it begins the sentence, is a *Copula.*

When the Copula precedes the Predicate, the question is categorical, and its answer is *Yes* or *No.*—Question. *Is John at home?* Answer. *Yes* or *no* as the case may be.

When the Predicate precedes the Copula the question is Indefinite, and the answer may be anything whatever. To *where is John?* we may answer *at home, abroad, in the garden, in London, I do not know,* &c., &c.

The Reciprocal Construction.—§ 295. In all sentences containing the statement of a reciprocal or mutual action there are in reality two assertions, one that A. *strikes* (or *loves*) B.; and another that B. *strikes* (or *loves*) A. Hence, if the expression exactly coincided with the fact signified, there would always be two full propositions. This, however, is not the habit of language. Hence arises a more compendious form of expression, giving origin to an ellipsis of a peculiar kind. Phrases like *Eteocles and Polynices killed each other* are elliptic, for *Eteocles and Polynices killed—each the other.* Here the second proposition expands and explains the first, whilst the first supplies the verb to the second; so that each clause is elliptic. The first is without the object, the second without the verb. That the verb must be in the plural number, that one of the nouns must be in the nominative case, and the other in the objective, is self-evident from the structure of the sentence.

This is the syntax. As to the power of the words *each* and *one*, I am not prepared to say that in the common practice of the English language there is any distinction between them. A distinction, however, if it existed, would give precision to our language. Where *two* persons performed a reciprocal action, the expression might be, *one another*; as, *Eteocles and Polynices killed one another.* Where *more than two* persons were engaged on each side of a reciprocal action, the expression might be, *each other*; as, *the ten champions praised each other.* This amount of perspicuity is attained, by different

processes, in the French, Spanish, and Scandinavian languages.

(1.) French.—*Ils* (*i. e.* A. and B.) *se battaient—l'un
l'autre. Ils* (A. B. C.) *se battaient—les uns les autres.*

(2.) In Spanish, *uno otro* = *l'un l'autre,* and *unos otros* =
les uns les autres.

(3.) Danish.—*Hinander* = the French *l'un l'autre ;*
whilst *hverandre* = *les uns les autres.*

PART V.

PROSODY.

§ 296. The term *Prosody*, derived from a Greek word (*prosodia*) signifying *accent*, includes not only the doctrines of accent and quantity, but also the rules of metre and versification.

Take the sentence last written, count the syllables, and mark those that are accented.

The térm Prósody, derived from a Greék wórd signifýing áccent, inclúdes nót only the dóctrines of áccent and quántity, but álso the rúles of métre and vérsificátion.

Here the accented syllables are the 2nd, 3rd, 7th, 10th, 11th, 12th, 14th, 16th, &c.; that is, between two accented syllables there are sometimes one, sometimes two, and sometimes no unaccented syllables intervening. In other words, there is no regularity in the recurrence of the accent.

Proceed in the same way with the following lines.

The wáy was lóng, the wind was cóld,
The minstrel wás infirm and óld.

Here the syllables accented are the 2nd, 4th, 6th, and 8th; that is, every other syllable.—Again, in

At the clóse of the dáy, when the hámlet is stíll,

the syllables accented are the 3rd, 6th, 9th, and 12th; that is, every third syllable.

Now, the extract where there was no regularity in the recurrence of the accent was prose; and the extracts where

the accent recurred at regular intervals formed metre—
*metre being a general term for the recurrence within certain
intervals of syllables similarly accented.*

§ 297. *Measures.*—For every accented syllable in the
following line, write *a*, and for every unaccented one *x*, so
that *a* may stand for an accent, *x* for the absence of one—
The wáy was lóng, the wind was cóld—or expressed sym-
bolically, *x a x a x a x a*, where *x* coincides with *the*, *a*
with *way*, &c.

§ 298. Determine the length of the line in question.—
It is plain that this may be done in two ways. We may
either measure by the syllables, and say that the line consists of eight syllables; or by the accents, and say that it
consists of four accents. In this latter case we take the
accented syllable with its corresponding unaccented one,
and, grouping the two together, deal with the pair as one.
Now, a group of syllables thus taken together is called
a *measure*. In the line in question *the way* (*x a*) is one
measure; *was long* (*x a*) another.

In lines like the following the measure is the reverse
of the preceding. The accented syllable comes first, the
unaccented one follows; the formula being *a x*.

> Láy thy bów of peárl apárt,
> A'nd thy sílver shíning quíver.

The number of dissyllabic measures is necessarily
limited to two, expressed by *a x* and *x a* respectively. The
number of trisyllabic measures is necessarily limited to
three, viz.: *a x x, x a x* and *x x a*.

§ 299. *Rhyme.*—Observe, in each of the following
couplets, the last syllable of each line. These are said to
rhyme to each other, or to constitute *rhymes*.

> O'er the glad waters of the dark blue sea,
> Our thoughts as boundless, and our souls as free;
> Far as the breeze can bear, the billows foam,
> Survey our empire and behold our home;
> These are our realms; no limits to our sway;
> Our flag the sceptre all who meet obey.—BYRON.

Syllables may be similar in their sound, and yet fail in furnishing full, true, and perfect rhymes.

I.

The soft-flowing outline that steals from the *eye*
Who threw o'er the surface,—did you or did *I* ?

WHITEHEAD.

II.

'Tis with our judgments as our watches; *none*
Go just alike, yet each believes his *own*.—POPE.

III.

Soft o'er the shrouds aërial whispers *breathe*,
That seem'd but zephyrs to the train *beneath*.—POPE.

§ 300. *Analysis of a pair of Rhyming Syllables.*—Let the syllables *told* and *bold* be taken to pieces. Viewed in reference to metre, they consist of three parts or elements: 1. The vowel (*o*); 2. the parts *preceding* the vowel (*t* and *b* respectively); 3. the parts *following* the vowel (*ld*). Now the vowel and the parts following the vowel are alike in both words; but the part preceding the vowel is different in the different words (*told, bold*). This difference between the parts preceding the vowel is essential; since, if it were not for this, the two words would be identical, or rather there would be but one word altogether. This is the case with *I* and *eye*. Sound for sound, although different in spelling, the two words are identical, and, consequently, the rhyme is faulty.

Again—compared with the words *bold* and *told*, the words *teeth* and *breeze* have two of the elements necessary to constitute a rhyme. The vowels are alike, whilst the parts preceding the vowels are different, and, as far as these two matters are concerned, the rhyme is a good one, *tee* and *bree*. Notwithstanding this, there is anything rather than a rhyme; since the parts following the vowel, instead of agreeing, differ. *Breathe* and *beneath* are in the same predicament, because the *th* is not sounded alike in the two words.

Again—the words *feel* and *mill* constitute only a false and imperfect rhyme. Sound for sound, the letters *f* and *m* are different. This is as it should be. Also, sound for sound, *l* and *ll* are identical; and this is as it should be also: but *ee* and *i* are different, and this difference spoils the rhyme. *None* and *own* are in the same predicament; since one *o* is sounded as *o* in *note*, and the other as the *u* in *but*.

We have now got the notion of full, true, and perfect rhymes as opposed to false and imperfect ones. For two words to fully, truly, and perfectly rhyme to each other, it is necessary—

1. That the vowel be the same in both.
2. That the parts following the vowel be the same.
3. That the parts preceding the vowel be different.

Beyond this it is necessary that the syllables should be accented. *Sky* and *lie* give good rhymes, but *sky* and merri*ly* bad ones, and *merrily* and *stony* worse.

§ 301. *Varieties of imperfect Rhymes.*—*None* and *own* are better rhymes than *none* and *man*; because there are degrees in the amount to which sounds differ from one another; and the sounds of the *o* in *none* and the *o* in *own* are more alike than the sounds of the *o* in *none* and the *a* in *man*. In like manner *breathe* and *teeth* are nearer to rhymes than *breathe* and *teal*. In imperfect rhymes there are degrees, and some approach the nature of true ones more closely than others.

In matters of rhyme the letter *h*, being no articulate sound, counts as nothing. *High* and *I*, *hair* and *air*, are imperfect rhymes:

> Whose generous children narrow'd not their *hearts*
> With commerce, giv'n alone to arms and *arts*.—BYRON.

Words where the letters coincide, but the sounds differ, are only rhymes to the eye. *Breathe* and *beneath* are in this predicament; so also are *cease* and *ease* (*eaze*).

In the fat age of pleasure, wealth, and *ease*,
Sprang the rank weed, and thrived with large *increase.*—POPE.

On the other hand, if the sounds coincide the difference of the letters is unimportant.

Bold in the practice of mistaken *rules*,
Prescribe, apply, and call their masters *fools.*—POPE.

§ 302. Accent is essential to English metre. Rhyme, on the other hand, is only an ornament. Of all the ornaments of English versification it is undoubtedly the most important. Still it is not essential. Metres where there is no rhyme are called Blank Metres.

§ 303. The English measures are as follows :—

1. *a x.—týrant, sílly*,	} Disyllabic.
2. *x a.—presúme, detér*,	
3. *a x x.—mérrily, fórtify*,	} Trisyllabic.
4. *x a x.—disáble, preférring*,	
5. *x x a.—refugée, cavaliér*,	

§ 304. *The last measure in a line or verse is indifferent as to its length.*—By referring to the section upon single rhymes, we shall find that the number of syllables is just double the number of accents. Hence, with five accents, there are to each line ten syllables. This is not the case when the rhymes are double, and the last accented syllable has *two* unaccented ones to follow it. With five accents there are to each line *eleven* syllables. In the last measure, however, of any verse, supernumerary unaccented syllables can be admitted without destroying the original character of the measure.

Now in the last pair of couplets in § 305 the original character of the measure is *x a* throughout, until we get to the words *disséver* and *for éver*; when a change takes place, and the line contains an *extra* syllable. At the first view it seems proper to say that in these last-mentioned cases *x a* is converted into *x a x*. A different view, however, is the more correct one. *Disséver*, and *for éver*, are rather *x a* with a syllable over. This extra syllable may be expressed by the sign *plus* (+), so that the words in point may be expressed by *x a* +, rather than by *x a x*. It is very clear that a measure whereof the last syllable is accented can only vary from its original character on the side of excess; that is, it can only be altered by the *addition* of fresh syllables.

With the measures *a x*, *a x x*, *x a x*, the case is different. Here a syllable or syllables may be subtracted.

> Queén and huntress, cháste and fair,
>   Nów the sun is laid to sleep,
> Seáted in thy silver chair,
>   Státe in wónted spléndour keép.
> Hésperús invókes thy light,
>   Góddess, éxquisítely bright.—BEN JONSON.

In all these lines the last measure is deficient in a syllable, yet the deficiency is allowable, because each measure is the last one of the line. The formula for expressing *fair*, *sleép*, *chair*, &c. is not *a*, but rather *a x* followed by the *minus* sign (−), or *a x* −.

A little consideration will show, that *x a* and *x x a* naturally form single, *a x* and *x a x* double, and *a x x* treble rhymes.

§ 305. *Measure.*—Dissyllabic.
Four measures :—

> And a gentle consort made he;
>   And her gentle mind was such,
> That she grew a noble lady,
>   And the people loved her much.
> But a trouble weigh'd upon her,
>   And perplex'd her night and morn
> With the burden of an honour
>   Unto which she was not born.—TENNYSON.

Five measures :—

> Then methought I heard a hollow sound,
> Gath'ring up from all the lower ground.
> Narrowing in to where they sat assembled,
> Low voluptuous music winding trembled.—*Id.*

Six measures:—

> O'n a moúntain, strétch'd beneáth a hoáry willow,
> Láy a shépherd swáin, and view'd the rólling billow.

Seven measures:—

> Wé have hád enoúgh of áction ánd of mótion; wé--
> Lét us sweár an oáth, and kéep it, with an équal mind.
>
> Id.

Eight measures:—

Cómrades, leáve me hére a líttle, whíle as yét 'tis eárly mórn :
Leáve me hére ; and, whén you wánt me, sóund upón the búgle hórn.

Id.

Accent on the *even* syllables.

Two measures :—

Unheárd, unknówn,	The straíns decáy,
He mákes his móan—	And mélt awáy.
What soúnds were héard !	Upón a moúntain,
What scénes appéar'd—	Beside a foúntain.

> 'Twas when the seas were roaring
> With hollow blasts of wind,
> A damsel lay deploring,
> All on a rock reclined.—GAY.

Four measures :—

> His aspect and his air imprest
> A troubled memory on my breast;
> And long upon my startled ear
> Rung his dark courser's hoofs of fear.—BYRON.

Five measures :—

> Fond fool ! six feet of earth is all thy store,
> And he that seeks for all shall have no more.--BISHOP HALL.

> The meeting points the sacred hair dissever
> From her fair head for ever and for ever.—POPE.

§ 306. The general term for metres of five accents, with the accent on the even syllables, is Heroic. The first division into which the heroic metres fall is into, *a*. Blank heroics ; *b*. Rhyming heroics.

Blank Heroics.—Blank heroics, or blank verse, as it is generally called, falls into two varieties, determined by the nature of the subject-matter; *a.* Dramatic blank verse; *b.* Narrative blank verse.

Dramatic Blank Verse.—With the exception of the earliest dramas in the language, and some rhyming tragedies written in imitation of the French in the time of Charles II., the works for the English stage consist chiefly of either prose or blank verse. It is in blank verse that most tragedies and many comedies are either wholly or partially written.

Dramatic blank verse not only admits, but calls for supernumerary syllables. In rhyming metres these would constitute double rhymes.

OTHELLO'S SPEECH BEFORE THE SENATORS.

Most potent, grave, and reverend seigniors,
My very noble and approved good *masters*,
That I have ta'en away this old man's *daughter*,
It is most true: true, I have married her:
The very head and front of my *offending*
Hath this extent, no more.—SHAKESPEAR.

Narrative Blank Verse.—The metre of Paradise Lost, Paradise Regained, Young's Night Thoughts, Cowper's Task, Cowper's Homer, &c.

Nine times the space that measures day and night
To mortal men, he, with his horrid crew,
Lay vanquish'd, rolling in the fiery gulf
Confounded, though immortal.—MILTON.

Here the admission of a supernumerary final syllable is rare; lines of *eleven* syllables like the following being uncommon.

Of sovran power with awful ceremony.—MILTON.

Six measures:—

He lifted úp his hánd that báck agáin did stárt.

Seven measures :—

The Lórd descénded fróm abóve, and bówed the heávens most hígh,
And únderneáth his feét he cást the dárkness óf the ský.

STERNHOLD AND HOPKINS.

Eight measures :—

Where vírtue wánts, and více abóunds, and weálth is bút a baíted hoók
Wherewíth men swállow dówn the báne befóre on dánger dárk they loók.

§ 307. The Three Trisyllabic Measures—Accent on the
1st, 4th, &c., syllables.

Two measures :—

Píbroch o' Dónuil Dhu!
  Píbroch o' Dónuil!
Wáke thy shrill voíce anew.
  Súmmon Clan Cónnuil.
Cóme away, cóme away,
  Hárk to the súmmons!
Cóme in your wár array,
  Géntles and cómmons.—

Cóme every híll-plaid, and
  Trúe heart that wéars one;
Cóme every steél-blade, and
  Stróng hand that beárs one.—
Leáve the deer, leáve the steer,
  Leáve nets and bárges:
Cóme with your fíghting-gear,
  Broádswords and tárges.

SCOTT.

Three measures :—

Peáce to thee, ísle of the ócean,
  Peáce to thy bréezes and bíllows.—BYRON.

Four measures :—

Wárriors or chiéfs, should the sháft or the swórd
Piérce me in leáding the hóst of the Lórd,
Heéd not the córpse, though a kíng's in your páth,
Búry your steél in the bósoms of Gáth.—BYRON.

Two measures :—

Besíde her are laíd
Her máttock and spáde—
Alóne she is thére,
Her shoúlders are báre—
Éver alone
She máketh her moán.
TENNYSON.

But vaínly thou wárrest;
For thís is alóne in
Thy pówer to décláre,
That, in the dím fórest,
Thou heárd'st a low moáning.
COLERIDGE.

The bláck bands came óver | The Boúrbon! the Boúrbon!
  The A'lps and their snów; | Sans coúntry or hóme,
With Boúrbon, the róver, | We 'll fóllow the Boúrbon
  They pássed the broad Pó. | To plúnder old Róme.

BYRON.

Four measures :—

> Oh, húsh thee, my bábie, thy síre was a knight,
> Thy móther a lády both lóvely and bright :
> The woóds and the gléns and the tówers which we seé,
> They áll are bélonging, dear bábie, to theé.

One measure :—

> As ye sweép
> Through the deép.—CAMPBELL.

Two measures :—

> In my ráge shall be seén
> The revénge of a queén.—ADDISON.

Three measures :—

> And the spárkles they flásh from their éyes !

Mixed.

> See the snákes, how they reár,
> How they híss in the áir,
> And the spárkles they flásh from their éyes.—DRYDEN.

Four measures :—

> And the kíng seized a flámbeau with zeál to destróy.—DRYDEN.

§ 308. Lines or verses grouped together constitute stanzas, couplets, triplets, &c. It is only a few of the English metres that are known by fixed names. These are as follows :—

1. *Octosyllabics.*—Butler's Hudibras, Scott's poems, The Giaour, and other poems of Lord Byron—*eight* measures.

> The way was long, the wind was cold,
> The minstrel was infirm and old ;
> His haggard cheek and tresses gray
> Seem'd to have known a better day ;
> The harp, his sole remaining joy,
> Was carried by an orphan boy,
> The last of all the bards was he
> That sung of ancient chivalry.—SCOTT.

2. *Octosyllabics.*—Same as the last; except that the rhymes are regularly alternate, and the verses arranged in stanzas.

> And on her lover's arm she leant,
>   And round her waist she felt it fold,
> And far across the hills they went,
>   In that new world which now is old:
> Across the hills and far away,
>   Beyond their utmost purple rim,
> And deep into the dying day
>   The happy princess follow'd him.—TENNYSON.

3. *Octosyllabic Triplets.*—Three rhymes in succession. Generally arranged as stanzas.

> I blest them, and they wander'd on;
> I spoke, but answer came there none:
> The dull and bitter voice was gone.—TENNYSON.

4. *Blank Verse.*—*Five* dissyllabic measures, with accents on the even syllable, without rhyme.

> All these and more came flocking; but with looks
> Downcast and damp, yet such wherein appear'd
> Obscure some glimpse of joy to have found their chief
> Not in despair, to have found themselves not lost
> In loss itself.—MILTON.

5. *Heroic Couplets.*—Five measures, as before, with pairs of rhymes.

> O'er the glad waters of the dark blue sea,
> Our thoughts as boundless, and our souls as free;
> Far as the breeze can bear, the billows foam,
> Survey our empire and behold our home:
> These are our realms; no limits to our sway;
> Our flag the sceptre all who meet obey.—BYRON.

6. *Heroic Triplets.*—Five measures, as before. Three rhymes in succession. Arranged in stanzas.

7. *Elegiacs.*—Five measures, as before; with regularly alternate rhymes, and arranged in stanzas.

> The curfew tolls the knell of parting day,
>   The lowing herds wind slowly o'er the lea,
> The ploughman homewards plods his weary way,
>   And leaves the world to darkness and to me.—GRAY.

P

8. *Rhymes Royal.*—Seven lines of heroics, with the last two rhymes in succession, and the first five recurring at intervals.

> This Troilus, in gift of curtesie,
>   With hauk on hond, and with a huge rout
> Of knightes, rode, and did her company,
>   Passing all through the valley far about;
>   And further would have ridden out of doubt.
> Full faine and woe was him to gone so sone;
> But turn he must, and it was eke to doen.—CHAUCER.

This metre was common with the writers of the earlier part of Queen Elizabeth's reign. It admits of varieties according to the distribution of the first five rhymes.

9. *Ottava Rima.*—A metre with an Italian name, and borrowed from Italy, where it is used generally for narrative poetry. The Morgante Maggiore of Pulci, the Orlando Innamorato of Bojardo, the Orlando Furioso of Ariosto, the Gierusalemme Liberata of Tasso, are all written in this metre. Besides this, the two chief epics of Spain and Portugal respectively, the Araucana and the Lusiados, are thus composed. Hence it is a form of poetry which is Continental rather than English, and naturalized rather than indigenous. The stanza consists of eight lines of heroics, the six first rhyming alternately, the two last in succession.

> Arrived there, a prodigious noise he hears,
>   Which suddenly along the forest spread;
> Whereat from out his quiver he prepares
>   An arrow for his bow, and lifts his head;
> And lo! a monstrous herd of swine appears,
>   And onward rushes with tempestuous tread,
> And to the fountain's brink precisely pours,
> So that the giant's join'd by all the boars.—BYRON.

10. *Terza Rima.*—Like the last, borrowed both in name and nature from the Italian, and scarcely yet naturalized in England.

The Spirit of the fervent days of old,
  When words were things that came to pass, and Thought
  Flash'd o'er the future, bidding men behold
Their children's children's doom already brought
  Forth from the abyss of Time which is to be,
  The chaos of events where lie half-wrought
Shapes that must undergo mortality :
  What the great seers of Israel wore within,
  That Spirit was on them and is on me ;
And if, Cassandra-like, amidst the din
  Of conflicts, none will hear, or hearing, heed
  This voice from out the Wilderness, the sin
Be theirs, and my own feelings be my meed,
  The only guerdon I have ever known.—BYRON.

11. *Alexandrines.*—Six measures ; like the last, generally, perhaps always, with rhyme. The name is said to be taken from the fact that early romances upon the deeds of Alexander of Macedon, of great popularity, were written in this metre. One of the longest poems in the English language is in Alexandrines, viz. Drayton's Poly-olbion.

Ye sácred bárds that tó your hárps' melódious strings
Sung th' áncient héroes' deeds, the mónuménts of kings ;
If, ás those Drúids taúght who képt the British rites,
And dwélt in dárksome gróves, there cóunselling with sprites,
When thése our soúls by deáth our bódies dó forsáke,
They instantly again to óther bódies táke,
I coúld have wísh'd your soúls redóubled ín my breást,
To give my vérse applaúse to time's etérnal rést.—DRAYTON.

12. *Spenserian Stanza.*—A stanza consisting of nine lines, the eight first heroics, the last an Alexandrine.

It hath been through all ages ever seen,
That with the prize of arms and chivalrie
The prize of beauty still hath joined been,
And that for reason's special privitie :
For either doth on other much rely.
For he meseems most fit the fair to serve
That can her best defend from villanie ;
And she most fit his service doth deserve,
That fairest is, and from her faith will never swerve.
                      SPENSER.

P 2

Childe Harold and other important poems are composed in the Spenserian stanza.

13. *Service Metre.*—Couplets of seven measures. This is the common metre of the Psalm versions. It is also called Common Measure, or Long Measure. In this metre there is always a pause after the fourth measure, and many grammarians consider that with that pause the line ends. According to this view, the service metre does not consist of two long lines with seven measures each; but of four short ones, with four and three measures each alternately. The Psalm versions are printed so as to exhibit this pause or break.

> The Lord descended from above, | and bow'd the heavens most high,
> And underneath his feet He cast | the darkness of the sky.
> On Cherubs and on Seraphim | full royally He rode,
> And on the wings of mighty winds | came flying all abroad.
>   STERNHOLD AND HOPKINS.

In this matter the following rule is convenient. When the last syllable of the fourth measure in the one verse *rhymes* with the corresponding syllable in the other, the long verse should be looked upon as broken up into two short ones; in other words, the couplets should be dealt with as a stanza. Where there is no rhyme except at the seventh measure, the verse should remain undivided. Thus :—

> Turn, gentle hermit of the glen, | and guide thy lonely way
> To where you taper cheers the vale | with hospitable ray—

constitute a single couplet of two lines, the number of rhymes being two. But,

> Turn, gentle hermit of the dale,
>   And guide thy lonely way
> To where yon taper cheers the vale
>   With hospitable ray.—GOLDSMITH.

constitute a stanza of four lines, the number of rhymes being four.

14. *Ballad Stanza.*—Service metre broken up in the way just indicated. Goldsmith's Edwin and Angelina, &c., from which the last stanza was an extract.

15. *Poulterer's Measure.*—Alexandrines and Service metre alternately.

§ 309. *Symmetrical Metres.*—Allowing for the indifference of the number of syllables in the last measure, it is evident that in all lines where the measures are dissyllabic the syllables will be a multiple of the accents, *i.e.* they will be *twice* as numerous.

Similarly, in all lines where the measures are trisyllabic, the syllables will also be multiples of the accents, *i.e.* they will be *thrice* as numerous.

Lines of this sort may be called symmetrical.

§ 310. *Unsymmetrical Metres.*—Lines, where the syllables are *not* a multiple of the accents, may be called Unsymmetrical. Occasional specimens of such lines occur (as may be seen from several of the examples already quoted) interspersed amongst others of symmetrical character. Where this occurs the general character of the versification may be considered as symmetrical also.

The case, however, is different where the whole character of the versification is unsymmetrical.

> In the yéar since Jésus diéd for mén,
> Eighteen húndred yeárs and tén,
> Wé were a gállant cómpaný,
> Ríding o'er lánd and sáiling o'er séa.
> O'h! but wé went mérriló!
> We fórded the ríver, and clómb the high hill,
> Néver our steéds for a dáy stood still.
> Whéther we láy in the cáve or the shéd,
> Our sleép fell sóft on the hárdest béd;
> Whéther we cóuch'd on our róugh capóte,
> Or the róugher plánk of our glíding bóat;
> Or strétch'd on the beách or our sáddles spréad
> As a pillow beneáth the résting héad,
> Frésh we wóke upón the mórrow.
> A'll our thóughts and wórds had scópe,
> Wé had heálth and wé had hópe,
> Tóil and trável, bút no sórrow.

These lines are naturally trisyllabic; from any measure of
which one of the unaccented syllables may be ejected.
Where they are symmetrical they are so by accident. A
metrical fiction, that conveniently illustrates their structure, is the doctrine that they are *lines formed upon measure x a x, for which either x x a or a x x may be substituted,
and from which either a x or x a may be formed by ejection
of either the first or last unaccented syllable.*

§ 311. *Convertible Metres.*—Such a line as

Ere her faithless sons betray'd her

may be read in two ways. We may either lay full stress
upon the word *ere*, and read

E're her faithless sóns betráy'd her;

or we may lay little or no stress upon either *ere* or *her*,
reserving the full accentuation for the syllable *faith-* in
faithless, in which case the reading would be

Ere her fáithless sóns betráy'd her.

Lines of this sort may be called examples of *convertible
metres*, since by changing the accent a dissyllabic line may
be converted into one partially trisyllabic, and *vice versâ.*

This property of convertibility is explained by the fact
of accentuation being *a relative quality.* In the example
before us *ere* is sufficiently strongly accented to stand in
contrast to *her*, but it is not sufficiently strongly accented
to stand upon a par with the *faith-* in *faithless* if decidedly
pronounced.

The real character of convertible lines is determined from
the character of the lines with which they are associated.
That the second mode of reading the line in question is
the proper one, may be shown by reference to the stanza
wherein it occurs.

Let E'rin remémber her dáys of óld,
Ere her faithless sóns betráy'd her,
When Málachi wóre the cóllar of góld,
Which he wón from the próud inváder.

Again, such a line as

> Fór the glóry I' have lóst,

although it may be read

> For the glóry I' have lóst,

would be read improperly. The stanza wherein it occurs is essentially dissyllabic (*a x*).

> Heéd, oh heéd my fátal stóry!
> I' am Hósier's injured ghóst,
> Cóme to seék for fame and glóry—
> Fór the glory I' have lóst.

§ 312. *Metrical and Grammatical Combinations.*—Words, or parts of words, that are combined as measures, are words, or parts of words, combined *metrically*, or in *metrical combination*. Syllables combined as words, or words combined as portions of a sentence, are syllables and words *grammatically combined*, or in *grammatical combination*.

The syllables *ere her faith-* form a metrical combination.

The words *her faithless sons* form a grammatical combination.

When the syllables contained in the same measure are also contained in the same construction, the metrical and the grammatical combinations coincide. Such is the case with the line

> Remémber | the glóries | of Brían | the Bráve;

where the same division separates both the measure and the subdivisions of the sense, inasmuch as the word *the* is connected with the word *glories* equally in grammar and in metre, in syntax and in prosody. So is *of* with *Brian*, and *the* with *Brave*.

Contrast with this such a line as

> Lay vanquished, rolling in the fiery gulf.

Here the metrical division is one thing, the grammatical division another, and there is no coincidence.

Metrical,

> Lay ván | quished, róll | ing ín | the fiér | y gúlf.

Grammatical,

> Lay vanquished, | rolling |·in the fiery gulf.

The variety which arises in versification from the different degrees of the coincidence and non-coincidence between the metrical and grammatical combinations may be called *Rhythm*.

§ 313. *English Metres and Classical.* — The English metres are based upon *Accent*, the Latin and Greek metres upon *Quantity*. By treating an accented syllable as the equivalent to a long, and an unaccented syllable as the equivalent to a short one, we get a loose kind of analogy, which, from the fact of its having been, to some extent, recognized, requires notice. Subject to this view, the metrical notation for—

> The wày was lóng, the wind was cóld—
> Mérrily, mérrily, shàll I live nòw—

would be, not—

> *x a, x a, x a, x a,*
> *a x x, a x x, a x x, a*

respectively, but—

> ∪ − ∪ − ∪ − ∪ −
> − ∪ ∪ − ∪ ∪ − ∪ −

Again—

> As they splásh in the blóod of the slíppery streét,

is not—

> *x x a, x x a, x x a, x x a,*

but—

> ∪ ∪ − ∪ ∪ − ∪ ∪ − ∪ ∪ −

From this point of view there is a certain number of Latin and Greek *feet* with their syllables affected in the way of *quantity*, to which there are equivalent English *measures* with their syllables affected in the way of *accent*. Thus if the formula

¯ ⌣ be a classical, the formula *a x* is an English *trochee*.

⌣ ¯	„	„	*x a*	„	*iambus*.
¯ ⌣ ⌣	„	„	*a x x*	„	*dactyle*.
⌣ ¯ ⌣	„	„	*x a x*	„	*amphibrachys*.
⌣ ⌣ ¯	„	„	*x x a*	„	*anapæst*.

And so on in respect to the larger groups of similarly affected syllables which constitute whole lines and stanzas; verses like

> Cóme to séek for fáme and glóry—
> The wáy was lóng, the wind was cold—
> Mérrily, mérrily, sháll I live nów—
> But váinly thou wárrest—
> At the clóse of the dáy when the hámlet is still—

are (*a*) trochaic; (*b*) iambic; (*c*) dactylic; (*d*) amphi-brachych; and (*e*) anapæstic, respectively. And thus, with the exception of the word *amphibrachych* (which I do not remember to have seen), the terms have been used. And on this principle, with the same exception, systems of versification have been classified.

To show, however, that this view is exceptionable, let us compare a so-called English anapæst like—

> As they splásh in the blóod of the slippery stréet—

with

> Δέκατον μὲν ἔτος τόδ' ἐπεὶ Πριάμου.

For the latter line to have the same movement as the former, it must be read thus —

> Dekatón men etós to d' epéi Priamóu.

Now we well know that, whatever may be an English scholar's notions of the Greek accents, this is not the way in which he reads Greek anapæsts. In applying Latin names to English metres we can get a 'loose analogy,' but we can get nothing more.

§ 314. *Alliteration of the Anglo-Saxon and other Metres.* In Anglo-Saxon, the metres were, what is called, Allitera-tive, *i.e.* a certain number of accented initial syllables,

rithin the space of either a single line or a couplet, beg
rith the same letter: the vowels passing for identic
'his system was not only Anglo-Saxon, but Norse as w
nd in a less degree, German also.

§ 315. Specimens.

Anglo-Saxon.

OPENING OF BEOWULF. (*Tenth Century.*)

Hwæt we *Gár*-Dena,	Lo! we of the-Gar-Denes
in *gear*-dagum,	In the days-of-yore,
þeód-cýninga,	Of the people-kings,
þrým ge-frunon—	Glory have-heard—
hú ða Æþelingas	How the Athelings
ellen fremedon	Strength promoted —
oft *Scýld Scéfing*,	Of Scyld Scefing
sceaþen(a) þreátum,	Of enemies to-the-hosts,
monegum mægþum,	To many nations,
meodo-setla of-teáh—	The mead-settles off-drove—
egsode eorl—	The earl terrified—
syððan æ'rest wearð	Since erst was
feá-sceaft *f*unden;	Fee-ship found—
he þæs *f*rófre ge-bá(d),	He for this prosperous bided,
weóx under *w*olcnum,	Waxed under welkin,
weorð-mýndum þáh;	With worth-memorials throve,
oð þæt him æ'g-hwýlc	Till him each
þára ymb-sittendra,	Of the around-sitters,
ofer *h*ron-ráde,	Over the whale-road,
hýran scolde,	Hear should,
gomban *g*ýldan—	Tribute pay—
þæt wæ's *g*ód cyning.	That was good king.

Middle English.

LANGLAND'S PIERS PLOWMAN. (*Thirteenth Century.*)

n a somer sesun,	Wende I wydene in þis world,
Whon softe was the sonne,	Wondres to here.
: schop me into a schroud,	Bote on a Mayes morwnynge,
I scheep as I were;	On Maluerne heilles,
n habit of a hermite,	Me bifel a ferly,
Vnholy of werkes,	A feyrie, me þouhte;

I was weori of wandringe,
And wente me to reste,
Vndur a brod banke,
Bi a bourne syde;
And as I lay and leonede,
And lokede on the watres,
I slumberde in a slepyng,
Hit sownede so muerie.
þenne gon I meeten
A meruelous sweuene,

þat I was in a Wildernesse;
Wuste I neuer where.
And as I be beo-heold into þe Est,
An-heigh to þe sonne,
I saub a tour on a toft,
Trizely i-maket,
A deop dale bi-neoþe,
A dungun þer-inne,
With deop deck and derk,
And dredful of siht.

§ 316. OLD SAXON OF GERMANY.

HELIAND, pp. 12, 13. (*Schmeller's edition.*)

LUC. II. 8-13.

Tho uuard managun cud,
Obar thesa uuidon uuerold.
Uuardos antfundun,
Thea thar, ebuscalcos,
Uta uuarun,
Uueros an uuahtu,
Uuiggeo gomean,
Fehas aftar felda.
Gisahun finistri an tuue
Telatan an lufte;
Endi quam lioht Godes,
Uuanum thurh thui uuolcan;
Endi thea uuardos thar
Bifeng an them felda.
Sie uurdun an forhtun tho,
Thea man an ira moda.
Gisahun thar mahtigna
Godes Engil cuman;
The im tegegnes sprac.
Het that im thea uuardos—
'Uuiht ne antdredin
Ledes fon them liohta.
Ic scal eu quadhe liobora thing,
Suido uuarlico
Uuilleon seggean.
Cudean craft mikil.
Nu is Krist geboran,
An thesero selbun naht,
Salig barn Godes,

Then it was to many known,
Over this wide world.
The words they discovered,
Those that there, as horse-grooms,
Without were,
Men at watch,
Horses to tend,
Cattle on the field.
They saw the darkness in two
Dissipated in the atmosphere,
And came a light of God
—through the welkin;
And the words there
Caught on the field.
They were in fright then
The men in their mood.
They saw there mighty
God's angel come;
That to them face-to-face spake.
It bade thus them these words—
'Dread not a whit
Of mischief from the light.
I shall to you speak glad things.
Very true;
Say commands;
Show strength great.
Now is Christ born.
In this self-same night;
The blessed child of God,

An thera Davides burg,	In the David's city,
Drohtin the godo.	The Lord the good.
That is mendislo	That is exultation
Manno cunneas,	To the races of men,
Allaro firiho fruma.	Of all men the advancement.
Thar gi ina fidan mugun,	There ye may find him
An Bethlema burg,	In the city of Bethlehem,
Barno rikiost.	The noblest of children.
Hebbiath that te teena,	Ye have as a token
That ic eu gitellean mag,	That I tell ye
Uuarun uuordun,	True words,
That he thar biuundan ligid,	That he there swathed lieth,
That kind an enera cribbium,	The child in a crib,
Tho he si cuning obar al	Though he be king over all
Erdun endi himiles,	Earth and Heaven,
Endi obar eldeo barn,	And over the sons of men,
Uueroldes uualdand.'	Of the world the Ruler.'

§ 317. OLD HIGH GERMAN.

Daz hort ih rahhon,	That have I heard relate
Dia werolt rehtwison	The worldwise
Daz sculi der Antichristo	That should the Antichrist
Mit Eliase pâgen.	With Elias struggle.
Der warch ist kiwâfinit;	The traitor is armed;
Denne wirdit untar in	Then becomes between them
Wik arhapan;	War raised.
Khensun sind so kreftec;	The champions are so strong;
Diu kosa ist so mihhil,	The case is so great.
Elias stritit	Elias strives
Pi den euigon lîp;	For the everlasting life,
Will den rehtkernon	Will by the right-doing
Daz rihhi kistarkan:	The kingdom strengthen;
Pidiu scal imo halfan	Therein shall him help
Der himiles kiwaltit.	Who rules heaven,
Der Antichristo stêt	The Antichrist stands
Pi dem altflante;	By the old Fiend;
Stêt pî demo Satanase;	Stands by Satanas;
Der inan farsenkan scal;	Who shall sink him.
Podiu scal er in der wroksteti	Both shall in fight
Wunt pivallan;	Wounded fall,
Enti in demo sinde	And on that occasion
Sigalos werdan.	Be without victory.

§ 318. Old High German.
Weissobrun Hymn.

Dat chifregin ih mit firahim	That have I heard among men,
Firiuuizzo meista ;	Of the fore-wise most,
Dat ero ni uuas, noh ufhimil,	That erst neither was, nor heaven above,
Noh paum noh pereg,	Nor tree, nor berg,
Ni (sterro) nohheinig,	Nor [star] nor . . .
Noh sunna noh scein.	Nor sun shone.
Noh mana ni liuhta.	Nor moon gave light.

§ 319. Old Norse.
THE OLDER EDDA,
Völuspa.

1.

Hlióðs bið ek allar	Silence ask I of all,
helgar kindir,	Holy children,
meiri ok minni,	Lesser and greater,
mögu Heimdallar;	Sons of Heimdall ;
vildu at ek Valföðrs	Wilt theu that I Valfader's
tél framtelja ?	Weal forth-tell ?
fornspjöll fíra,	Fore-spells of men,
þau er ek fremst um man.	They (whom) I first mind.

2.

Ek man jötna	I mind of Yotuns
ár um borna,	Years ago born,
þá er forðum	They (who) fore-times
mik fœdda höfðu ;	Me fed have :
niu man ek heims,	Nine mind I homes,
níu íviðjur,	Nine * * *
mjötvið mœran	The mid-wood great,
fyr mold neðan.	Before the mould nether.

3.

Ár var alda	Yore was of ages
þar er Y'mir byggði,	Then when Ymer built,
vara sandr né sær	Was (nor) sand nor sea,
né svalar unnir,	Nor cool waters ;
jörð fannsk æva	Earth found-its-self never,
né upphiminn,	Nor up-heaven,
gap var ginnunga,	Gaping was yawning,
en gras hvergi.	And grass nowhere.

The following is from Thorlakson's Translation
Paradise Lost' :—

MODERN ICELANDIC.

Um fyrsta manns	Sŷng þú, Menta-
felda hlyŏni	móŏir himneska !
ok átlystíng	þú sem Hórebs fyrr
af epli forboŏnu,	á huldum toppi,
hvaŏan óvægr	eŏa Sínai,
upp kom dauŏi,	sauŏaverŏi
Edens missir,	innblèst fræŏanda
ok allt böl manna ;	útvalit sæŏi,
þartil annarr einn,	hve alheimr skópst
særŏi maŏr,	af alls samblandi ;
aptr fær	Eŏa lysti þik
oss viŏreista,	lángtum heldr
ok afrekar nŷan	at Zíons hæŏ
oss til handa	ok Sílóa brunni,
fullsælustaŏ	sem framstreymdi
fögrum sigri ;	hjá Frètt guŏligri, &c.

Of Man's first disobedience, and the fruit
Of that forbidden tree, whose mortal taste
Brought death into the world, and all our woe,
With loss of Eden, till one greater Man
Restore us, and regain the blissful seat,
Sing, heavenly Muse, that on the secret top
Of Oreb, or of Sinai, didst inspire
That shepherd, who first taught the chosen seed,
In the beginning how the Heavens and Earth
Rose out of Chaos : or if Sion's hill
Delight thee more, and Siloa's brook that flow'd
Fast by the oracle of God, &c.

§ 320. SWEDISH (Present Century.)

FROM TEGNÉR—FRITHIOF'S SAGA.

1.	1.
Sitter i högen,	Sits on high,
högättad hofding ;	High-ancestered, noble ;
slagsvärd vid sidan	Sword-guard by side,
sköldan på arm	Shield on arm.
Gångaren gode	Steed good
gnäggar derinne	Neighs therein ;
skrapar med gullhof	Scrapes with gold hoof
grundmurad graf.	Turf-raised grave.

2.   2.

Nu rider rike	Now rides rich
Ring öfver Bifrost	Ring over Bifrost (*The rainbow*)
svigtar för bördan	Sways for the burthen
bågiga bron.	The bowlike bridge.
Upp springa Vallhalls	Up spring Valhalla's
hvalfdörrar vida;	Valve-doors wide
Asarnas händer	The Asas hands
hänga in hans.	Hang on his.

It is in the Icelandic, Scandinavian, or Norse where
the Alliterative Metres are the commonest; and next to
the Norse, the Anglo-Saxon. In the High German they
are, comparatively, rare.

ADDENDUM (*omitted in p.* 19).

Now we should praise	He erst shaped,
Heaven's-kingdom's guardian,	For earth's bairns,
The might of the Lord,	Heaven to roof;
And his mood-thought;	Holy shaper.
The glory-father of works;	Then mid-earth,
As he, of wonder each,	Mankind's home,
Everlasting Lord,	Everlasting Lord,
Erst established:	After formed,

For the homes of men,
Lord Almighty.

ERRATUM.

Page 4, § 11, *for* 'Mamertinus' *read* 'Eumenius.'

LONDON : PRINTED BY
SPOTTISWOODE AND CO., NEW-STREET SQUARE
AND PARLIAMENT STREET

Lightning Source UK Ltd.
Milton Keynes UK
UKHW020632291021
393021UK00003B/133